Properties and behaviour in clothing use

B T Batsford Ltd London

© Edward Miller 1968, 1984, 1989 and 1992

First Published 1968
New edition 1992
Reprinted 1995

Typeset by
Tek-Art Ltd, West Wickham, Kent
Printed in Great Britain by
Redwood Books, Trowbridge, Wiltshire
for the publishers
B T Batsford Ltd
4 Fitzhardinge Street
London WIH 0AH

ISBN 0 7134 7235 9

Contents

Note
Before going to press it was announced that Du Pont of the USA has taken over ICI Fibres but it is not yet known what will happen to the brand names *Terylene* and *Tactel*.

Introduction

Many books have been written on textiles, but most of them are specialist technical works primarily written for the benefit of those either actively engaged in some branch of the textile industry or learning textile manufacture.

Knowledge of textile fabrics is essential for those who are concerned, either domestically or industrially, with the making-up of fabrics into garments.

This book, which deals mainly with clothing fabrics, has been written for fabric users who need knowledge of fabric properties and behaviour but who are not greatly concerned with technical details of manufacturing processes.

Obviously some technical explanation is necessary to enable a user to understand why fabrics differ in appearance, texture and properties. This explanation has been confined to basic principles which, even when fibres and yarns are being dealt with, constantly keeps fabrics in mind with the object of relating technical processes to fabric appearance and behaviour.

During the past twenty years the range of fabrics available for clothing has widened tremendously. New fibres have been produced; existing fibres have been modified and changed; new types of yarn and fabric processing have been developed; new fabric structures have been devised. The fabric user is continually being faced with new names and claims; there is profusion — and confusion — of materials.

The basic knowledge necessary to be able to select, use and understand present-day textile fabrics correctly can only be acquired by deliberate study and the object of this book is to provide this knowledge without irrelevant technicalities.

Appropriate bibliographical references are given to assist those who require additional or perhaps more detailed information.

What is a textile?

If any study of textile fabrics is to be made, the meaning of the word *textile* must be made quite clear.

The dictionary states that the word is derived from the Latin word *texere* — to weave; but a wider meaning than simply that of weaving must be accepted since that is only one of various ways of making textile fabrics.

It is now generally accepted that a textile is a fabric *made* from fibres but, as diagram 1 shows, the fibres may either be converted into yarn first and then the yarns put together in one of a variety of ways to make fabrics, or the fibres can be converted directly into a fabric.

This definition excludes clothing materials such as fur, leather, suede and unsupported plastic sheeting. The first three are natural materials and are not *made* from fibres although the fibres of fur can be detached from the skin and used as textile fibres. Leather and suede are fibrous in structure but the fibres have no separate identity in a textile sense, and plastic sheeting has no fibre content at all. Fur, leather and suede can be simulated in textile structures and in combinations of textile and plastic materials.

Textile fibres

The word *fibre* creates a mental picture of a long, thin, hair-like object, and indeed textile fibres are like that in general physical shape.

Not all fibres though are suitable for textile purposes because a textile fibre must possess sufficient length, fineness, strength and flexibility to be suitable for manufacture into fabrics. It will be seen later on how they vary in these respects and how the variations are responsible for the differing character of materials. It will be seen also that this definition can apply both to natural and to man-made fibres.

Filament and staple These two terms represent the two basic forms of textile fibres.

Filament is the name given to a fibre of continuous length, that is to say it is long enough to be used in a fabric without increasing its length by adding other fibres on to it.

An example of a natural filament is silk; the cocoon of a silk-worm can contain about 3000 m of continuous twin filaments. Man-made

8

filaments produced by extrusion machines can be many times longer.

Staple is the name given to fibres of shorter length. To make a continuous length of yarn, staple fibres have to be twisted together. Staple fibres can range from about 10 mm to many centimetres in length, but in no case do they ever become long enough to be classed as filament, so the two terms are quite separate except for the fact that man-made filaments can be converted into staple fibres by deliberately cutting them into short lengths. This is a very common way of processing man-made fibres, but the reverse process is never carried out.

An example of a natural staple fibre is cotton. If a yarn from an ordinary cotton fabric is untwisted, it will be seen to break down into fine fibres about two or three centimetres long.

Yarn can consist of either staple fibres, or of filaments put together. Filaments merely need grouping in order to produce the thickness of yarn required, the length is already there in the individual filaments. Grouping of filaments is achieved by twisting them together. The twist, usually quite a small amount, merely serves to keep the filaments reasonably together.

Staple fibres *have* to be twisted to make them cohere into a continuous length of yarn. The action of twisting forces the fibre surfaces into contact with each other setting up friction between them which enables a lengthwise tension on the yarn to be resisted. In this way a continuous length of yarn can be made even from very short fibres.

The type of yarn exerts a strong influence on the texture and appearance of the fabric. In general, filament yarns are thin, smooth and lustrous and staple fibre yarns are thicker, fibrous and non-lustrous. An excellent example of these different characteristics can be seen by comparing the fibrous nature of the outer wool fabric of a coat or suit jacket with the smooth lustrous surface of the lining of the garment, the wool fabric being staple and the lining being filament.

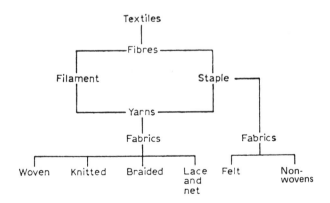

1   The four main types of structure

Fabrics

Most fabrics are made from yarns and diagram 1 shows the four main types of structure. Unquestionably the two most common structures are *woven* and *knitted*. In this chapter only their fundamental forms are dealt with. Chapter V deals more fully with variations of these structures.

Woven fabrics

In their simple form these consist of two series of threads, *warp* and *weft*, interlaced at right angles to each other (2). The *warp* threads (or 'ends') run the length of the fabric and the *weft* threads (or 'picks') run across the width.

The edge at each long side of a woven fabric is called the *selvedge* and it is usually in a firmer construction than the rest of the fabric, to provide a firm neat edge and a secure grip for finishing machinery. This often makes small groups of pin-holes along the edge, although newer types of machines use clips which do not mark the selvedge. However, fabrics such as synthetic filament linings woven by the fast water jet systems do not produce conventional selvedges and are often left with short projecting yarn ends.

The diagram shows *plain weave*, which is the simplest form of inter-lacing. The section drawings at the side and the bottom of the plan show that warp and weft interlace with each other in a similar manner. If the threads are closely spaced it can be seen that this form of interlacing

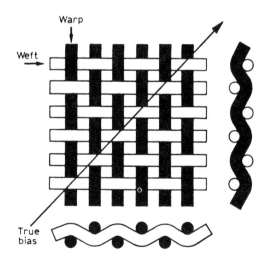

2   Woven fabric: plain weave

10

gives a very tight structure because the alternate interlacings give no room for sideways movement of the threads. The draping properties of such a structure would depend entirely on the flexibility of the fibres and yarns.

For example, a square of wire gauze, as used in a laboratory, is formed by interlacing steel wire in plain weave. As a result a fairly rigid piece of fabric is produced—which is the intention. This fabric is too rigid to be used for any normal fabric purpose because steel wire is far less flexible than any extile fibre or yarn. A fine cotton calico can be made by interlacing cotton yarns in plain weave much more closely than the wire gauze, but because of the softness and flexibility of the cotton, the resulting fabric is quite supple and is flexible enough for many fabric purposes. The *toile* used by dressmakers for making preliminary models of dresses is often a calico of this type.

As will be seen later, woven structures can vary in density and in interlacing, and this can make them differ in appearance and handle, but in their simple forms they represent a very stable material.

By this it is meant that unless a woven fabric is deliberately made otherwise (such as in a 'stretch' fabric) it does not extend a great deal in warp and weft directions because of the interlacings—which resist an attempt to pull warp or weft straight. The natural elasticity of the material will produce a reasonable amount of 'give' in warp or weft directions. This will vary according to the tightness of the structure and the amount of elasticity in fibre and yarn. The amount of movement is usually small enough to ensure that a piece of woven fabric cut to shape, as part of a garment is not too easily distorted, but yet in wear it will 'give' enough to be comfortable if the garment is cut and styled properly.

If tension is exerted diagonally much more movement is obtained because the force is not now directly along a yarn direction but is pulling across both series of threads causing a 'scissor' action. This diagonal direction is known as *bias*. True bias is an angle of 45°, ie exactly between warp and weft, and smaller angles of bias can be used if necessary, but the greatest amount of movement is along the true bias line.

In using a woven fabric for clothing, due regard must be paid to the *grain* of the fabric. The grain is represented by warp and weft. If the fabric is true, the warp runs straight lengthways and the weft runs across the fabric at 90° to the warp. Garments are usually made up so that the warp runs vertically down the garment as it is worn and the weft horizontally across it. Care must be taken to ensure firstly that the fabric is 'true' and then that the pattern pieces are correctly related to grain. Sometimes it is found necessary to cut *off grain*, but this should only be done deliberately and grain will be again referred to in chapter IX.

Knitted fabrics

These consist of a structure formed by interlocking loops of yarn. Diagram 3 shows a simple *weft-knitted* structure. This term is used because the yarn is fed horizontally to form rows of loops which are individually locked vertically with the corresponding loop in the next horizontal row. This is the type of knitting which can be produced by hand using two knitting 'needles' and one ball of yarn. Knitting machines can produce either a flat fabric or a tubular fabric according to type.

It will be seen that the interlocked loops form vertical rows which are called *wales* and horizontal rows which are called *courses*. If the fabric is correctly on grain, *wales* and *courses* intersect at 90° and are thus the directional equivalent of warp and weft, as far as grain is concerned.

The stability of a simple knitted fabric is much less than that of an ordinary woven fabric because any tension exerted on it will never be along the line of a yarn, but will distort the loop structure so that the fabric can be stretched in any direction.

This simple structure can also be unravelled very easily from the top downwards, and if the yarn forming a loop is broken it immediately releases loops so that a 'ladder' quickly forms which will widen and lengthen under tension.

The instability of simple types of knitted fabric was a limiting factor in their use for garments. At one time hosiery and underwear formed the main bulk of garments made from this type of fabric because shapes

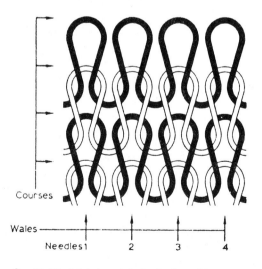

3   Knitted fabric: plain knit, face side

could be kept simple and the stretch of the knitted structure enabled a close fit to be obtained without complicated cutting or styling.

Knitted fabrics are now strenuously competing with woven fabrics in many clothing uses due to the fact that improved machines and techniques have produced knitted fabrics in complex structures which in some cases are equal to woven fabrics in stability and in addition makers-up and consumers are more accustomed to handling and using stretchable materials.

Techniques of fabric lamination and bonding, referred to in chapter V also serve to make knitted fabrics easier to handle by the maker-up and to give them more stability for garment use when required.

Lace and net fabrics

The manufacture of these was formerly a hand technique but they are now mostly machine made. The basic net structure is shown in diagram 4 and two basic structural points are important at this stage. The first is that in this form of fabric yarns are actually twisted round each other and do not form straight lines. The second point is that lace and net are 'open' type structures which tend to be dimensionally unstable if tension is exerted on them. In this respect these fabrics behave similarly to simple knitted fabrics, but whereas compound knitted structures can be made close, compact and stable, lace structures must remain rela-

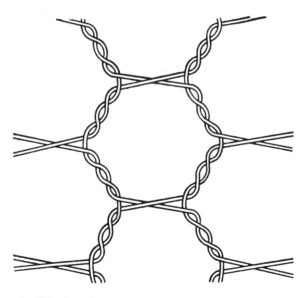

4   *Simple net*

tively open to preserve their character. So lace is mostly used for decoration in the form of flouncings, edgings and inserts. Many laces for inserts are made partly with stretch yarns to help with the fitting of 'bodywear' and swimwear. Lace can also be used as a basic dress fabric but the easily distorted and open structure produces problems in cutting and lining. It can be stabilised by 'bonding' to a fine tricot (chapter V).

Lace-type fabrics are frequently made on a special type of knitting machine called a *Raschel* where the lace formation is produced by a loop structure instead of by twisting threads around each other.

Braided fabrics

These are produced by interlacing yarns diagonally in a form of 'plaiting' (5). This type of structure is confined to narrow flat fabrics or to relatively small tubular structures because the machine must keep all the constituent threads in motion simultaneously, and separately, so that a very large or wide structure would need an extremely complicated and uneconomic machine.

A common example of braid use is the normal shoe lace which can be either a flattened or a rounded tube according to type. The rounded effect is sometimes enhanced by filling the tube with packing yarns which lie perfectly straight.

Apart from use as shoe laces and various forms of cord, such as sash cord and blind cord, braid is used for decorations in either flat, rounded or in more elaborate ruched or zigzag forms.

The diagonal course of the yarns normally makes braid easily extended in the length direction with a corresponding contraction in

5   *Braid*

width but setting in finishing processes can produce stability to length-ways stretch if necessary.

The term *braid* is also used in general to describe narrow fabrics which have actually been woven, or even knitted. Woven 'braid' is of course quite compact and stable in dimensions and is often used for edge bindings and for stabilising edges of knitted garments. Knitted 'braids' are usually used for girdles and other minor uses where length instability is not important. The manufacture of braids, ribbons and tapes, known as *narrow fabrics* is carried out by a specialised section of the textile industry.

All the fabric types so far dealt with are those in which the textile fibres have been converted into yarns first and then the yarns used in various ways to form the fabrics. On sheer common sense grounds the idea of converting fibres directly into fabrics, by-passing the yarn stage, seems economically attractive providing some means of consolidating the fibres is available.

Felt

Felt has been used by man for centuries and its manufacture is made possible by the fact that wool, and some other animal fibres, possess a natural tendency to felt or mat together under the influence of heat, moisture and mechanical pressure. In this way, webs of wool fibres can be consolidated into a fabric.

A fabric produced in this way is entirely without grain because the flat webs of fibres are non-directional, ie the fibres point in all directions. Felt can be cut in any direction without fraying or unravelling because of the compact fibre arrangement.

Unfortunately this convenience is marred by distinct deficiencies in drape, stability and durability so that felt is of very little use for normal garment making.

If felt is to be strong and stable the fibres must be so consolidated that the material is stiff and heavy with very little draping property.

If felt is made soft and supple its properties of tensile strength, resistance to abrasion and distortion are too low to be of practical value for normal garment use.

The main apparel use of felt is in the manufacture of hats where its capacity to be shaped by heat and moisture can be exploited. Its lack of grain makes it suitable for handicraft and appliqué work where cutting of intricate shapes is possible and certain types of soft bulky felts are used as padding in garment interlinings.

Certain types of woven or knitted wool fabrics are given a felted finish which gives them the appearance of felt in that no yarn structure is apparent and the fabric appears to be composed entirely of fibres. However, closer examination, tearing or cutting the fabric will show the basic yarn structure and will prevent confusion with true felt. This type of finish will be referred to in chapter VI.

Non-woven fabrics

In spite of the disadvantages of felt, referred to above, the idea of making fabrics directly from fibres has remained economically attractive. It was really the conditions following the Second World War which prompted the Germans to start copying woven fabrics by a faster, cheaper way. Now it is a world-wide industry and it would be a mistake to look on non-wovens as cheap substitute materials, for they have their own character and properties. But at the start the producers were unsure of their direction. They tried short-life garments including quite attractive printed fabrics, some for underwear and nightwear, which was not a success because the manufacturing costs of the garments were too high for the type of product. Then they settled down to develop interlinings for clothing and industrial fabrics for protective clothing in hospitals and factories, resulting in the production of filter fabrics, face masks, airline head-rest covers, sheets, table cloths, overalls, medical materials and household cleaning cloths, in which they are now very well established. More recently non-woven fabrics for the armed services, made to NATO specifications, provide 24 hour protection against chemical attack involving toxic gases and liquids, also made with a flame retardent finish.

The fibres most commonly used for non-wovens are nylon, polyester and viscose. There are several different methods used for the formation of the web and a variety of ways in which the fibres are compacted and held together to become a non-woven fabric which, dependent on the fibres and processes used, can sometimes be washed for a limited number of times and sometimes indefinitely before showing signs of breakdown. If made in 100% synthetic fibres which have been heat-bonded by sophisticated methods they can compete on equal terms with many woven and knitted fabrics. In particular non-wovens made by 'lacing', arranging thousands of fine filaments immediately after extrusion and allowing them to set in this intermingled form, gives a strong fabric which can be used for children's anoraks, protective clothing, even book covers. However, with most of the standard non-wovens produced today the abrasion resistance is low compared with other textiles and this is generally the factor which limits their use. Yet there is considerable scope for future development within the non-woven sector—more so than in weaving or knitting.

In general, therefore, very few non-wovens are suitable as top fabrics unless they have been given a surface coating of some hard wearing substance such as polyurethane, the filaments spun-bonded or laced or the web needled to a woven scrim or stitch bonded with thread.

Chapter V provides a more detailed description of the various techniques being employed to make the new generation of fabrics in this sector of the textile industry.

Factors affecting the properties and behaviour of textile fabrics

Every textile fabric is the result of a combination of materials and processes so that any understanding of fabrics must include some knowledge of materials and processes involved in fabric production since no single stage of production is entirely responsible for the appearance and performance of a fabric. It is also important to know what can be altered, on request.

Each stage of processing has its variables so that in the complete sequence of manufacture the number of possible combinations is enormous. This is a very simple explanation of the wide variety of fabrics available.

Once the principles of the common variations in the separate stages of manufacture are understood, the effects of the usual combinations of them in fabrics soon form a pattern of fabric appreciation. These are the 'basic' fabrics referred to in chapter VIII, and knowledge of these makes the uncommon fabric easier to comprehend because it can be compared with the usual 'pattern' and, with some experience, the points of difference will be perceived so that the probable behaviour of the fabric can be assessed.

Diagram 6 sets out the sequence of production and in the following chapters the influence of each stage on the finished fabric will be made clear because this is the sole reason for study of manufacturing processes.

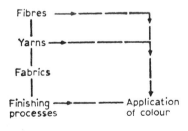

6   *Sequence of production*

II Foundations of fabrics: natural fibres

The quality and properties of the fibre, or blend of fibres used are the foundations of the fabric quality and properties.

The processes of yarn manufacture, formation of fabric structure, and finishing may serve either to enhance or to suppress certain fibre properties but no properties can be created in any type of fibre by any form of process if the potential is not there.

Selection of fibre, or fibres, to be used depends on the quality, intended use, performance requirements and price of the ultimate fabric. All these factors are considered before a fabric is made because the textile manufacturer is normally aiming at a specific market when designing fabrics.

It must be accepted that no textile fibre is perfect for all purposes because the use and performance requirements of fabrics vary so widely that the 'perfect' fibre would need to be instantly changeable in appearance, handle, texture and many other properties. This is clearly impossible so that the necessary variety of fibres can only be obtained by having a range of different fibres from which to select those required for a particular purpose or effect.

Until approximately the beginning of this century the *natural* textile fibres were the only fibres available. These fibres have been used by man for thousands of years; samples of fabrics over 5,000 years old have been found in Egyptian tombs showing that a high degree of technical skill in fabric manufacture and processing was evident at that time. Discoveries of textile equipment in even earlier civilisations show that man must have begun to make some form of textiles in the very dawn of his civilised history

It is important for this reason alone that the general characteristics of *natural* fibres should be studied first and when it is also appreciated that the natural fibres still remain an important and necessary source of the world's textile fabrics in spite of increasing competition from *man-made* fibres it becomes even more appropriate.

Diagram 7 shows the main natural fibres used in all forms of textiles. It is by no means exhaustive but it does include the main clothing fibres as well as some of the less well-known speciality fibres.

The *animal* and *vegetable* groups are the most significant as far as conventional clothing is concerned. It will be noticed that the *animal*

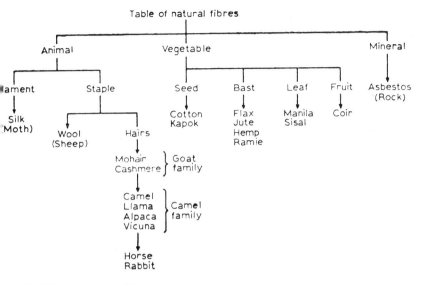

7 *Table of natural fibres*

group is subdivided into *filament* and *staple*. This is necessary because of the presence of *silk* which is the only natural filament in consistent commercial use.

It is not necessary to use the term *staple* in many of the other main groups because all the other fibres are staple fibres.

The use-pattern of natural fibres

Statistics indicate that nearly 25 million tonnes of textile fibres of all kinds, both natural and man-made, were used world wide in 1990. Of this total the natural fibres account for approximately 35%. The general tendency is for the total amount of fibres to increase yearly, the increase being mainly in man-made fibres. This means that the proportion of man-made fibres is rising yearly, not entirely at the expense of natural fibres, but in terms of total textile fibre use.

Accurate statistics of the use of textile fibres in clothing are difficult to obtain and in any case vary from one country to another for economic, social and climate reasons. It is unquestionably true that *cotton* is the most widely used textile fibre in the world. No other fibre comes anywhere near it in total use nor is likely to within the near future.

Next, and a good way behind, comes *wool*, and these two fibres between them comprise the bulk of natural apparel fibres. Hairs such as

19

mohair, camel, cashmere, llama, alpaca, vicuna, are grouped statistically with *wool* for convenience, as they only represent a very small percentage.

Flax and *silk* are the only other natural fibres used widely in any significant quantity for clothing and they fall well behind the two major fibres.

Fibre 'qualities'

The word *quality* is a relative term indicating class or degree of excellence and it can either be used loosely to describe the combined effect of general impressions, or it can be a more precise term referring to expert observations of specific properties. (This should not be confused with the term *Fabric Quality No*, generally used by textile houses to denote a base cloth, which may then have a series of *Design Nos* to identify variations.)

All natural fibres are produced in a range of qualities because variable growing conditions, such as varieties of plants, breeds of animals, soil, climate and cultivation methods, prevent uniformity.

Producers aim at consistent quality production but influences beyond their control can cause variations and fibres from the same area can vary in their position in the quality range from one year to another. Normally these variations are not great but it means that each crop of fibres has to be examined and appraised by experts for accurate quality assessment.

Each fibre type named in the table possesses certain general characteristics which distinguish it from the other fibres. The difference between fibre types in different main groups is usually wide enough to be obvious to casual examination once the general characteristics are appreciated (eg wool and cotton).

Differences between fibre types within the same main group may not be as obvious, and usually demand more detailed observation and knowledge (eg wool and mohair).

Highly specialised expert knowledge is needed to detect the small differences between adjacent qualities within the range of one fibre type but broad quality differences can be perceived if some knowledge of handle, appearance and fabric processing is possessed.

The quality range of a fibre type represents significant degrees of variation in the properties of the fibre, which influence its cost, use and fabric value.

To simplify the study of fibres only broad quality groups will be described in any one fibre type.

Physical and chemical properties of fibres

The *characteristics* which are responsible for the individuality of a fibre are produced by a combination of the physical and chemical properties of the fibre. In detail they form quite a lengthy list but for convenience and brevity they are collected into two groups.

Group 1

Represents mainly physical properties, apparent to sight and touch, in fact the properties which can be appraised by the hand and eye of the expert when accurate quality assessment and evaluation is being made:

Range of fibre lengths and thicknesses.
Fibre strength, elasticity and resilience.
Fibre lustre, colour and handle.
Amounts of impurities present in the 'raw' fibre.

The length of natural staple fibres is usually expressed as 'staple length'. The fibres in a lock of wool, or attached to a cotton seed, will be of varying lengths so that the 'staple length' represents the average length of such a representative group of fibres of similar quality.

With the exception of colour, lustre and handle, these properties can be measured accurately by scientific methods, but even if this is done the interpretation of the combined results in terms of quality and fabric is still a matter of expert opinion.

Group 2

Represents mainly chemical properties, all of which can be scientifically measured.

The chemical stability and composition of the fibre.
The effect of heat, moisture, acids, alkalis, solvents and other chemicals on the fibre.
The affinity of the fibre for dyestuffs.

These properties, unlike those in group 1, are not obvious to visual examination and generally speaking they do not vary greatly within the quality range of one fibre type. They have an important influence on the adaptability of the fibre to processing and on the versatility of the fibre in fabric use.

Factors affecting the fabric use of natural fibres

The use of widely differing amounts of individual fibres can only be satisfactorily explained by relating the practical significance of the fibre qualities and properties to fabric manufacturing processes.

The cost of a fabric is always an important factor and it is based on the initial cost of the fibre plus the cost of converting it into a fabric. Cost, therefore, enters into each aspect of fabric manufacture and can be described as the *consequence* of the effect of fibre quality, properties and manufacturing processes combined.

The processing factors which, together with quality and properties, influence the fabric use value and cost of converting a fibre into fabrics are:

1 Availability.
2 Adaptability to processing.
3 Versatility.

Availability

The initial cost of a fibre depends upon its availability in relation to demand.

Natural fibres are agricultural products which require the use of land and labour for their production and collection. The majority of textile fabrics are made in industrial areas which are usually far away from the growing areas so that transport charges add to the basic production costs.

In highly developed countries where land and labour are expensive productivity must be high for efficient economic production. The scientific methods used to ensure this usually produce fibres which are reasonably uniform in quality and which can be classified conveniently in bulk. In these countries the transport systems are well organised so that large quantities of fibres can be moved quickly and relatively cheaply.

In this way these countries can compete in price and quality with the less well-developed countries where land and labour are cheaper but production methods and transport systems are less efficient.

It is significant that, with a few exceptions, the fibres which are widely used can be obtained from many different countries. This ensures continuity and competition in supply of a wide range of fibre qualities at varying prices and prevents undesirable monopoly by any one country.

The 'best' qualities in any fibre type normally represent deliberate development of the best characteristics of that fibre and it is logical that these qualities should be less widely available and therefore more expensive than the greater bulk of the 'ordinary' qualities.

There are numerous instances though where it can be shown that the best qualities are not always the correct choice for every purpose so that it does not necessarily follow that the lower, or 'ordinary' qualities are always 'second-best' choice.

If wide demand can be matched by wide and competing production sources then the basic cost of the fibre will be low. If production cannot be adequately matched to demand by reason of difficulties of land, location, transport, labour, climate or artificial restrictions, then the basic cost of the fibre will tend to be high.

Adaptability to processing

The conversion of fibres into yarns and fabrics is now a highly organised industry in which, for the majority of textiles, machines are used at every processing stage.

There are few instances nowadays where it can be proved that traditional hand methods produce a better quality textile product. Production entirely by hand methods is slow, costly and limited to textiles which have a high aesthetic or artistic individuality and therefore are not suitable for bulk production methods.

In the production of textiles in any degree of bulk hand operations are slow and expensive, particularly so if they have to be combined with machine operations. The aims of textile production development are, to reduce the conversion of fibres to fabrics into as few operations as possible, to speed up the operations, to introduce automated sequences and to replace fallible human judgement in high speed control by ingenious electronic and mechanical devices. Machine processes are, however, not only concerned with mere bulk but also the desirability of being able to produce a wide variety of textiles by machine methods.

The adaptability of a fibre toward machine processing, for purposes of bulk and variety, is governed by the properties of the fibre and the cost of processing the fibre is a direct reflection of its adaptability.

Versatility

The versatility of a fibre type is a measure of the extent of variety of textile structures which can be made from it and the variety of use and suitability of these structures.

Every fibre has *some* degree of versatility but limitations imposed by physical and chemical properties, in response and adaptability to processing, and widely differing use requirements cause certain fibres to have a narrower more specialised range of uses than others.

The more specialised fibres possess marked characteristics, usually of handle and appearance, which are enhanced by appropriate fabric structures and finishing processes. These outstanding characteristics are usually accompanied by limitations in other directions which restrict the versatility of these fibres in uses which are not exploiting their special virtures.

As the production of fabrics from specialised fibres tends to be expensive and troublesome it is inevitable that attempts to imitate them should be made by using cheaper and more versatile fibres, by using re-manufactured forms, or by using man-made copies of the specialised fibres. It is perhaps unfortunate that the term 'imitation' is often thought to be connected with 'deception', because imitations can provide lower-priced fabrics which possess in some degree the desirable characteristics of appearance and handle of more expensive structures. These fabrics are useful providing that the element of deliberate deception is not present and that the fabrics are used, with full knowledge of their limitations, in the appropriate market.

It will be seen later that imitation was the basic idea which eventually led to what is now known as the Man-made Fibre Industry. In addition the continued efforts to develop and improve fibre production and fibre processes, in both natural and man-made fibres, are partly inspired by the desire to imitate attractive features and properties.

Characteristics

Now that the factors affecting the fabric use of fibres have been outlined individual fibres can be studied more closely so that the reasons for their use can be more clearly understood. The fibres will be dealt with in their order of importance as clothing fibres and details of their production will not be given because this information can be obtained from the books quoted at the end of the chapter.

Cotton

This is the most versatile and the most widely used textile fibre, possessing more 'ideal' properties than any other fibre.

Availability

Cotton is widely available and is the cheapest natural fibre used for clothing.

It is produced on a bush which is widely grown in sub-tropical regions throughout the world, lying roughly between the parallels of latitude of 35° North and South of the Equator.

The bolls, which are the flower seed capsules, open when ripe revealing a fluffy mass of fibres and they are picked either by hand or by machine. The fibres are separated from the seeds by 'ginning', a machine process, which quickly and conveniently makes the fibres available for textile use. The fibres are then graded for quality and press-packed into large bales of about 225 kg weight for despatch to textile manufacturing areas.

The major cotton producing areas are the southern states of the USA, Russia, China, India, Pakistan, Brazil, Egypt, Turkey, Mexico and Argentina, in that order. Sea Island cotton, a very high quality fibre, sometimes 55 cm long, is grown in the West Indies but only in small quantities. However, cotton is reasonably easy to acquire in usable form, available from a wide area, with assured continuity and competitive supply.

Qualities

There are hundreds of different qualities of cotton, but they can be conveniently grouped into three quality types.

1 Long-staple cottons This is the best quality type which goes up to about 55 mm in staple length. These are the finest, softest and strongest cottons comprising Sea Island, which is the best quality of all, and Egyptian types which are the next best. This is the most expensive type of cotton and is used for the finest types of fabrics and sewing threads.

2 Medium-staple cottons This is the largest group comprising well over 50% of cotton and is dominated by the American types. These cottons are about 25 mm or just over 25 mm long, not as fine, soft or strong as the long-staple types but much cheaper and much more plentiful. The bulk of the world's clothing cotton fabrics are made from this quality type.

3 Short-staple cottons This type of cotton is mostly less than 25 mm in staple length and is coarser and harsher than medium cotton. Indian and other Asiatic cottons belong to this group. They are used in cheap fabrics and in fabrics where the lack of softness will give some semblance of warmth of handle. Being associated with the Ethnic look they have fashion appeal.

Adaptability to processing

The short, fine, straight fibres of cotton can be conveniently handled by machines when being converted into yarns. The unique combination of length, fineness and strength possessed by the long-staple cottons enables exceedingly fine even yarns to be spun so that very fine lightweight fabrics may be made which are still strong and durable. Even in the medium qualities reasonably fine fabrics can be produced. This versatility of strength and fineness enables a very wide range of fabric structures in light, medium and heavy weights to be made.

All natural fibres contain impurities which could hinder or prevent spinning into yarns and some form of cleansing is an essential preliminary to preparation for spinning. Cotton, however, can be cleansed sufficiently by mechanical means during preparation for spinning so that the raw fibre can be converted into yarns and fabrics. Final purification is deferred until yarn or fabric stage and it can be conveniently done in bulk without further disturbance of the fibres. This combination of properties means that cotton processing can be done in bulk by machines and yet produce a wide range of fabrics and that the efficiency of the machine processes helps to reduce costs.

Cotton in its raw state is composed of about 90% cellulose and a small amount of wax, it is usually a creamy off-white colour although there are some varieties which are almost brown. The raw fibre is water-repellent, due to the wax content, and can be used for that purpose to some extent. When purified the fibre is pure white, highly absorbent, tasteless and odourless, very smooth and soft, non-irritant and cool to the touch. It is ideal therefore for all clothing uses because the properties just mentioned make it comfortable and it has no objectionable wearing properties. In addition to its purity the fibre is very chemically stable when purified. It can be boiled, or sterilised, without disintegration, it is resistant to damage by alkalis so that severe laundering treatments can be withstood. It has good resistance to heat so that abnormal care in ironing, pressing or drying is not necessary. The absorbency of the pure fibre and its chemical stability give it a good affinity for dyes and its whiteness enables a wide range of colours to be applied. The fibre in its normal state is not lustrous but the chemical treatment known as *mercerisation* can produce a permanent lustre on yarns or fabrics when required. The chemical stability of cotton enables a wide range of finishing treatments to be applied to produce specific performance properties such as water-repellency, flame-resistance, crease-resistance, 'drip-dry' properties, weather and rot resistance, and 'permanent set' properties. Cotton has two main disadvantages:

1 Lack of resilience Though cotton is strong it has very little elasticity and the fibre does not resist deformation so that cotton fabrics tend to crease easily and do not 'give' much in wear. As mentioned above chemical assistance can be given in this respect but usually at the expense of softness and draping properties to some extent.

2 Flammability Cotton burns very readily and once ignited a fabric will carry flame; fabrics with a raised fibrous surface, such as flannelette and winceyette are particularly dangerous in this respect. Chemical treatments which will make cotton fabrics flame-resistant can be applied, and some of these will withstand washing, but again some adverse effect on softness of handle is very difficult to avoid.

The commercial manufacture of childrens' night-wear from untreated cotton fabric (or fabric made from any other inherently flammable fibre) is forbidden by law. The term 'Flammability' is now generally preferred as being less ambiguous than the term 'Inflammability' in describing the tendency of a material to flare.

Versatility

Cotton can be seen as a fibre without outstanding properties of handle and drape but with many useful physical and chemical properties. These structures can be further varied in appearance, handle, colour and performance by virtue of the processing and chemical adaptability of the fibre, and every type of fabric use can be catered for to some extent, by the use of cotton. Different qualities, treatments and processes can produce a fine, light, semi-transparent lawn, a heavy, tough, water-proof tent canvas, a smooth lustrous dress fabric, a colourful corduroy, all from cotton.

Most cotton fabrics need no special care or attention and can be safely washed and do not need elaborate drying or finishing treatments after washing and they are reasonably durable in wear.

Wool

This is the second most widely used natural clothing fibre. It is more specialised and restricted in use than cotton.

Availability

Wool is widely available but the quantity produced is much smaller and more expensive than cotton.

Wool grows on the body of the sheep forming a protective covering known as a *fleece*. Wool is obtained either by shearing the fleece from the live animal, usually once a year, or by pulling the wool, after chemical loosening, from the skin of the dead animal. It can therefore, be either fleece wool or 'skin' or 'slipe' wool. The weight of wool in a fleece varies according to the breed of sheep but the average will be under 4 kg per sheep.

Every country in the world, except desert, has some sheep but the main producing areas are Australia, New Zealand, South Africa, South America, India, China, Russia, USA, Canada and the United Kingdom. The first five countries export large quantities of wool to this country and elsewhere, Russia, USA, Canada use the wool they produce themselves.

Though wool is produced in many countries it is more difficult and more expensive to produce than cotton so that the total quantity is considerably smaller than that of cotton, therefore, the basic price is more than three times that of cotton on average because demand is always high.

Qualities

Again, the many different qualities can be grouped into three basic types:

1 *Merino or botany* These are the best quality types, produced by Merino sheep which are bred entirely for their wool, their meat having small commercial value. These wools are about 50-100 mm in length and are the finest, softest and most crimpy wools. They are the warmest types of wool but they are not the strongest nor the most durable. In general the better the quality the shorter and finer the fibre.

Australia is the largest producer of these types, but South Africa, South America and other countries also produce quantities of these fine wools.

They are used for the best quality wool fabrics where maximum softness and warmth are desired.

2 Cross-bred types This is a very large group of qualities ranging from about 75-200 mm in length. In general these wools are thicker, longer, not as soft, nor as crimpy as the fine wools. As the quality types get longer in length they increase in strength and resilience but diminish in softness and crimpiness. Some types have quite a high lustre and the whole range is much more varied than the Merino group. These wools come from many breeds of sheep, mainly British breeds crossed with Merino sheep, and represent types of sheep deliberately bred both for wool and meat.

Countries such as New Zealand and South America, which have a large frozen-meat industry, are large producers of these types.

They are used for wool fabrics where economy, extra strength, resilience, lustre and durability are more important than fineness and softness.

3 Carpet types These are long coarse wools about 150-400 mm in length. They are strong and resilient but lacking in softness so that they are not suitable for clothing fabrics and as the name implies they are used in carpets where their lustre and superb resilience can be exploited. These types of wools are produced by Asiatic breeds of sheep, which have not been greatly improved by selective breeding and by mountain and hill breeds whose rigorous life does not lead to the production of soft fine wools.

Adaptability to processing

It is immediately apparent that wool is a much longer fibre than cotton, the shortest wools are about the same length as long staple cotton. The wool fibre possesses a feature called *crimp* which is a 'permanent wave'. Fine wools are very crimpy, the crimp becomes less evident as the wool gets coarser and longer in quality. Very fine wool is similar to cotton in length and fineness but is very crimpy whereas cotton fibres are straight. The majority of wool qualities are therefore much thicker and longer than cotton particularly since the relationship between length, fineness and quality in cotton and wool runs in opposite directions.

It will be clear from this that the longer crimpy wool fibres will not be as convenient to handle by machinery as are the shorter fine straight cotton fibres. Wool fibres need a much more complicated series of processes than cotton fibres to convert them into yarns and fabrics. The expense of these processes together with the higher basic price of wool makes wool fabrics considerably more expensive than cotton fabrics.

Each fleece contains wool fibres of varying quality and must be divided by hand, by a skilled sorter, into various quality 'matchings' which are grouped together for separate use. In addition, raw wool contains impurities such as grease, dirt and vegetable matter and any form of preparation is impossible until the fibres have been thoroughly washed. This operation however carefully done tends to tangle the fibres and makes the work of preparing for spinning more difficult. Some of the better quality wools contain 50% of impurities and a chemical treatment is sometimes necessary to eliminate burrs and other vegetable matter tangled in the fibres. The grease is refined and useful cosmetic ingredients, such as Lanolin, are recovered from it.

The spinning of fine wool yarns is difficult because of the crimpy resilient nature of fine wool and the useful limit of fineness is reached much sooner than for cotton because wool has only about one third of the strength of cotton. Fine wool yarns are therefore expensive to produce because of the physical difficulties involved and the strength limitations.

Wool fibres tend to 'felt' or mat together when under the influence of heat, moisture and movement. This can be an inconvenience when not required, as in the washing of wool fibres referred to above, but when brought about deliberately it can produce close compact structures such as felts and thick coating fabrics, or this faculty can be skilfully used by the tailor to create and shape into garments.

Wool is much more sensitive to heat, moisture and chemicals than cotton and processes involving these agencies have to be carried out with great care and control if unwanted felting and other damage is to be avoided. Wool is less sensitive to acid than cotton but it can easily be irreparably damaged by alkalis. This general sensitivity must be borne in mind in all dyeing and finishing processes. Very little natural wool is pure white, and bleaching is difficult owing to its chemical sensitivity in this respect and is only done when absolutely necessary, not as a routine as with cotton. However, the fibre has a good dye affinity and a wide range of colours can be applied with appropriate chemical control.

Versatility

Wool can be seen then as a fibre with outstanding clothing properties of softness, warmth, resilience and drape.

The warmth of fine wool fabrics is produced by the thousands of tiny air pockets trapped in the yarns because the crimpy resilient fibres 'stand away' from each other, and the fibre itself being protein does not transmit heat quickly.

A wool fabric acts as an insulating medium preventing a quick escape of body heat so that a feeling of warmth is engendered. A further aid to comfort is that wool can absorb excess moisture without feeling cold and clammy as cotton does in similar circumstances. Fine wool is usually soft enough not to irritate the skin and individual sensitivity varies, but cross-bred and coarse wools are too rough for reasonable comfort in this respect. Washing processes have to be done with great care if unwanted felting is to be avoided so that a wide range of washable wool fabrics, such as underwear, is not produced although modern treatments have improved wool in this respect and are referred to in a later chapter. The high cost of these garments, relative to cotton, is a further inhibiting factor.

Fine wools possess 'comfort' qualities at their best but they are not the strongest and most durable wools. The lower, or crossbred qualities have superior durability but less softness so that selection of quality or qualities to be used depends on appearance, durability and cost requirements which naturally vary according to purpose.

Variety in structure of fabric and appearance is possible with wool but wool is restricted in versatility because of physical and chemical limitations and its higher cost. The texture of wool fabrics relies on the 'natural' appearance and handle so that a wide range of chemical finishes, as applied to cotton, is not practicable because these would spoil the 'natural' characteristics.

The practical limit of lightweight wool fabrics is reached at about 135 grams per square metre because of the low strength of the fibre, but cotton fabrics weighing less than half this amount can be made.

Wool fabrics are not highly flammable, they do not ignite easily, nor do they carry flame readily. But so that wool fabrics can meet the most recent and severe textile flammability legislation, a special flame-retardent treatment has been developed which can be applied to wool fibre or wool fabric by a simple and inexpensive process. In addition the insulating properties of wool cloths give some measure of heat protection.

Hairs

Certain animals other than sheep produce fibres, with special properties, used in clothing fabrics which are called *hairs* to distinguish them from wool. In general these speciality hairs are more expensive than wool particularly in their better qualities, and they are available in much smaller quantities than wool.

Mohair

This is the name given to the long wavy lustrous hair of the angora goat. It is a white hair up to 250 mm long, smooth and very resilient. It is used in fabrics for its lustre and resilience possessing both these properties in a much more marked degree than wool. As well as being decorative it is a very hard-wearing fibre. It is used in suitings, coatings, dress-goods, knitwear, rugs and upholstery. The best qualities are expensive, and it is a difficult fibre to spin.

Mohair is chiefly produced in Turkey (where the goat originated) and in South Africa.

Cashmere

This is the undercoat hair of the cashmere goat, a domestic animal living in mountainous districts of northern India and other parts of Asia. This animal grows two coats, a fine soft undercoat and a coarse outer coat of long hairs. Every spring the goats moult and shed lumps of hair, or the hair is plucked from the animals when it is loose, and the annual yield per goat is only about 250 gm. The undercoat hairs are about 40-90 mm long and vary in colour from white, grey and tan. The outer coat or beard hairs are longer and coarser and must be separated from the fine hairs.

Cashmere is beautifully soft and lustrous and has a smooth slightly slippery handle and it is used in high quality knitwear, dress-goods, coatings and suitings. Fabrics made from 100% cashmere are expensive so that mixtures with wool are quite common; the addition of wool detracts from the softness according to amount, but improves durability. The characteristic pale fawn colour of some types of cashmere has led to imitation by dyeing botany wool to this colour.

Camel

This hair is produced by the Bactrian (two-humped) camel which is the key transport animal in all desert regions of Central Asia. Like the cashmere goat it is a two-coat animal but instead of moulting completely in spring these animals shed lumps of hair all the year round.

The fine undercoat hairs vary in length from 25-125 mm and they are very soft. The outer beard hairs are up to 375 mm in length and are very coarse and tough. The fine hairs are a characteristic reddish fawn colour and unlike cashmere there is no clear division between them and the outer coat hairs because the coat contains intermediate hairs so that separation is difficult and the qualities of camel hair vary considerably in softness because of this.

This hair is used mainly in high quality coatings, scarves and travelling rugs. The fine soft qualities are expensive, and mixed qualities less so. Mixtures with wool are common, as with cashmere, and the fact that the hair has a distinctive colour makes inferior imitation easy.

Llama and alpaca

These two hairs come from very similar types of animals, which are members of the camel family. They live in the Andean mountain regions of South America, Equador, Peru and Bolivia. The llama is slightly larger than the alpaca and is used as a transport animal in high mountain regions.

These animals produce long hair, up to 300 mm, but the length depends on shearing interval. The hair is mixed in quality and colour, white, grey, fawn brown and even black. In general the hair is softer and less resilient than mohair, but not as soft as camel or cashmere and has a pleasing lustre. It is used in suitings and coatings, blankets and rugs, and makes attractive fabrics which are not as expensive as those made from camel and cashmere hair. Before the wide use of man-made fibres these hairs, particularly alpaca, were used extensively in dress goods and clothing lining fabrics, their lustre and resilience making them very suitable for this purpose and the traditional black or grey alpaca jacket once extensively worn in summer dates from the same era.

Vicuña

This is the finest, softest and most rare animal hair. It is produced by the vicuña, the smallest of the llama species, which lives wild at very high altitudes in the Andes mountains, mainly in Peru. The hair is 25-50 mm long and varies in colour from deep fawn to almost white. Unfortunately the vicuña must be killed to obtain the hair because domestication of these animals has met with limited success. Since 1971 a total ban on vicuña hunting has made supplies of hair completely unobtainable. All importing countries have agreed to support this conservation measure.

It was used mainly in high quality men's coatings and was very expensive more perhaps for its 'status' than its textile value, up to £50 being paid for one metre of coating fabric even in the 1960s.

These special hairs are similar in other general properties to wool, but in general the very soft fine hairs are more sensitive than wool both physically and chemically. Resilient hairs such as mohair, llama and alpaca are in general stronger and more hardwearing than the fine quality wools.

Horse hair

This is long coarse tough hair from the manes and tails of horses. At one time it was a cheap strong material used widely for upholstery, carpets and interlining fabrics but it is now becoming much more scarce and the best qualities are quite expensive. Its fabric use is mainly as weft in interlining fabrics and hair cloths for the tailoring use exploiting the resilience of the hair, but due to the expense and scarcity of new horse hair it is gradually being replaced in general use by special types of man-made fibres.

Rabbit hair

This is the hair of the rabbit detached from the skin. It is a fine, soft, short rather slippery fibre. Only the longer types such as angora rabbit hair are suitable for conventional spinning and then only mixed with wool. It is used in such mixtures for its decorative effect and its lustre and softness in knitwear and dress goods. Larger quantities are used in the manufacture of fine quality millinery felts.

Re-manufactured wool

This is wool which has been used or processed before, as opposed to *virgin wool* or *pure new wool* which is wool being used for the first time.

Wool, and, to some extent, hairs, have the capacity to be used more than once and in view of the cost of new wool, this is a distinct practical advantage which is not shared by any other textile fibre type.

There are three main sources of raw materials for this industry:

1 Shoddy Fibres obtained by shredding 'soft' rags, ie knitted or loosely woven wool fabrics.

2 Mungo Fibres obtained by shredding 'hard' rags, ie closely woven or thick heavily milled fabrics.

3 Noils The shorter fibres of the wool staple extracted during the worsted combing process.

The term *shoddy* will be familiar to many as a word signifying something which looks inferior or poor in quality. The rags used to obtain shoddy and mungo fibres are either old fabrics or new clippings but in reducing the rags to fibres there is considerable fibre damage and breakage. These fibres then are short, and vary considerably in thickness and quality and lack the full qualities of resilience and softness which new wool possesses. Noils are better in that the fibres are merely shorter than average and not damaged, but they are not fully representative of the quality of wool from which they were extracted.

Due to the shortness of shoddy and mungo fibres they would be difficult to hold securely in a yarn and would easily be rubbed out in use so that the fabric would gradually disintegrate in wear. It is easy to see therefore how the term 'shoddy' came to represent something poor in quality.

These fibres are mostly blended with new wool in order to prevent rapid loss of fibres. In this use they are a valuable contribution to the textile industry because if they are skilfully used, attractive medium and low priced woollen fabrics can be made which have sufficient durability, particularly for fashion garments. Fabrics so made are not obviously inferior and at the present state of legislature can be labelled 'all wool' in this country. Hair noils can be used as a fibre content in a fabric and labelled as the hair so that the fibre name in itself on a label is no clear guarantee of quality. The United States of America demands clear labelling distinguishing between new, re-used, and re-processed fibres.

The adoption of the 'Woolmark' is a step in that direction as far as this country is concerned, but ambiguity still exists.

Whereas the Woolmark symbol is used to identify products made 'in pure new wool', a licensed quality mark carefully controlled by wool growers, an additional symbol the Woolblendmark was recently introduced to certify that selected blends of wool and other fibres, usually polyester, contain at least 60% wool and meet specified performance standards. This acknowledges that the use of synthetics improves the mechanical performance of some lightweight wool fabrics for certain end uses such as trousers, because high tensile strength and tear strength are not always obtainable in lightweight wool. The bulk of Woolblendmark fabrics are in the range of 200-300 gm per sq metre.

Flax (linen)

Flax is the name of the fibre from which linen fabrics are made. Although it would appear that flax has been used by man for textiles far longer than cotton, this fibre is more restricted and specialised in use, does not have the versatility of cotton and is a more expensive fibre because of the difficulties of processing, also because of its rarity value. It is, however, one of nature's luxury fibres.

Availability

Flax is a bast fibre, being obtained from the stalks of the linen plant which can be grown in many parts of the world in almost any climate. The fibres are loosened from the stalk by a process known as *retting*, the immersion of bundles of stalks in slow-moving water or, more likely today, laid on the ground to allow bacteria in the soil and the natural elements including dew to rot and disintegrate the woody core, helping to separate the fibres. The latest development is to spray the plant with a chemical which removes moisture, causing the core to crumble. Then after retting the bundles are dried and *scutching* takes place. This is a mechanical beating or breaking process whereby the woody parts of the stalks are broken, leaving the long bundles of fibres intact.

The main flax-producing areas are: Russia and other eastern European countries: France, Belgium and the Netherlands.

Adaptability to processing

Flax fibres, formed of bundles of cells cemented together, are very long, up to 900 mm in length. They are much longer and coarser than cotton fibres and their thickness is irregular. Preparation of the fibres consists of splitting the bundles of fibres, as obtained from the stalks, into individual long fibres and removing waste and broken fibres. Yarns produced from the long fibres are known as *line* and those produced from the shorter irregular and broken fibres are *tow*.

It will be obvious that preparation of these long fibres is much more involved than the processing of the short fine fibres of cotton. Yarns spun from flax tend to be uneven because of the length and variable thickness of the fibres. A special technique of spinning has to be used for the yarns, whereby the fibre cells are loosened so that the yarn can be drawn out to the requisite fineness, because it is impossible to draw out the long fibres in their entirety. Recent processing of linen can alter the molecular structure of the fibres which enables them to be purified, bleached, crimped and cut to staple lengths ready for blending as spun yarns with other fibres such as wool, cotton, polyester or acrylic. But the traditional method of bleaching the yarn or finished fabric rather than the fibres is in greater use worldwide.

Flax is a cellulosic fibre, as is cotton, but it has a higher wax content which, together with a higher degree of crystallinity of the fibre, gives this distinctive lustre associated with linen. Purification of the fibre requires a plurality of treatments which make a more expensive process than cotton. Fabric structures are limited by the degree of fineness and inextensibility of the fibre which in turn determine the fineness of the yarn. It is not possible to spin it as finely as cotton yarn. These and other processing difficulties prevent the production of a wide range of structures at low prices.

Versatility

In view of the processing difficulties already mentioned, the versatility of flax is limited. The natural lustre of flax is developed and exploited in linen damask fabrics used for table wear. The beauty and natural lustre of these fabrics is well known and appreciated but their use has declined because they require skilled treatment after washing to preserve their appearance and the tendency is now to use 'easy-care' materials which are less expensive to look after.

The unevenness of linen yarn is an attractive textural feature in dress fabrics, coupled with the lustre of the fibre. The strength and durability of the fibre make the fabrics an attractive proposition. These features of appearance can be simulated by man-made fibres more cheaply, although without the strength and durability. The high strength of flax made it suitable for industrial uses in strong threads and twines and heavy canvases and tarpaulins. Stronger, lighter, man-made fibre products compete with flax in these uses.

It would appear from all this that though flax is an excellent fibre it has difficulty in competing with other textile materials in cost, convenience and easy-care performance, although many of its properties are infinitely superior. For instance, whereas most fibres become weaker when wet, linen becomes 20% stronger. It is highly absorbent but disperses the moisture into the atmosphere again, and does not absorb body odours. It is therefore a very comfortable fabric in tropical climates.

Silk

If textile fibres were only studied from a statistical point of view silk would be hardly worth a mention because only a relatively small amount is produced. However, as a textile fibre it occupies a unique position because no other fibre possesses such a combination of beauty and strength.

Silk is a fibre traditionally associated with rank or wealth because it has always been expensive and scarce so that as a clothing fibre it was a status symbol.

Silk is the only natural filament used for textile purposes and it is produced by the silk-worm, the caterpillar of a moth, in the form of two very fine filaments coated with gum. With this twin filament the caterpillar produces a protective casing known as a cocoon around itself before the chrysalis stage of its life.

Inside this casing it would normally change into a moth and emerge when the change had been completed.

Silk filaments are obtained by unwinding the cocoons in groups of six to eight at a time and reeling the resultant fine thread, after the silk-worms have been stifled by steam. This is a tedious operation requiring much skill, because to obtain a regular even thread the beginning and end parts have to be discarded, so that although a cocoon can contain about 3000 m of filament the amount of 'first quality' filament can be less than 1000 m.

The bulk of silk produced is cultivated, ie the silk-worms are reared on farms and cared for at every stage of development as carefully as any other animals. Production of silk requires a good supply of cheap skilled labour as well as a suitable climate so that very few countries can produce the fibre efficiently. China and Japan produce most of the world's cultivated silk; southern France, Italy and parts of Asia produce small amounts. Cultivation and care ensures the production of regular even filaments.

In addition there are *wild silks* which are produced in India, China and Japan, by undomesticated varieties of silk-worm. In general these types are coarser and more uneven than cultivated silk and produce fabric types such as *Shantung silk* where the unevenness of texture is a desired characteristic.

Waste filament from all stages of production is converted into *spun silk*, ie lengths of filament spun as staple fibres. This type of material lacks the lustre, fineness and general character of filament silk.

Silk is a strong fibre, having slightly less strength than cotton. It is,

36

in addition, an elastic and resilient fibre similar to wool but not quite as good. This combination of strength and elasticity was unique in textile fibres until certain man-made fibres were developed.

This combination of properties, together with fineness, high lustre, softness and superb drape enables silk to be converted into many beautiful types of fabrics, varying from delicate chiffons to beautiful heavy brocades. The fineness, regularity, strength and elasticity of silk make it suitable for fine screens for printing and sifting purposes and parachute fabrics. All these fabrics require careful maintenance because being an animal fibre silk has similar chemical sensitivity to wool and the fine delicate nature and high cost of most silk fabrics make extreme care in handling essential. Difficulties in production and processing have always meant high costs and limited production, so that it is understandable that for centuries Man dreamed of producing 'artificial silk' in order to be able to produce large quantities of this expensive fibre easily and cheaply. It was the partial realisation of this dream which led to the foundation of the man-made fibres industry.

III Foundations of fabrics: man-made fibres

Development

The man-made fibres industry developed from attempts to make 'artificial silk'. The beauty, scarcity and costliness of silk made the possibility of a man-made substitute attractive and potentially rewarding. Over centuries of observation, the apparent simplicity of the operation of the silk-worm seemed simple enough. The secretions which the silk-worm used seemed to be only a form of gum which when squeezed through a small hole dried in the air to produce a fine beautiful filament.

Very little practical progress appears to have been made towards this end until the latter part of the nineteenth century when knowledge of textile chemistry was rapidly advancing in European countries and the first filaments of artificial silk were produced in the late 1880s.

The apparent simplicity with which the silk-worm changes the cellulose of mulberry leaves into a protein gum which hardens after extrusion into silk hides a complex chemical process which even now cannot be duplicated by man. The first artificial silk filaments were based on cellulose, which was not radically changed in the process, and although lustrous filaments were produced which bore a superficial similarity to silk they had little of the warmth, resilience and beauty of handle of silk because they were still basically cellulose. However, the manufacture of 'artificial silk' persisted and by the beginning of this century it was commercially established, in spite of its obvious inferiority to silk, and constant efforts to improve the product and make it more like silk were made for twenty years or more.

Gradually it was realised that a more successful future lay in the development of these types of materials as textile fibres in their own right and not as inferior copies of silk. During the 1920s work was started in the deliberate use of man-made staple fibres; ie filaments cut into designated staple lengths. The term *rayon* was devised at this time to give a separate identity to these fibres and with the awakening of general textile interest in them the man-made fibres industry came into being and the term 'artificial silk' began to become, as it is now, obsolete.

The discovery of the first synthetic man-made fibre, *nylon,* during the late 1930s was a major break-through and the further types of synthetic fibres which followed closely after increased the importance of this expanding industry.

Once the conception of slavish imitation or cheap substitute has been dispelled man-made fibres can be seen to possess many economic and technical advantages.

In the previous chapter it was emphasised that the production of natural fibres cannot be completely controlled by man insofar as quantity and quality are concerned. Therefore from year to year quantities of specific qualities vary and this tends to cause price fluctuations according to variations in demand which cannot be foreseen until the fibres have been produced and, normally, production takes place once a year.

Man-made fibres are produced in factories, which need not be a great distance from textile manufacturing areas; specific qualities can be produced deliberately and quickly in accordance with demand. Filaments can be produced as fine or as thick as required, staple lengths can be cut exactly to order. Fibres can be produced with high lustre, with reduced lustre, or completely dull, as required. Impurities are eliminated during manufacture so that filament or staple is completely ready to use without purification. Most of the fibres are pure white, or colourless when produced, but if necessary colour can be incorporated in manufacture. Research and development in all types goes on ceaselessly so that many types of man-made fibre can be 'tailor-made' for specific purposes. At one time research was directed towards the discovery of the ideal all-purpose 'wonder fibre' and the tone of some of the publicity on nylon in its early days indicated that the 'wonder fibre' had been discovered! However, research and development is now concentrated on the improvement for existing types and the development of different varieties of existing types for specific purposes.

The control of quality and quantity that can be exercised in established man-made fibres tends to keep prices steady, improvements in production efficiency also assist in this direction. Man-made fibres vary in price, they are not all cheap because of the high capital costs of the complex equipment necessary to produce them, synthetic fibres in particular, but the prices do not fluctuate wildly and once production expands the price of an expensive fibre is often reduced. As the production of man-made fibres is industrial and not agricultural, increase in production can be rapidly achieved by acquiring more factory space. This does not require large areas of land and does not conflict with food production. For these reasons the man-made fibres industry is better able to expand with the growing textile needs of the world.

Classification

Man-made fibres are products of chemical engineering and to understand the differences between them the basic types must be recognised.

There are three main categories of fibres:

1 Regenerated fibres These are fibres made from natural fibre-forming materials such as cellulose and certain protein materials which have been chemically shaped by man into filament form. The old artificial silks were fibres of this type.

2 Synthetic fibres These are fibres made from substances which neither suggest fibres nor which form fibres in nature; eg coal and petroleum (gasolene).

These are two main types of man-made fibres and they are initially produced as filaments but are also used as staple fibre, in fact some are used only in staple form, and the use of staple in total exceeds the use of filament.

CELLULOSE

Standard viscose
Filament
Staple

Modified viscose
High-tenacity types:
Filament
Staple
Chemically crimped types:
Filament
Staple
Modal (high wet modulus) types:
Staple only
Hollow staple fibre

Cuprammonium
Filament
Staple

Acetate
Secondary acetate:
Filament
Staple
Latent crimp filament

Triacetate
Filament
Staple

8 Regenerated man-made fibres

In the case of each fibre in both categories a spinning liquid is prepared either in the form of a solution, or by melting a solid thermoplastic material. The liquid is then extruded through fine holes in a 'jet' or 'spinneret'. This is a mechanical copy of the silkworm's spinning glands but whereas the silkworm can only produce two filaments a man-made 'jet' can produce as many filaments as required, from a single one to a few thousand.

The thin streams of spinning liquid emerging from the jet holes are hardened into filaments by chemical action, evaporation or cooling, according to type, and then collected in suitable packages.

If staple fibre is required a rope of filaments is cut into the required lengths mechanically.

3 Miscellaneous types These are fibres made from substances such as metal and glass. Both these materials have been used by man for a long time in forms other than textile fibres. Their malleable and ductile nature suggested textile fibre use long ago but cost and technical difficulties hindered wide use. Modern developments in converting both these materials into textile fabrics have overcome the difficulties sufficiently to ensure modest regular use for household items eg curtains.

Regenerated fibres: properties and uses

Standard viscose

This is the modern form of one of the earliest types of artificial silk. The name 'viscose' was derived from the word *viscous* referring to the sticky spinning solution, looking like clear honey. The name *rayon* was the first generic term devised to replace 'artificial silk' but is now going out of use, being replaced by *viscose* as shown in figure 8.

It is produced in a wide range of filament thicknesses ranging from the fineness of natural silk to the thickness of coarse wool or hair. It is produced as continuous filament yarns, or in a wide range of staple lengths. Shaped filaments such as flat or 'straw' filaments can be produced for special purposes or decorative effects.

Ordinary viscose is reasonably strong, between wool and cotton when dry, and it has reasonable elasticity under moderate stress. When wet, however, it loses about half its strength and can easily be over-stretched, so that great care is necessary in handling wet fabrics. Being made from regenerated cellulose it is not a resilient fibre and fabrics tend to be rather limp in handle and crease easily, so that chemical assistance in the form of a crease-resist finish is essential for most viscose fabrics. This can give them some stiffness of drape and hardness of handle and is a question of compromise between drape, handle and crease-resistance required.

The lustre can be controlled during manufacture enabling smooth lustrous fabrics to be made from filament, or lustreless and more textured forms of fabric to be made from staple fibre. Some crimp can be imparted to staple fibres to assist texture and to produce fabrics with a fibrous 'lofty' handle similar in superficial appearance to wool. The variety of staple available enables a wide range of different types of fabric to be produced.

The coarse denier long staple fibres are used on a worsted spinning system, through a modified 'carding' process, blended with polyester, to weave fabrics with traditional suiting patterns such as twills, barathea, hopsack and herringbone. Lighter fabrics are also made from semi-worsted spun yarns, in particular the linen-look fabrics, with the yarns slubbed. Slub yarns are also used extensively in furnishing fabrics. The shorter, finer fibres are spun by the cotton system for blouse and dress fabrics.

Viscose, being a highly absorbent fibre, is suitable for all clothing and other uses requiring this property. It has similar dye affinity to cotton but it has not the same physical strength, durability and chemical stability, so that all processes requiring the use of heat, moisture and chemical substances have to be much more carefully controlled. Viscose, like cotton, is inherently flammable, but can be 'internally' processed with flame retardent additives which will not deteriorate in washing or wearing.

Viscose is sufficiently adaptable to processing and treatments to result in many fabric variations, mainly reasonably priced, for all types of clothing, not as a substitute for cotton or wool but as a useful alternative. It is also the main fibre used for lining men's suits and coats.

It is also widely used, in staple form, blended with various other fibres, both natural and man-made, but this special aspect of fibre use will be referred to later in more detail.

Modified fibres

Chemical crimp

As has been already mentioned in the previous chapter, the crimp in wool is an important textural feature conferring warmth and loftiness of handle to fabrics. When the uses of viscose in the form of staple fibre were being developed the desirability of imparting crimp to the otherwise straight fibres was felt to be necessary if versatility in textures was to be achieved. Various methods of crimping the fibres after manufacture were tried and some were moderately successful, but no successful method of giving permanent crimp was discovered until a way was found of crimping the fibres deeply and permanently during manufacture so that the crimp was actually built-in and not imposed afterwards.

When staple fibres of this type are spun into a yarn, either alone or blended with some other fibre such as polyester, a bulky warm handling fabric is produced with something of a wool-like texture. This texture is diminished when blended with a straighter colder synthetic fibre but the bulky effect is not reduced in wear because the crimp is permanent. The fibre is otherwise similar to ordinary viscose staple but the crimp improves fabric handle and appearance.

Modal

Standard viscose does not compare favourably with cotton in many ways, even though both are made from cellulose. The basic reason why viscose is inferior to cotton in performance is that the cellulose has been degraded during the fibre manufacturing process to the detriment of its physical and chemical properties. In addition to the piece-meal improvement of viscose properties already referred to above, development work in all-round improvement of properties was going on, the main basic research being carried out in Germany, USA and Japan.

This work culminated in the establishment of what were known originally as 'polynosic' types with properties more akin to cotton than any other man-made fibre. In fact if this form of expression was still used these fibres would be known as 'artificial cotton' and there would be more justification for this title than there was for artificial silk.

One of the most significant properties of these fibres is that the tendency to stretch easily when wet has been reduced to compare favourably with the performance of cotton in this respect and this is the main reason why the use of the term 'High Wet Modulus', often abbreviated to HWM, is now preferred. The term 'Modal' has been adopted by the EC as the standard generic term for these fibres. The similarities to cotton mean that whereas ordinary viscose fabrics cannot be processed, dyed and finished like cotton because of inferior physical and chemical properties, this type of fibre can be processed alone, or with cotton, without the modifications necessary for viscose in this respect. In handle and appearance the fibre is similar to a good quality mercerised cotton. The economic value of a man-made fibre which can 'stand-in' for cotton is considerable, because the raw materials to manufacture modal fibres can be imported far more cheaply than cotton. However, there are environmental problems with viscose production.

Hollow viscose fibres

A modified viscose fibre constructed in tubular form produces a softer yet bulkier fibre. It is a fine denier fibre, hot-stretched to improve its tenacity and inflated through its length by the internal generation of carbon dioxide, so increasing its outer diameter and giving it a bulky handle, whilst still remaining light in weight. It is often termed 'high bulk viscose'.

Fabrics knitted or woven from this fibre, spun with staple polyester or cotton, have better 'cover' than standard bulked viscose blends, with better draping properties and fuller handle, more opaque for the same weight. The Courtauld's fibre of this type, named *Viloft*, used for thermal underwear described in chapter IX, is also suitable for soft knitwear, nightwear and sportswear, competing with modal fibres because it produces a softer, more sympathetic handle. The hollow fibre has in fact enabled knitters to use viscose blend yarns which would have been too 'lean' with standard viscose. But it does not have the high wet modulus of modal, still being weak when wet, although in practice it is generally strengthened by polyester to give the garments suitable wash and wear properties.

Cuprammonium

This is the only other type of true rayon manufactured and its use is much smaller than that of viscose. It is not manufactured now in this country but the United States, Germany, Italy and Japan manufacture it and it is used in dress fabrics under such names as *Bemberg* and *Cuprama*. It is very similar to viscose except that the filaments produced are much finer and the lustre is more subdued. This gives better draping properties and a more silk-like appearance and until fibres like nylon came along it was considered to be the best man-made substitute for silk in stockings and underwear fabrics. It has not been developed in versatility in the way viscose rayon has so that it remains a minor fibre.

Cellulose acetate

This fibre was first produced in 1921 and was originally grouped with viscose under the common heading of 'rayon'. By the 1960s it had become the practice to use 'rayon' only for viscose, cuprammonium and modified types but today the collective term 'rayon' is avoided except in very general usage. There are very good reasons for this decision, based on the difference in properties and behaviour between acetate and viscose which make it undesirable and, to some extent, confusing to have them under one collective term.

Cellulose acetate is a completely different chemical compound to viscose except that both have cellulose in common. It is similar in superficial appearance to viscose but it is not quite as strong, nor quite as resistant to abrasion. It has more resilience and a pleasing more silk-like handle. It is acknowledged to be a better artificial silk than viscose, at the same time being less expensive. Fabrics made from it need less chemical crease-resist assistance. It is a much less absorbent fibre than viscose and is therefore not suitable for clothing and other uses which demand quick absorbency.

It is a thermoplastic fibre actually melting at about 230°C. At temperatures lower than actual melting point the fibres soften and can be damaged so that great care must be taken in processes which involve heat and pressure, such as ironing.

It is very similar to viscose in behaviour to heat and moisture; reasonable care in handling and temperatures well under boiling are necessary. As the fibre does not absorb or swell greatly when wet fabrics are more dimensionally stable to washing than those of viscose.

Its chemical properties differ from viscose in that it is sensitive to certain solvents, notably acetone which dissolves it very quickly. Its dye affinity is completely different from that of viscose and cotton, and this meant that special dyes, known as *disperse dyes*, had to be developed for this fibre.

These differences in properties mean that cellulose acetate cannot be as widely used as viscose because they reduce its versatility. It is used extensively for blouse and dress fabrics in both staple and filament forms and in woven and knitted structures. It has not been widely modified like viscose although high tenacity types can be made and special shaped and uneven filaments are made for novelty effects in dress fabrics. Its pleasing handle and lustre make it suitable for a wide range of clothing lining fabrics, but like viscose its lustre can be reduced or removed if required.

Like viscose it is flammable and it melts and drips as it burns, but special flame-resist types have been developed for furnishing use. Acetate has no natural crimp but filament yarn can be textured to improve the bulk of fabrics.

Cellulose triacetate

This fibre appeared during the 1950s but in actual fact it was originally made as early as 1914, before cellulose acetate, but at that time there were insoluble technical difficulties which prevented any commercial success. The present commercial success of the fibre is due to technological advances which have made production and processing commercially feasible.

The fibre is in most respects similar to cellulose acetate but it has two important differences which justify its use.

Firstly, although it is thermoplastic it is more resistant to heat than acetate, melting at approximately 300°C.

Secondly it can be 'heat-set' like a synthetic fibre by subjecting it to a heat of about 195°C. When it has been heat-set its absorbency is very low and it exhibits 'drip-dry' properties like synthetic fibres.

It is used for dress fabrics because in its 'heat-set' form it behaves like a synthetic fibre but it is considerably cheaper than most synthetics, so that reasonably low priced permanently pleated fabrics can be made from it.

Regenerated protein fibres

At various times these fibres have been made from the protein of peanuts, maize, soya beans and milk. They all possessed wool-like characteristics of softness, warmth and resilience but it has not yet been found possible to produce a fibre of this type sufficiently strong to be used alone. These fibres are slightly weaker than wool when dry but when wet the strength is almost negligible. These fibres are only suitable for blending with stronger fibres and they have had some success in blends with viscose or cotton, to give some warmth and softness to the fabric, and in blends with cross-bred wool to give softness. Very little of this type of fibre has been manufactured in bulk.

Synthetic fibres: properties and uses

The main types in clothing use are nylon (polyamide), polyester, acrylic, modacrylic, elastane, polypropylene, polyolefin, chlorofibre and aramid. They are completely synthetic fibre-forming substances.

It was discovered during research that natural fibres are made up of long, thin, complicated molecules of cellulose, or protein as the case may be, and that the long thin fibre shape results from the long thin shape of the molecules of which it is composed. These complicated molecules are called *polymers*, or *long chain polymers* to be more precise. When a natural substance such as cellulose is regenerated into viscose rayon the long chain polymers of cellulose are broken into shorter chains by the chemical process involved. They will still form fibres, but as is demonstrated by comparing the physical chemical properties of viscose rayon and cotton, the regenerated material is inferior because of the 'breaking down' of the long chains.

The discovery of the first synthetic fibre, nylon, arose out of research work carried out by a team of scientists, working for the American firm of Du Pont, led by Dr Wallace Carruthers, and their work started in 1928. It was known by this time that man could make these large complicated molecules which formed into synthetic substances, but no-one knew what to do with them because they were quite different from the usual chemical product in behaviour and properties, many of them could not be melted or dissolved. Carruthers and his team embarked on research mainly to find out more about these synthetic polymers and to investigate the possibility of using some of them.

The discovery of nylon came when it was proved that a certain type of synthetic long-chain polymer when melted could be formed into fibres. After a tremendous amount of development work nylon was announced as a commercial fibre at the end of the 1930s. Once the technique was understood it became possible to produce other different types of long-chain polymer, and it was obvious that man was now independent of natural fibre forming substances and that far from having to

accept 'broken-down' substances he could now make very long polymers which could form very strong fibres. A further advantage of this
type of process was that a wide variety of raw materials could be used,
since no fibre-forming properties were necessary in them, but for commercial convenience oil by-products and coal are the main sources
because these substances are plentiful.

Nylon

This name is now accepted as a generic or collective term covering a
'family' of fibre-forming polyamides. The two most important types are
Nylon 66 and *Nylon 6*, as far as clothing is concerned. The numbers
relate to the number of carbon atoms in the basic compounds which
form the polymer. Nylon 66 is made from two substances, adipic acid
and hexamethylene diamine, each of which has six carbon atoms. Nylon
6 is made from one substance, caprolactam, which has six carbon atoms.
These basic substances are made by complicated chemical processes
from coal-tar, or from oil products. Oil is by far the most widely used
source of nylon and other synthetic fibres.

As the first synthetic fibre Nylon 66 exhibited some unusual properties which distinguished it from all other fibres both natural and
man-made which existed at that time.

Firstly it combined strength, elasticity and toughness in a much
higher degree than any previous fibre, exceeding silk in all of these
respects and in sheer strength better than any of the fibres used for clothing at that time. In addition the fineness of filament and degree of lustre
were controllable in the same manner as other man-made fibres. This
meant that very fine filaments could be produced which were still very
strong, so that it had an excellent potential for very fine and light structures.

Secondly, although the fibre was thermoplastic and would melt at
250°C, it could be 'permanently set' by subjecting it to appropriate heat
treatment.

The basic idea of 'setting' a fabric was not in itself new, the pressing
of pleats and creases into wool fabrics by means of heat and pressure is a
'setting' process, but it is well-known that this 'set' is only temporary
and needs renewing from time to time. When nylon fabrics are pleated
or creased at temperatures above 100°C the internal structure of the
fibres is changed so that the crease or pleat is 'locked' in the fibres and
remains for the life of the garment. This technique was and is used to set
the shape of ladies' stockings — which were the first items of clothing
to be made from nylon, and it was found that the losing of shape in wear,
a common stocking fault at that time, was prevented. A 'set' imposed by
heat will remain so long as the temperature of setting is not approached
or exceeded in use. Nylon can be set in boiling water, or in steam, but as

these temperatures can be inadvertently approached in normal use and treatment the present-day method is to set at higher temperatures, under strict control, in the range of 150°C to 180°C. Fabric shrinkage in washing can also be prevented by 'setting' and the crease resistance improved. Very hot or boiling water will not harm 'set' nylon but temperatures are not allowed to get too high for fear of 'setting' unwanted creases in the fabric.

Thirdly, nylon had a very low moisture absorption capacity, much lower than any existing fibre, even cellulose acetate. This meant that when fabrics were washed they did not absorb large quantities of moisture which required a long drying period. The quick drying properties of nylon gave rise to the now common term *drip-dry*, which is rather a vague expression but is taken to mean a fabric which if left to hang in a wet state will dry in a few hours.

These unusual properties together with the good physical properties of strength and resilience, and the excellent chemical properties of the fibre gave an initial impression that here at last was the 'wonder fibre' which would supersede all others.

Nylon was not available for wide-scale civilian use until after the Second World War; its superiority and similarity to silk in physical properties had meant that it was confined to military uses for the war period, with the exception of relatively small quantities of ladies' stockings which were regarded as almost miraculous in their wear properties. However, when nylon burst on to a fabric-hungry civilian market it was tried in every conceivable form of fabric structure.

It was then apparent that this was no all-purpose fibre and that its unusual properties created some unusual problems.

Firstly, the handle of ordinary nylon is not one of its best features, the glassy synthetic appearance and rather 'soapy' handle of filament fabrics proved to be rather unattractive once the novelty had worn off. Closely woven fabrics proved to be very uncomfortable to wear because the lack of absorbency of the fibre prevented ventilation of body moisture. Fine fabrics tended to be translucent—a feature not always appropriate — and opacity was not always possible without undue density, which added to discomfort. The lack of absorbency also posed dyeing problems which took a long time to overcome.

The thermoplastic nature of the fibre made it sensitive to heat, in much the same way as cellulose acetate but with the added hazard of unwanted creases and crinkles being set into fabrics and not removable by ironing.

It was found also in making-up into clothing that nylon fabrics, and blends containing a high proportion of nylon, could not be manipulated and shaped by the use of shrinking techniques, and different methods of pattern cutting and styling had to be evolved to overcome these difficulties.

Nylon is quick to develop static electricity. All textile fibres develop it to some extent but until synthetic fibres came along users of fabrics rarely noticed this. The tendency of fabrics to cling to the body, and the speed of soiling because of electrical attraction of dirt particles are aspects of static electricity which are soon observed by the user; nylon and other synthetic fibres can be troublesome in this respect.

However, permanent anti-stat components are now being added during polymerization to several branded nylon fibres. There are also effective anti-stat finishes for polyester and nylon, although not as durable (p.152).

The warp-knitted structure was found to be very suitable for the manufacture of fine open nylon fabrics, which soon became the most common form of lingerie material. Methods of 'texturing' and 'bulking' of yarns enabled opaque and reasonably comfortable fabrics to be produced on a wide scale, particularly in knitted structures. The easy-care properties of nylon—its drip-dry properties, crease-resistance and durability have revolutionised the attitude of users in general to textile fabrics to such an extent that the natural fibres have had to develop 'easy-care' properties in order to compete successfully with nylon and other synthetics.

Nylon 6 is very similar in general properties to nylon 66, it is claimed that it is softer in handle than 66 and that it stays white and does not go yellow in the way that white nylon 66 sometimes does. It has a lower melting point (about 215°C) than nylon 66, but in spite of this, better stability to heat and easier dyeing is claimed.

Ordinary nylon filaments are circular in cross-section which does not help the handle. Different shapes of filament have been produced notably those with a rounded triangular cross-section. These fibres have been found to have a firmer and more pleasant handle when used in fabrics. The so-called *glitter nylon* is a variation of this technique whereby a trilobal shape of filament produces a higher degree of internal reflections in the fibres causing them to 'sparkle' (9) .

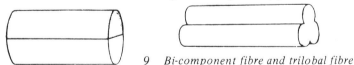

9   Bi-component fibre and trilobal fibre

Special high-tenacity types of nylon have been developed for industrial uses such as tyre cords, ropes, transmission belts and many other uses where high strength and toughness are required.

A development in nylon has been the bi-component fibre in which each fibre is made from two forms of the nylon polymer so that each fibre is composed of approximately half conventional material and the other half modified polymer joined lengthwise as in the diagram 10a. In wet treatments of fabric during finishing the modified polymer portion shrinks more than the conventional portion and the resulting stresses cause the fibres to crimp and produce bulk and softer texture.

Polyester fibres

This class of fibre was discovered in 1941 but was not in commercial production until the early 1950s. *Terylene* is a British invention developed from work carried out on polyester materials by Dr Carruthers prior to the discovery of nylon. *Dacron* is a polyester fibre similar to Terylene manufactured by Du Pont, who purchased the American patent rights.

In appearance and general properties polyester has many similarities to nylon. It is strong, elastic and tough. It can be heat-set and it has excellent drip-dry properties, being even less absorbent than nylon, and has good chemical properties. It melts at a slightly higher temperature than nylon 66 (about 260°C) but its sensitivity to heat in use is similar.

It is inevitable therefore that polyester should follow similar use-patterns to nylon in clothing, but certain small but significant differences between the two fibres have caused different use-patterns in certain directions to emerge. Polyester has a more pleasant handle and a rather less 'glassy' appearance than nylon — in an ordinary filament state. This has led to the use of polyester staple being preferred to nylon for blending with wool in the now familiar proportions of 55% polyester 45% wool.

Conversely, for ladies' stockings and tights nylon is the accepted better material because it has a lower initial resistance to stretch than polyester and is therefore more comfortable and responsive in wear. In uses where the extra stability given by a higher initial resistance to stretch is desirable, polyester would be preferred.

The high resistance of polyester to degradation by the action of daylight makes it suitable for curtain net and other materials to be used in and out of doors; it is superior to nylon in this respect.

Both polyester and nylon are not regarded as being dangerously flammable. They both melt when ignited and the flame tends to go out when the molten portion drops away. Certain open type structures like fine nets tend to flare and these are usually given an anti-flare finish, but ordinary materials are presumed not to need extra protection. There is, however, a flame-retardant polyester fibre *Trevira CS* which can be used for nightwear when suitably fine yarns are spun. The fibre is produced by Hoechst of West Germany and Teijin of Japan.

A 'sheath-core' type of polyester has been developed by ICI, known as Heterofil. This combination fibre consists of a core fibre with higher melting point, covered by a different polyester type with lower melting point which enables a mass of these fibres to be heat-bonded by surface contact of the sheath material, leaving the core unaffected. (See chapter V, *Non-woven fabrics*.)

50

Acrylic fibres

These fibres take their name from a synthetic long chain polymer substance called *polyacrylonitrile*, and although this substance was known during the time nylon was being developed, the first commerical acrylic fibre was not produced until about 1950. The reason for this delay was the difficulty in finding a suitable solvent for polyacrylonitrile, because although it is to some extent thermoplastic, it cannot be melted and spun in a molten state as can nylon and polyester, and it has to be spun from a solution.

Orlon was the first fibre of this type to be produced, by Du Pont, and when first made it was composed entirely of polyacrylonitrile but processing difficulties, dyeing in particular, were such that it was found necessary to combine a small proportion of another constituent to improve the fibre. Virtually all present-day acrylic fibres contain a small proportion of another substance, the identity of which is usually not disclosed by the manufacturer. The variation of these extra substances, in composition and proportion, causes different response to processes, such as dyeing, between various types of acrylic fibre much greater than with other types of synthetic fibre.

The most significant characteristic of this type of fibre is its handle, particularly when used in staple fibre form. It has a warmer more 'wool-like' handle than nylon and polyester. Staple fibre yarn can be 'bulked' and made to resemble the texture of a wool yarn, so that it is not surprising that most acrylic fibres are used in staple fibre form in knitwear which resembles wool and in woven fabrics of a wool character. This warmth of handle is accompanied by the normal synthetic fibre drip-dry properties, without the felting shrinkage tendencies of ordinary wool knitwear. A disadvantage is the sensitivity of these materials to stretching when in a warm moist condition which demands careful washing temperature control and flat drying. Ironing of these fabrics must be done carefully at a cool setting to avoid distortion and glazing. But some new acrylics have a higher melting point.

This type of fibre cannot be as completely heat-set as can nylon and polyester, but fabrics can be durably pleated. Acrylic fibres, particularly in staple form, do not have the very high strength and toughness of nylon and polyester, their strength and extension behaviour being nearer to that of wool, but, in view of their wool-like texture previously referred to, this is not considered to be a grave disadvantage.

Filament acrylic fibres are stronger and tougher but are not as yet very widely used. Fabrics made from them have an astonishing resistance to exposure to sunlight and weather, particularly useful for furnishing fabrics.

Many different types of staple fibre are made in each individual brand.

These vary somewhat in filament thickness, staple length, handle and dyeing capabilities. They are used either alone, or blended with other fibres in a wide variety of clothing fabrics, knitted and woven, blankets, furnishings, rugs and carpets. The range of types enables manufacturers to select whichever are suitable for the textures and colour effects desired.

Bi-component forms of acrylic fibre are being made, the method of make-up of the fibres being similar to that described for bi-component nylon. Wet treatments cause differential shrinkage and crimp in the fibres thus producing bulk and soft texture, which is particularly suitable for knitwear.

Acrylic fibres are flammable and could be dangerous, burning rapidly and emitting black smoke with gaseous fumes. Burning acrylic polymer melts and drips when tested by BS 5438 for upholstery and curtains. It is used very extensively for knitwear so these garments should be treated with care – kept away from lighted cigarettes.

Modacrylic fibres

These are 'modified' acrylic fibres containing 35% to 85% acrylonitrile (true acrylic fibres contain over 85%).

These fibres are very similar, in general characteristics, to acrylic fibres in that they have a warm handle and bulk well. Their outstanding property is flame resistance and in this respect they are superior to ordinary acrylic fibres. *Dynel* fibres are used in fur fabrics and give no risk of 'flaring' of the pile and *Teklan* is useful for warm textured nightwear fabrics, particularly for children where safety from fire-risk is absolutely essential.

Their washing properties are similar to those for acrylic fibres, but with particular attention to heat because they are even more sensitive than acrylic fibres.

Elastane fibres

All textile fibres possess some stretch, varying from the low stretch of flax and cotton to the high stretch of wool and nylon. Some stretch is essential for comfort and suitability of a fibre for clothing use. Very few fibres stretch more than 50% under any circumstances without breaking, and even then recovery is neither complete nor instantaneous. The high stretch and quick recovery of rubber has been integrated with normal textile use for a long time but the lack of durability of rubber, particularly to washing with synthetic detergents, was always disappointing. Since the power of stretch in a fibre is linked with the shape of the polymers from which it is formed it is not surprising that attempts to make high stretch fibres by modifying the synthetic polymers composing them

52

were made very early in the development of synthetic fibres in general. A form of elastic nylon was made but the fibres were not successful.

Elastane, or spandex fibres as they are called in the United States, are synthetic fibres which stretch 500% to 600% before breaking. They stretch easily and have a high rate of recovery from stretch up to 200%. Their stretch performance is not as good as rubber but they are not as heavy as rubber, and they are more durable in wear and can be washed easily, although the presence of chlorine bleach can cause yellowing and degradation. Elastane consists mainly of segmented polyurethane.

They have been widely used for all types of foundation and support garments, and swimwear, where the stretch capacity can be fully used. They have also been used in conventional fabrics to give stretch properties, but this use will be referred to later.

Special purpose fibres

Polyolefin fibres

Polyethylene and polypropylene come into the polyolefin group, otherwise known simply as olefins. Polyethylene, often termed polythene, is one of the polymers used for adhesives on fusible interlinings and because of its very good performance during washing it is the main adhesive for shirt collars and cuffs, applied either as high density or low density, the former having the greatest resistance to dry cleaning and commercial laundering. It is also used in thin sheet form for transparent bags to protect garments. But it is not produced as a fibre for weaving or knitting clothing textiles, although in coarse high denier filaments it is woven into deck chair canvas and similar hard-wearing fabrics. However, as non-woven fabric made directly from the filaments by the spun-bonded system (see chapter V) under the name *Tyvek* it has become an important type of fabric for hospital and clean air clothing. It can be successfully printed in colourful patterns for promotional garments or the fibre can be coloured during extrusion.

The other polyolefin fibre is polypropylene which to a certain extent has similar properties. Both have low water absorbency, are very strong and have high abrasion resistance. Polypropylene was first developed in 1954 but only came to prominence during the 1970s onwards, possibly because it has the advantage of being a waste by-product of oil rather than a direct product. It was only when the original form of polypropylene, only suitable for insulation panels, was modified by an Italian professor, who received the Nobel Prize for this work, that it was seen to have characteristics suitable for textile fibres. In 1960 the first quantities of staple fibre were put on the commercial market by the Italian company Montedison and by 1971 they had built a special plant to produce the fibre in bulk.

The main end-use for polypropylene textile fibres is in knitted fabrics for sports clothing and thermal clothing which means that as the fibre has virtually a nil moisture regain facility, that is almost total non-absorbency of liquids, the body's water vapour cannot be absorbed by the fabric. Moisture in any form passes through the fabric so that when an absorbent layer is worn over the polypropylene garment, the moisture is 'wicked' away into the absorbent layer and the skin is kept dry, providing the polypropylene is worn next to the skin, as the first layer. In addition to the Italian research the Czechoslovakians have carried out extensive wearing trials with this fibre, using it for items such as babies' nappy liners, relying on the wicking theory outlined above. But more will be said of its use, amongst other fibres, as thermal clothing in chapter IX.

However, there are difficulties in the production of polypropylene, for it cannot be piece dyed as a fabric or as knitted garments. It has to be coloured by the addition of pigments to the polymer before extrusion, so that it is sold virtually as coloured staple fibre in various deniers. The fibre blends well with other fibres such as cotton and wool and it can be crimped without difficulty. It can also be printed on the finished fabric surface but as the softening temperature is comparatively low, ie 150/155°C and the melting point is 170/176°C, pressing of any type is not recommended and therefore transfer printing can only be undertaken at low temperatures which reduce the colour fastness of the prints.

Polypropylene is very light, having low specific gravity, low thermal conductivity, very low moisture regain, good abrasion resistance and non-staining properties. It can be used in tufted, woven or non-woven form. Deep pile garments and, of course, blankets make good use of its low thermal conductivity and lightness. Its resistance to acids and alkalis makes it suitable for workwear. Although its main progress during the 1970s was for carpet backing, its future in clothing is thought to be good, providing it is used for washable garments.

Chlorofibres

Polyvinylchloride, better known as PVC when in film form, is another fibre which does not absorb moisture and has other properties similar to polypropylene. Whereas polypropylene is being developed by Italian and Eastern European countries, the chlorofibres, the generic name for polyvinylchloride fibres, are mainly backed by French interests. Once again the principal clothing use is for thermal wear, which has been established in Britain since the mid 1950s under the brand name *Damart*, consisting of nearly every type of garment from underwear to outer coats. The name of the French fibre from which these garments are produced is *Rhovyl* and its main advantage is the fibre's tendency to generate a negative electro-static charge. It is thought that it creates a barrier of electro-static air which increases and maintains body warmth. Chlorofibres are often blended with other fibres such as acrylic, polyester, nylon or wool and are made into woven and knitted fabrics. Being non-flammable the fibre is also used as the backing for deep pile imitation fur fabrics, to help counteract the flammability danger of acrylic fibre pile, which should contain the non-flammable mod-acrylic at least for the longer guard hairs, to reduce the danger of flaring. The chlorofibre has a very low softening temperature, at 75°C, but the actual melting point is relatively high, at 185°C. In effect this means that the fabrics should never be ironed and all the garments carry warning labels to this effect. They should not be cleaned in perchlorethylene, which is usually applied hot. Cold trichlorethylene, used with care, is normally a satisfactory solvent for the purpose.

Fibre type	Fibre	Softening Point °C	Melting Point °C
Natural	Cotton	nil	nil
	Silk	nil	nil
	Wool	nil	nil
	Linen	nil	nil
Regenerated	Viscose	nil	nil
	Acetate	190-205	260
	Triacetate	200-240	300
Synthetic	Acrylic	190-290	Decomposes
	Polyamide (Nylon 6)	160-195	215-220
	Polyamide (Nylon 66)	230-240	250
	Polyester	230-240	250-260
	Polyester (*Kodel*)	220	290-295
	Polyethylene	80-120	110-135
	Polypropylene	140-150	160-17 0
	Polyurethane	175	200-230
	Polyvinylchloride	60-80	180-210

10 Thermal sensitivity of fibres

Aramid fibres

The term 'aramid' was adopted as a generic name in the USA in 1974 to describe a new class of high strength fibres which were chemically termed aromatic polyamides, quite different from the more standard polyamides which include the better known nylon 6 and 66. Within the aramid category is Du Pont's fibre *Nomex* which is specially resistant to high temperatures. It consists of four basic elements—carbon, hydrogen, nitrogen and oxygen. Known at first in 1963 as HT-1, it was immediately used by the clothing industry for ironing board covers and the 'cladding' of high temperature presses, despite its high price. However, the major use for which it was developed is protective clothing worn by jet fighter pilots, tank crews and other military personnel, also certain industrial uses. Later it was incorporated into the Apollo space suits. Trials by racing car drivers have proved that an assembly of knitted *Nomex* underwear and woven *Nomex* fabric for the outer layer would provide the wearer with 17 seconds protection before skin blistering occurs through burning fuel flames which could reach a temperature of 1370°C.

Nomex starts to char at 378°C, then disintegrates but will not burn in normal atmosphere, ie it will flame with difficulty at about 500°C but this goes out when the flame source is removed. There is no molten polymer to damage the skin as with most synthetics. Tests have proved that the fibre retains 50% of its original strength after a million hours at 200°C.

The fibre is sold as staple fibre for spun yarns and as continuous filament, also in paper form. Its physical properties include high tenacity, high resistance to flexing and abrasion, and resistance to stretching. Although the initial cost of these garments is high they have a longer wear-life than conventional fabrics and can be washed in the usual way. Having a normal clothing handle they are comfortable to wear.

Another aramid fibre is *Kevlar*, this being petroleum based, also developed by Du Pont for industrial uses needing a fabric with extremely high strength and tenacity yet at the same time very light. It has saved many lives in combat zones, in the form of bullet-proof vests, officially known as 'ballistic protective jackets'. This particular fabric is woven from a coarse yarn, then many layers are superimposed as a composite fabric assembly to resist most low and medium energy bullets and metal fragments. In simpler form it is used for gloves, aprons and overalls because of its resistance to cuts, punctures and abrasion. The fibre is flame resistant and self extinguishing, only starting to carbonise at 425°C; it has low thermal conductivity. Woven *Kevlar* is immersed in strong plastic, used to re-inforce helmets, shields and even aircraft panels, the combined moulding replacing steel. *Kevlar* is much lighter than steel for the same strength, in this way increasing mobility without loss of protection. Tests have shown that it is three times as stiff and two and a half times as strong as glass, on a weight basis.

Metallic filaments

Decorative threads made from precious metals such as gold and silver were probably the first man-made textile materials. They were very expensive and tended to tarnish on prolonged exposure to air, silver particularly. From time to time cheaper forms of metal were used but these tarnished very quickly and tended to be hard, brittle and uncomfortable in wear.

Modern metallic filaments are available in a wide range of tarnish free glittering colours. Aluminium foil is the metal used and the filaments are composed of a thin strip of foil coated each side with clear plastic film. Colour is incorporated in the adhesive used to secure the film which protects the aluminium from tarnish. The laminated construction gives flexibility and special types of polyester film can produce reasonably high strength, although the strength of normal type metallic filaments is fairly low. The most common brand used in this country is *Lurex*, and several different types of filament are produced under this name.

These filaments are used for their decorative effect in many types of clothing fabrics, woven, knitted and lace. They usually give a glitter effect but a more subtle effect can be obtained by the use of opaque colours which reduce the brightness of the aluminium foil. Their hardness can cause some discomfort in wear unless lined, and care must be taken in dry cleaning to prevent de-lamination by unsuitable solvents.

Blends and mixtures of fibres

The variety of natural and man-made fibres available offers a wide selection of fibres for fabric use. Looking at textile fibres as a whole, certain broad general trends of use emerge which help to simplify the many complications.

Versatile fibres such as cotton and viscose rayon are not expensive; the two fibres vary in properties but in general their value is in all-over usefulness without outstanding features.

Cellulose acetate and triacetate are both somewhat cheaper than cotton and viscose rayon but, as has been explained, their properties restrict their versatility. Their good handle properties and the heat-setting property of triacetate coupled with its lower price as compared with synthetic fibres, make them useful fibres for clothing fabrics.

The remaining natural and man-made fibres are in general more expensive than the fibres referred to above and this, together with their more distinctive properties of handle, appearance or performance, tends to restrict their use versatility. In the case of man-made fibres development of special types of fibres, processes and treatments goes on continually in an attempt to widen the sphere of use of synthetic fibres with the main aim of improving 'natural' qualities of handle and texture. Development of natural fibre use, particularly in cotton and wool, and in viscose rayon, aims at easy-care properties such as are possessed by the synthetic fibres.

The whole field of fibres can be seen to provide variety in price, appearance, handle and performance. Man-made fibres have moved completely out of the artificial silk era and are accepted and used as textile fibres in their own right. At the same time natural and man-made fibres mutually stimulate development which can only be to the eventual advantage of the user.

Fabric requirements vary so widely in cost, appearance, handle and performance that even with the wide range of fibre types and qualities now available it is understandable that mixtures and blends should be used widely.

The terms *mixture* and *blend* are similar in general meaning, but in the present context *mixture* refers to the use of two or more different fibres in a fabric, each fibre being spun into a separate yarn, ie the fabric is composed of a mixture of yarns made from different fibres, eg, a cheap blazer cloth could be made having a cotton warp and a wool weft; it is therefore a mixture of wool and cotton.

The term *blend* in this context refers to a more intimate mixing of fibres before or during spinning so that individual yarns contain two or more different fibres, eg a polyester and wool suiting or dress fabric, where all the yarns are spun from a blend of polyester staple fibre and wool.

There are three basic reasons why mixtures and blends of fibres are used, and the reasons can apply in combination as well as separately.

1 For economy To reduce the cost of a fabric by the use of a cheap fibre mixed or blended with a more expensive fibre.

2 For combination of properties To effect a compromise where no one fibre is ideal by combining two or more fibres each contributing something to the whole.

3 For decorative or colour effect Some fibres have a distinctive appearance, lustre or texture, and fibres vary in their affinity for dye. Fibres can be combined to give certain decorative textural or colour effects arising from the differences referred to. Different coloured yarns of the same type of fibre can be used in fabrics for decorative purposes but this type of colour effect is excluded from consideration at present.

The practice of mixing and blending was firmly established long before man-made fibres were produced, for each of the three reasons set out above.

The practice of combining cotton and wool is old established. Primarily the basic reason is economy, cotton is cheap and strong, wool is more expensive and not very strong, re-manufactured wool is cheaper than new wool but tends to be weaker than new wool because of shortness of fibre. A cotton warp will give added strength and the wool weft will give texture and cover. With this combination a cheap form of wool-type fabric can be made which is actually stronger than if it was made from all wool of the re-manufactured type. Cotton and wool fibres can be blended and the resultant blend made into yarns for economy and the strengthening effect of the cotton. Again, re-manufactured wool is usually used because most new wool qualities and cotton are not compatible in length and would not blend well. Certain high qualities of wool are blended with cotton to make lightweight warm washable fabrics of the 'Viyella' type. This is not a case of 'economy' blending because great care must be taken to select the compatible qualities of wool and cotton. This is 'combination of properties' blending to combine the warmth and comfort of wool with the strength and good washing properties of cotton. Mercerised cotton coloured striping yarns can be incorporated in wool suiting and blazer cloths. When the fabric is dyed the wool dye only affects the wool and leaves the cotton unaffected, so that a range of ground colours can be dyed having the same colour cotton stripings. This is an example of 'colour effect' mixture of fibres. Viscose striping yarns can be used with the same effect because viscose has similar dye affinity to cotton. In fact viscose can substitute for cotton in any of the above examples for the same reason, except that if strength is required a modified viscose would be required.

Blends or mixtures of wool with special hair fibres or with spun silk are usually used to exploit the lustre and the handle of the more expensive fibre, or the wool is used as a measure of economy because hairs and silk are expensive. In the case of very soft hairs like cashmere the wool content makes for some durability, although with some loss of softness.

Where fibres are used for economy, special textural effect or strengthening effect in blends the amount of the 'key' fibre to be used is a question of compromise particularly where its handle is greatly different from the other fibre in the blend.

Generally speaking a quantity of less than 10% of a 'key' fibre in a blend will have little noticeable effect. The effect of increases above 10% depends on the textural and handling differences between the 'key' fibre and its companion, but it is rare that less than 15% of the 'key' fibre will show any marked difference in economy, texture, or strength improvement. Above 20% the handle and appearance of the 'key' fibre begin to be noticeable. In the case of cashmere as a 'key' fibre with wool, this could not be considered in any way undesirable, but where cellulosic fibres like cotton or viscose are 'key' fibres with wool—for economy reasons—this point would have to be closely watched unless economy was to be pursued at the expense of handle.

As the 'key' fibre increases in proportion over 50% it will gradually and increasingly dominate in characteristics until at 90% the consideration set out above regarding 10% 'key' content will be reversed.

Owing to the fact that unstated but 'insignificant' quantities of expensive fibres in a blend can have merely an 'academic' value, certain countries and many large buying organisations insist on correct percentage labelling of blends and mixtures. See chapter IX *Identification: Labelling*.

Nylon and polyester have excellent strength and abrasion resistance and can be used to strengthen wool fabrics. The effect of such blends on the handle of the wool depends on the amount of strengthening fibre used above the minimum requirement mentioned above. If the heat-setting properties of the synthetic fibre are required then at least 50% synthetic fibre content is required and this can affect the appearance and handle of the fabric as pointed out in the note on polyester.

This percentage factor affects nylon, polyester and cellulose triacetate when used for heat-setting properties in combination with fibres which do not possess this property.

Another factor in blending fibres for strength is fibre compatibility in elasticity and extension; because of this factor the resultant strength of a blend is not just a simple proportion sum based on the strength of the fibre types in the blend. If a yarn was made from 50% cotton and 50% nylon staple the strength of the resultant blended yarn would *not* be mid-way between cotton and nylon— it would actually be *lower* than the strength of a cotton yarn of equivalent size because as the two fibres differ greatly in elasticity and extension the cotton breaks before the nylon has taken much of the strain at all.

Viscose rayon and cellulose acetate are used in mixtures and blends for decorative purposes. They have different dye affinities, and also the addition of acetate to viscose helps the handle and the stability of the fabric to washing.

Blends of wool with acrylic fibres are used but not to the same extent as polyester and wool blends. Acrylic fibres and wool blend well together because there is not the amount of difference between them in appearance and handle as there is between wool and nylon or polyester. At the same time since acrylic fibres are not as strong as nylon or polyester the strengthening effect of acrylic fibres in a blend with wool is not as great.

Nylon and polyester are used in mixtures of yarns in fabrics to obtain 'cross-dye' effects arising from their differing dye affinity. This technique of colouring is referred to again in chapter VII.

So far reference has been made to mixtures involving the use of yarns made from different fibres. These yarns can be either in filament or in staple fibre form. Blending of fibres is done in the form of staple during preparation for spinning. At one time it would have been considered unlikely to find a *filament* yarn comprised of a blend of different type filaments. But such a yarn now exists in *Tricelon*, a yarn produced by Courtaulds which is a combination of *Tricel triacetate* filaments and nylon filaments in the same yarn. The idea is to combine the strength and abrasion resistance of nylon with the good handling properties of Tricel, and as the nylon shrinks more than the triacetate in finishing, a bulky handle results.

New fibre generation

Probably the most important development of the 1980s and 90s has been the universal acceptance of the microfibres, a change in construction which has provided a more sympathetic handle, particularly for nylon, also for polyester. The Japanese started the trend with very low decitex polyester fibres, much finer than a human hair and generally finer than pure silk filaments. Originally the microfibres were used for lightweight dress and blouse fabrics with a very soft handle, draping like silk.

Meanwhile, in the early 1980s, ICI Fibres had started research on polyamide 66 and eventually produced a new version named *Tactel,* with a dry cotton-type handle for outerwear and silk handle for lingerie. Quite apart from the low decitex the fibre had been re-engineered by introducing variations into the polymer, changing the extrusion methods and applying different texturising processes. In fact there have been changes in technology right through the production line, involving the throwsters, spinners, weavers, knitters, dyers and finishers. By the late 1980s the original *Tactel* fibres had been expanded into a series of yarns, including *Tactel Micro,* engineered for active sports wear, leisurewear, hosiery and lingerie. The fabrics have a fashionable appearance such as a dry crinkle surface for rainwear and ski anoraks. Sometimes a flat filament warp is combined with a *Tactel* weft yarn.

Parallel with ICI's work on polyamide, the German fibre producer Hoechst had by 1987 re-structured their polyester fibre into microfilament yarns under the brand names *Trevira Finesse* (breathable yet rain repellent) and *Trevira Micronesse* (soft silk-like fabrics). Brand names of principal producers are applied not so much to the fibres as to the several fabrics which can be made from them, required to conform to strict specifications before the trade mark can be used. In some cases this quality control extends through to the finished garment. Microfibre brand names have also been registered by producers Akzo/Enka (*Diolen Micro*), Montefibre (*Zero 4*), Rhone Poulenc (*Meryl and Setila*) and Du Pont (*Micromattique*). These last two companies restructured their nylon fibres, stressing the hard wearing properties whereas the others are promoting polyester microfibres.

By mid 1990 there had been considerable misuse of the term 'micro' by other companies, so to avoid confusing the public the German producers decided the term should be precisely defined. Hoechst led the way with a widely-agreed definition for textile processors, makers-up and retailers which specified 1.0 dtex and finer for polyester microfibres in staple fibre or filament yarn. For unblended filament yarns the optimum economical limit should be 0.5 to 0.6 dtex per filament. In the case of staple fibres mainly used in mixtures, the lower limit is considered to be 0.9 dtex. The most important aspect for monofilament yarns is said to be the number of filaments; in the case of staple fibre blends it is the compatibility and the homogenous result. For comparison it is stated that the finest fibres of wool are about 4 to 6 dtex, cotton 1.5 to 2.5 dtex and silk filament around 1 dtex.

When microfibre fabrics are densely woven they can provide a good degree of water repellency – adequate for most leisure and sports activities – yet are not waterproof. For a real downpour some type of waterproof finish is still required. The finest filament yarn produced in Europe (up to 1992) is Montefibre's *Terital Zero 4*, which consists of a large number of 0.4 dtex filaments. It has various uses from tents for Antarctic explorers to 'oilskins' for sailing crews in the Americas Cup race. The important point is that the body's water vapour and perspiration can pass away from the skin through the fibre filaments whereas raindrops cannot enter. There is also a good windproof factor created by the fabric construction, making the garments suitable for inclement outdoor conditions. They are claimed to be temperature compensating (outside to inside and vice versa) dependent on the dry temperature streams generated by the body and the ambient temperature.

The appearance of the microfibre fabrics can be varied by using bright or dull yarns, with round or trilobal cross sections, and textured variations for both woven and knitted fabrics. The finish can be rubbed or sanded for a doeskin look or given a ciré finish. Clothing made from these fibres – even with a rainproof finish – are softer and more supple than the earlier stiff protective garments which were difficult to use for really active sports. However, there are synthetic (sheet) membranes which are even more water impermeable yet made to be water vapour porous (see page 213). For extra warmth in anoraks, microfibres can be brushed into a fleece for fillings.

Novelty innovations

In recent years Japanese fibre producers have added novelty features to nylon and polyester, calling them 'intelligent fibres', but regarded by some as gimmicks. They contain microscopic capsules which can alter the fibre according to temperature or light; a perfume or even an insect repellent can be released. These novelties have been used for active and spectator sportswear, a market which is growing worldwide. Such innovation can add a 20% to 50% financial bonus in the higher price brackets. For example, fabric colours can change from white when above 23°C to vivid colours when below 14°C. Swimwear, which is subjected to various temperatures within a few minutes, has proved a very successful end-use. However, the fragrance in fibres used for tights, where the perfume is activated by leg movements, withstands only three washes. Other tights contain seaweed essence and vitamin C.

After the 'intelligent fibres' came the 'artificial intelligence fibres' which automatically adjust the garment properties from black to white or vice versa in order to make the wearer feel warmer or cooler according to temperature. Inorganic carbon particles are also being added to warm the body by converting near infra-red radiation from sunlight into thermal energy. All these fibre modifications by Teijin, Toray and Kanebo amongst others are used to compete against Chinese and Western producers; they fetch high prices in Japan and some export markets.

Whilst continually refining the processing techniques, all producers are searching for variations to give improved performance for the more standard fibres. Kanebo and Akzo/Enka have devised anti-bacteria fibres; Kanebo's contains a deodoriser which absorbs perspiration and assists speed of drying. Such fabrics were originally intended for uniforms and workwear. Generally, however, the trend in synthetic fibres has been towards softness and comfort in wear now that fabric performance is already so well established.

Table of comparative fibre properties (overleaf)

Explanatory note This table deals with the general average properties of the main natural and man-made fibres. As exp!ained in chapters II and III, natural fibres are obtained in various qualities which show differences in properties and price, and subsequent yarn and fabric treatments may modify inherent fibre disadvantages. Man-made fibres can be modified in manufacture to some extent to overcome some disadvantages, and some of the modifications have been included.

It is, however, impossible to produce a concise table covering all fibre qualities, modifications and treatments, so that the table is intended as a general guide only and should be used in conjunction with the text and bearing in mind subsequent treatment variation.

Fibre	Length range	Fineness	Strength	Resilience and elasticity	Resistance to abrasion	Absorbency
Cotton	10 mm-55 mm	Fine	Strong	Fair	Good	Very good
Wool	50 mm-400 mm	Fine to coarse	Moderate	Very good	Moderate	Good
Mohair	75 mm 250 mm	Moderately fine to coarse	Moderate	Very good	Moderate	Good
Cashmere	40 mm-90 mm	Fine	Moderate	Very good	Fair	Good
Flax (Linen)	150 mm-900 mm	Moderately fine to coarse	Very strong	Poor Poor	Moderate	Very good
Silk	Filament	Very fine	Strong	Very good	Good	Very good
Standard viscose	Filament and staple as required	Fine to coarse as required	Fairly strong	Moderate	Moderate	Very good
Modified viscose (crimped)	Staple only	Fine	Fairly stong	Moderate to good	Moderate	Very good
Modal	Staple only	Fine	Strong	Fair	Good	Good

Effect of heat	Flammability	General handle characteristics	Main use advantages	Main use disadvantages	Basic cost
Good resistance	Burns readily	Soft, cool to touch	Very versatile fibre	Creases easily, flammable	Moderate
Moderate resistance	Does not burn easily	Soft, warm, resilient	Good handle, drape and tailoring properties	Needs careful treatment: use range limited	Moderately expensive
Moderate resistance	Does not burn easily	Fairly soft, warm, very resilient	Lustre and resilience	Difficult to spin evenly	Expensive
Fair resistance	Does not burn easily	Very soft and warm	Fineness, softness and lustre	Expensive and not very durable	Expensive
Very good resistance	Burns readily	Similar to cotton	Natural lustre and durability	Creases easily, needs special care to preserve appearance	Expensive
Fair resistance	Does not burn easily	Very soft, warm, resilient	Beautiful lustre, handle and drape	Expensive: needs very careful treatment	Very expensive
Moderate resistance	Burns readily	Soft, rather limp, cool to touch	Very versatile	Low wet strength, creases easily, flammable	Moderate
Moderate resistance	Burns readily	Warmer in handle than ordinary rayon	Warmer, deeper texture	Similar to ordinary rayon	Moderate
Moderate resistance	Burns readily	Soft, between rayon and cotton in handle	Good dimensional stability similar to cotton	Creases easily, flammable	Moderate

continued ...

Fibre	Length range	Fineness	Strength	Resilience and elasticity	Resistance to abrasion	Absorbency
Acetate	Filament and staple as required	Fine to coarse as required	Moderate	Moderately good	Fair	Fair
Triacetate	Filament and staple as required	Fine to coarse as required	Moderate	Moderately good	Fair	Low
Polyamides	Filament and staples as required	Fine to coarse as required	Very strong	Very good	Excellent	Very low
Polyesters	Filament and staple as required	Fine to coarse as required	Very strong	Very good	Very good	Negligible
Polyesters (FR)	Filament and staple as required	Fine to coarse as required	Very strong	Very good	Very good	Negligible
Acrylics	Mostly staple	Fine to coarse as required	Fairly strong	Good	Fairly good	Very low
Modacrylics	Filament and staple as required	Fine to coarse as required	Fairly strong	Good	Fairly good	Very low
Elastane	Filament	Fine	Moderate	Excellent	Fairly good	Negligible
Metallic	Flat filament	Coarse	Fair	Fair	Fair	Negligible

Effect of heat	Flamma-bility	General handle characteristics	Main use advantages	Main use disadvantages	Basic cost
Thermo-plastic, cannot be 'set'	Burns and melts	Soft, fairly resilient	Good handle and drape for dress purposes	Heat sensitive, moderately durable	Moderately low
Thermo-plastic *can* be set	Burns and melts	Similar to Acetate	As Acetate, but can be heat-set and is 'drip-dry'	Moderately durable	Moderate
Thermo-plastic *can* be set	Burns and melts	'Classy' and rather 'slithery'	Strong, tough, can be heat-set and is 'drip-dry'	Unabsorbent, uncomfortable in 'close' textures	Moderately expensive
Thermo-plastic *can* be set	Burns and melts	Similar to nylon but not quite as 'glassy'	Similar to nylon	Similar to nylon	Moderately expensive
Thermo-plastic *can* be set	Resists flame	Slightly stiffer than standard	Flame resist nightwear	Not readily available	Higher than standard
Thermo-plastic *can* be set	Burns and melts	Soft and warm and resilient	'Wool-like' in texture	Sensitive to heat and moisture. Tendency to stretch	Moderately expensive
Thermo-plastic	Resists flame	Similar to Acrylic	Flame-resist properties	As Acrylic	Moderately expensive
Thermo-plastic	Resists flame	Rather 'hard' in handle	Excellent stretch and recovery	Sensitive to heat and chlorine (bleach)	Expensive
Thermo-plastic (plastic coating)	Burns and melts (coating)	Rather hard and 'scratchy'	Colour and 'glitter' effect	Not very resilient or comfortable	Moderately expensive

IV Yarns

Basic types of staple fibre yarns

It was shown in chapter I that staple fibres are converted into yarns for the construction of most types of fabrics. This is essential because the limited length of staple fibres necessitates numbers of fibres being twisted together to convert them into a continuous length of yarn. The appearance, strength and texture of the fabric depends on the nature of the fibres and the way in which they have been twisted together to form the yarn.

In chapter II it was stated that natural fibres are produced in 'staples' of varying fibre lengths, and that all fibres contain impurities of some kind which need removal before spinning preparation can take place.

The conditions of collection and transport of natural fibres usually present a tangled haphazard mass of fibres for cleaning and processing. Preparation for spinning consists basically of removing very short and clotted lumps of fibres. The opening out process, called *carding*, first of all converts the mass of fibres into a thin web. The fibres in this web are still pointing in all directions but they are evenly opened out and not in lumps. The web is then converted into a *sliver*, a thick soft rope of fibres, by passing it through a funnel, or it can be divided into strips and the strips rubbed into fine slivers depending on the particular system being used, but the main idea is the conversion of a flat web of fibres into a rope-like form.

The sliver is then drawn out in length and as it becomes finer in diameter twist is inserted by a spindle as the material is being wound on to it. The *drawing* and *twisting* operations are repeated until a yarn of the desired fineness has been spun.

The machines used for spinning perform the same actions as the fingers and spindle of the hand spinner, except that whereas the hand spinner can convert a prepared sliver into the final yarn in one operation the spinning machines usually need several, but machines are far more productive because they work at much higher speeds and make many yarns at the same time.

The haphazard arrangement of the fibres referred to above produces a fibrous yarn because the fibres are not lying all the same way and numerous fibre ends project from the sides of the yarn. When these yarns are made into a fabric the surface of the fabric will be fibrous and not smooth. The haphazard nature of the fibres also prevents them from lying closely packed together so the fibres tend to stand away from each other and produce a 'lofty' texture of yarn because of the air spaces in between the fibres. The degree to which this loftiness and fibrous appearance is visible depends on the type and quality of fibres used. Cotton yarns made this way do not look obviously fibrous and lofty because cotton fibres are very fine, straight and not resilient. Woollen yarns when made this way look very fibrous and lofty because the crimpy resilient fibres of wool emphasise their haphazard arrangement.

If a smoother and more compact type of yarn is required additional preparatory processes are necessary. The sliver of fibres prepared by the carding machine is subjected to a *combing* action. In this process the fibres are deliberately combed straight and parallel, and in addition, the shorter fibres of the staple are removed. This leaves the longer fibres in a more uniform length arrangement and the work of combing them straight is easier.

The combed sliver is then drawn out and spun into yarn. The parallel nature of the fibres enables a much smoother and more compact yarn to be spun, with relatively few fibre ends sticking out. It also enables much finer yarns to be spun because the fibres are more ideally arranged. When these yarns are made into fabric a much smoother surface and a more compact texture is produced.

There are then these basic types of yarn; the fibrous yarn produced from *carded* fibres and the smoother and more compact *combed* yarn. The terms *carded* and *combed* are used to describe these yarn types in the case of cotton but they are called *woollen* and *worsted* when made from wool fibres. Combed cotton yarns and worsted wool yarns are more expensive to produce than carded cotton or woollen yarns. The appearance and textural differences between woollen and worsted are much more obvious than the differences between carded and combed cotton because the crimpy resilient wool fibres lend themselves to the woollen appearance, so that the relatively smooth worsted appearance and texture is in abrupt contrast.

It is easy to see that if a fibrous lofty surfaced fabric is required the obvious choice of yarn will be the carded type, and it is also plain that subsequent processes will be directed towards enhancing and developing this fibrous nature of the yarns. Wool is the logical choice for this type of fabric, but for reasons of cost and variety it cannot be the automatic choice every time, and so this type of appearance can be developed in varying degrees, from other fibres both natural and man-made.

The use-development of man-made fibres in staple form is aimed at producing the variety of texture and appearance which can be obtained by using cotton or wool spun in one or the other of these basic ways. The idea of putting crimp into rayon staple was to produce a loftiness and texture more like that of wool than that of cotton because crimp increases the 'stand-away' effect mentioned earlier. The techniques of 'bulking' and 'texturing' synthetic fibre yarns, described later in this chapter, were also aimed at a more natural or wool-like texture. Man-made staple fibre does not need the same amount of preparation as a natural staple fibre because the impurities and very short and tangled lumps of fibres are not present. In fact, by the latest methods of staple-cutting a rope of filaments can be converted into a sliver of staple fibres without breaking the continuity, and it is not necessary to cut a rope of filaments into loose staple and then card it and process it back into a sliver, although this is sometimes done.

The influence of twist

The idea of twisting staple fibres into a yarn is to force fibre surfaces into contact and thus set up frictional forces which bond the fibres together and produce a yarn which will withstand tension along its length. If a loose thick rope of fibres is twisted it becomes thinner and harder as twist is increased because the twist is forcing the fibres closer together. If an open textured yarn is required the amount of twist put in will be the minimum required to give some strength to the yarn, ie the lower the twist the softer or weaker the yarn will be. If a firm strong yarn is required then more twist will be necessary to obtain compactness and strength. It will be found that in many woven cloths the warp yarns are firm, compact and strong, and the weft yarns are softer twisted and more lofty in texture. The reason for this is that the warp yarns need to be of reasonable strength to withstand weaving tension whereas weft yarns are not subject to great tension. The softer weft yarn acts as a textural 'filling' for the fabric and the warp yarns provide strength. This is possibly why some countries (such as the USA) call weft filling.

There is an optimum amount of twist for any size of yarn at which the maximum yarn strength is developed. If twist is prolonged past this point the yarn becomes harder but not stronger because the stresses set up by continued twisting begin to weaken the fibres in much the same way as a piece of wire can be broken if continually twisted at one point. If a hard crisp texture is required twist above the strength maximum is required. If this is done it will be noticed that hard twisted yarn shows a tendency to kink or 'snarl' unless held under tension. This force is used in very hard twisted, 'crepe' yarns to produce the characteristic crinkled surface of these fabrics.

Direction of twist

It will be noticed that if a bunch of parallel fibres is taken it can be twisted in two directions only, and whichever direction the twist takes

70

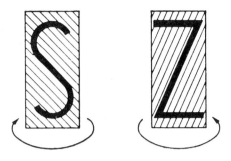

11 Directions of twist

the fibres incline in that direction. These two directions are indicated by letter symbols 'S' and 'Z' (11). In many instances the direction of twist of the yarns has little effect in fabric appearance, but the direction of inclination of the fibres can accentuate certain weave effects and the use of opposing twists in regular sequences in one set of yarns can produce shadow effects by the difference in light reflection in opposing fibre directions. In crepe fabrics opposing twists are used alternately because the two twists 'kink' in opposite directions and so give a more uniform crinkle effect to the fabric.

Folded or 'ply' yarns

The spinning process as already described converts fibres into a 'single' yarn. For reasons of strength and texture or colour effect, it is often necessary to combine yarns together by 'folding' or 'plying'.

It is impossible to spin a 'perfect' yarn from staple fibres in the absolute sense. Every single yarn contains unevenness in some degree because perfect conditions of all the factors involved cannot be produced simultaneously. If two yarns are twisted together it is highly unlikely that the thicker places in each yarn will coincide exactly, there is bound to be some fitting-in of thick and thin places in the two yarns so that two single yarns twisted together will produce a stronger and more even result than one single yarn of the equivalent thickness. A two-fold yarn is more 'balanced' in the twist sense also because two yarns of the same twist are taken and then folded together by being twisted in the *opposite* direction. This produces a balanced supple yarn of good strength development. Worsted yarns are most frequently used in two-fold form because the relatively low strength of wool needs all the strength assistance possible, particularly in fine yarns. For textural reasons it is sometimes necessary to insert doubling twist in the same direction as singles twist. This produces a firm yarn, not as flexible as the ordinary type but useful if a harder texture is required. The folding together of three or more single yarns produces a much rounder combination than two yarns can, as well as a stronger result so that very strong yarns, and yarns required to be round and even such as sewing threads, are produced in this manner. If roundness and evenness is required the three or more yarns are all twisted together in the same direction, but if a particular colour effect is required the folding can be done in two stages, ie two yarns twisted together with 'Z' twist and then a third yarn combined with these two in 'S' twist. This produces a regular mottled colour effect because of the twist differences.

Sewing threads

Sewing threads represent specialist spinning at perhaps its highest level. The 'perfect' sewing thread must be strong, round, even and balanced in twist (ie when allowed to hang slack in a loop it must not twist round itself, or only very slightly). These properties are necessary in order that first of all when the thread is being sewn in it can withstand the sudden strains and tensions to which it is subjected in the sewing machine. In a high speed lock-stitch machine sudden accelerations of thread movement to over fifty miles an hour occur a few thousand times a *minute* so that any kinking due to unbalanced twist, or weakness due to unevenness would cause endless trouble under these conditions. The thread must be even, unobtrusive and durable when the seam has been formed. The skill necessary to produce a wide range of different sizes and types of sewing threads from strong fibres, such as cotton, linen, silk and man-made synthetic fibres, can only be acquired by specialists who produce nothing but sewing threads and allied materials; it would not be either practicable or economic for them to be produced by an ordinary spinner producing a range of normal yarns in addition.

Basically ordinary cotton sewing threads are made from three yarns twisted together—to achieve the roundness and evenness mentioned above. Thicker and heavier sewing threads are made by *cording,* ie, in a 6-cord thread three two-fold yarns are twisted together instead of three single yarns, and so on up to 12-cord. This ensures that evenness and roundness is preserved even in thick threads.

Man-made fibres such as nylon and polyester can be used for sewing threads in either filament or in staple fibre form. Filament yarns (mentioned later in this chapter) can be monofilament or multifilament, plain or textured, or can be *cored* yarns, ie a core of continuous filament surrounded by a covering of spun staple fibres. The core gives strength (nylon or polyester) and the surrounding staple fibres give texture and 'cover' and need not be of the same material as the core. The surrounding staple fibres can also protect the core from the effects of heat developed by friction in high speed sewing.

Fancy yarns

The practice of folding yarns to remove unevenness is the basis of folding of ordinary yarns. This unevenness consists of thick and thin places because staple fibres cannot be so perfectly arranged that exactly the same number and thickness of fibres will be drawn into every part of the yarn length. With the variations of length and thickness found in natural fibres this is understandable, but it still obtains even with man-made staple fibre where length and thickness of individual fibres can be accurately controlled and tangled lumps of fibres are not likely to be present. Certain fibres, however, are extremely difficult to spin in a level manner, due to inherent unevenness in the fibres. Examples of this type of fibre are flax and certain types of wool where the whole staple is used without separation and selection of fibres. Unless extraordinary steps are taken a lumpy uneven yarn is produced from these fibres which communicates its appearance to the fabric. If these slubs, as the thick places are called, are numerous the fabric surface presents an all-over uneven or knobbly surface, the degree depending on the size of the slubs. This type of surface appearance is accepted as being the character of the material, such as is seen in the appearance of a linen fabric, or a tweed and is a useful alternative to plain smoothness. The usefulness is such that these imperfections are deliberately introduced into yarns which would otherwise be smooth and level in order to create this appearance. The slubs can be made as long, and as thick and numerous as required. Fancy yarns are therefore examples of deliberate uneven-ness in many forms in order to produce more interesting textures and colour effects, or to display or bring into prominence distinctive fibres. Fancy yarns combine individual yarns of varying thickness, and by feeding the yarns at different speeds or sporadically, spiral, loop, chain or gimp effects can be produced which add interest to fabric texture and colour, and a very wide variety of fancy yarns is produced by specialists.

Filament yarns

These are constructed either by combining the required number of fila-ments together, as in the silk throwing process, or by producing the required number and thickness of filaments simultaneously in one spin-ning operation, as in man-made fibres. The continuity in length required in a yarn already exists in individual filaments so that yarn construction is merely a matter of grouping the required number of them together by means of a small amount of twist. The average filament yarn is therefore a collection of parallel filaments lying close together and almost straight. This formation is ideal for display of lustre because the fila-ments are almost undistorted and can display their lustre effectively. At the same time the presence of a number of fibre filaments in one yarn contributes to suppleness and 'cover' in the fabric. A pure natural silk yarn provides an excellent example of this arrangement of fibres. Filament yarns are more regular and even than staple fibre yarns because the number of fibres in the yarn is the same throughout and filaments are normally regular in their thickness. Silk filaments are fairly uniform, so that yarns are built up by combining the required number of filaments. Man-made filaments can be deliberately varied in thickness, so that the required thickness or weight of a yarn can be achieved in a variety of ways ranging from one 'monofilament' to a number of fine filaments, and between these extremes a varying number of different filament thicknesses can be used. The number and size of filaments to be used in a man-made yarn depends on texture, appearance, and use requirements of the fabric. A monofilament yarn is theoretically the most effective way to display lustre. This is utterly impracticable in silk but is quite feasible in man-made fibres. Monofilament yarns are not effective in flexibility, nor do they give any fabric 'cover'; they produce a rather stiff wire-gauze effect which is of limited clothing suitability. Synthetic fibres such as nylon and polyester are strong enough to be produced in fairly fine monofilament form, but produce rather glassy and rigid fabric structures.

Multifilament yarns give more flexibility and cover, the finer and more numerous the filaments are in the yarn the better it is in this respect, but the more vulnerable the filaments are individually to being broken by abrasion.

The use of greater amounts of twist than the few turns required to group the filaments produces a firmer, and harder yarn and diminishes the lustre. Crepe yarns can be produced from very hard twisted filament yarns and, indeed, silk fabrics were probably the first crepe fabrics of any kind to be produced. The hard twist produces a crisp handle as well as the characteristic surface crinkle mentioned earlier.

Certain types of silk filaments are very uneven due to peculiarities in the life and habits of the types of silk-worms which produce them. This unevenness produces characteristic fabric types such as *shantung* and *tussah* silk. These characteristics can be duplicated in rayon and acetate by deliberately making uneven filament yarns which give *shantung* characteristics to otherwise plain smooth fabrics, and the rougher appearance of wild silk fabrics can be produced.

The evenness of the fine strong filament yarns produced from nylon was a significant factor in the rapid growth of the high-speed warp-knitting industry. This type of yarn can be produced much more cheaply than any staple yarn of equivalent fineness and its regularity is far superior to that which could be achieved in staple form.

Texture and stretch in man-made fibre yarns

Earlier references have been made to the importance attached to 'texture versatility' in the widening of fabric scope in man-made fibres. Interest in this matter, and active development, started when staple fibre uses of man-made fibres in general, and viscose rayon in particular, were being investigated. Earlier references to the desirability of crimp in man-made staple fibre underline the importance attached to texture.

It was found that if filaments were cut into staple lengths and the staple then spun in the same manner as cotton fibres a yarn of completely different texture and appearance to that of filament was produced. This deliberate cutting of filament into staple was found to be much more satisfactory than merely using filament waste, as in 'spun' silk fabrics, and since any desired filament thickness could be produced it became possible to produce a man-made staple, similar in length and thickness to any natural fibre.

Crimp The textural factor missing of course was crimp, because straight filaments produce straight staple, and although there would be some deformation of fibres in the mass it would be accidental and not permanent. Attempts were made in various ways to introduce crimp into viscose rayon staple in order to create fabrics with deeper texture more like that of wool. Some degree of success was reached but it was not until the comparatively recent discovery of chemical crimping – as referred to in modified rayon in chapter III – that a permanent deep crimp could be imposed in rayon. In the meantime synthetic fibres were developed and their use in staple form was an essential part of their development. The heat-setting properties of nylon enabled staple to be crimped and heat-set into a permanent state. This gave much needed textural assistance to nylon, but it was not the complete answer, because staple fibre yarns could not be spun to the necessary degree of fineness and regularity demanded by certain methods of fabric construction, such as fine gauge warp-knitting, so the textural values and uses of staple were limited in both nylon and later polyester.

The development of acrylic fibres followed on closely after nylon and the warmer and more wool-like handle of these fibres, particularly in staple form, was a clear pointer to development. As already mentioned in chapter III these fibres cannot be heat-set in just the same manner as nylon and so a different texturing technique was developed.

Newly formed acrylic fibres shrink up to 20% in boiling water unless they are heat-stabilised—which is the normal practice. A yarn is spun which contains 50% or more of fibres which have deliberately not been stabilised and the remainder are stabilised fibres. When the yarn is treated with steam or boiling water the un-stabilised fibres will shrink their full amount and in so doing will draw the stabilised fibres into a crimped or buckled form. This will give the yarn much greater bulk in order to accommodate the distortion caused by the shrinkage of a large proportion of the fibres. In this way fabrics having a wool type texture and appearance are made from acrylic staple fibres. Bi-component fibres can also be used. See chapter III.

Filament yarns Reference has been made above to the ease with which fine even yarns can be made from filaments, in complete contrast to the difficulty and expense of making fine even yarns from staple fibres. Whilst it can be accepted that for textural reason the less smooth and even appearance of staple fibres is desirable and essential, the processes of making a rope of man-made filaments, cutting them into staple, and then restoring continuity by conventional drawing and twisting methods, have an air of absurdity if studied in detachment. The thought occurs: 'Wouldn't it save a lot of time and trouble if some method of crimping or texturing the filaments could be devised without cutting them into staple'. This thought did occur, because methods of texturing rayon filament yarns were evolved before synthetic fibres were discovered, but they had limited success, much the same as staple crimping methods at that time.

Crimping by twist If staple fibres or filaments are twisted together the effect is to impart spiral crimp to each fibre, which becomes tighter and more cork-screw like as twist increases.

This is the basis of the *Helanca* method, one of the earliest texturing processes. A filament yarn of nylon was tightly twisted and then the yarn was heat-set. This had the effect of setting the spiral crimp in the filaments. After setting the yarn was untwisted and because of the set crimp the yarn increased in bulk as the crimps pushed the filaments away from each other. Stretch was obtained when the filaments were pulled straight and when the tension was removed the heat-set crimp reasserted itself and the yarn became bulky again.

Bulk and *stretch* are not necessarily always companion properties. The amount of bulk would depend on the degree of crimp which in turn depended on the amount of twist in the yarn. A modest amount of twist would crimp the filaments sufficiently to give added bulk to the yarn, but would not give an extension which could be called *stretch*, ie, over 100%. This type of yarn would be merely bulked and when made into fabric it would not exhibit stretch properties. A very high amount of twist would produce a very deep deformation of the filaments, which when set would produce 400 to 500% extension which could truly be called *stretch*.

Therefore whilst stretch produced in this manner results in a very bulky yarn in the relaxed state, a bulky yarn can be produced which does not have stretch properties. This is very convenient because whereas *bulk* is desirable for improvement in texture, handle and comfort, stretch properties are not always necessary or desirable.

This 'crimping by twist' method was originally slow and expensive, needing three separate operations. Eventually 'false-twist' methods were developed which enabled bulked yarns to be produced quickly in one operation, ie, a continuous process whereby the filament yarn was twisted, set, and untwisted as it passed from one package to another. The development of this type of process enabled bulking of nylon yarns to be carried out cheaply and quickly and it widened the scope and usefulness of nylon knitwear, and warp-knitted men's shirtings, because in addition to producing a deep texture with accompanying handle and wear comfort improvement, the process could produce light opaque fabrics, because of the 'cover' provided by the bulking, which were reasonably comfortable to wear because of the ventilation provided by the bulking and the knitted structure. This type of process can be applied to nylon or polyester.

Other methods of creating bulk without stretch or twisting are the 'stuffer box' systems in which filament yarn is closely compressed into the confined space of a heated chamber or box, which imparts a wavy random crimp once it is heat-set in that state, then cooled. In one version, frequently used, the filament is compressed into a tube by being fed in at a faster rate than it is withdrawn. The 'concertina' crimp imposed is heat-set, then the bulked yarn withdrawn from the other end of the tube. In fact moderate stretch can be obtained with this process if desired, but it is more often used for bulk alone. Other processes involve crimping the filaments by passing them through intermeshing gear wheels or fluted rollers and setting the resulting deformation. In another, known as 'knife edge', the filaments are passed over a heated roller, then pulled over a sharp edge at an acute angle. When relaxed, the filaments take the form of coiled springs, but the spiral direction reverses itself at random which helps produce a balanced yarn.

A popular method of texturing is the *knit-de-knit* process in which a thermoplastic yarn is knitted on a fine gauge knitting machine—usually a circular machine of a few inches diameter. The knitted fabric is then heat-set. This sets the yarn in the loops formed by the knitting machine. The fabric is then unravelled and the yarn re-knitted in a machine of different gauge so that there is no coincidence of stitches. When the resulting fabric is relaxed the yarns try to return to their original configuration and this distorts the loop structure and produces a resilient textured surface with an attractive chunky look. The process has been used with nylon glitter yarns to produce interesting colour and sparkle effects.

All the above methods involve the use of heat and demand a yarn which can be heat-set. However, one method of texturing has been devised which does not rely on heat. This is the successful air-jet texturising for which non-thermoplastic filaments such as viscose or cellulose acetate can be used in addition to polyester, nylon, etc. The yarn is passed, with overfeed, into a high pressure airjet in which turbulence is maintained. The filaments are blown apart, curled into loops and then recombined and intermingled into a yarn which, due to the presence of loops, has body and cover but without a great increase in extension, having little more than that of an ordinary staple fibre yarn (diagram 11a)

Versatile effects can be produced by Taslan, Du Pont's patented process, through combining yarns with varied characteristics. For example, two similar yarns may be combined or else two different types. In the latter case a cross-dyeable product is obtained. Also the two yarns may be supplied with an *equal* rate of overfeed or with *different* rates of feed. In the former case the product will have uniform bulk whereas in the latter case a whole family of products up to chenille-like yarns may be obtained. Non-uniform over-feeding of one component leads to slub and nub effects.

An important disadvantage of textured yarns is their tendency to snag on broken fingernails, chair seats and similar objects. Because it is a long filament rather than a short-spun fibre which snags, the likelihood of damaging the fabric is high. Textured yarns should, therefore, be avoided in such garments as children's playwear where some hard, rough use is likely.

The appearance of synthetic filament fabrics, either in plain or textured yarns, can be altered by the shape of the filament's cross section, produced by altering the shape of the spinaret's extrusion holes. Trilobal cross-section to the fibre produces a greater reflection of light, intentionally making the glitter yarns mentioned earlier. The ordinary round cross-section is normally more matt, but during false twist texturing there is a certain amount of pressure which flattens part of the fibre, making it reflect light and so give a shiny look which may not be required. Heat-setting the fabric tends to increase the shine still further, but it has been found that when the fibre is given an octalobal structure ie a cross section which has eight lobes, it is a much smaller side which is flattened, by this means giving much less reflection of light. The fabric has a de-lustred look, the irregular surface of the fibre gives a more natural feel to the fabric and its breathability is increased.

For polyester fibres there are different types of octalobal fibre, each taking a different dyestuff. One accepts only disperse dyestuffs whilst another will accept both basic and disperse, taking up the basic first and foremost and, when saturated, will not take up the disperse dye at all. If the two are woven together in patterns such as checks, they can be differentially dyed (ie cross dyed) by this method. When the two fibre types are mixed in one yarn and dyed in this manner after weaving or knitting, a marl or melange effect is produced. Nearly all the work carried out with these filament fibres is to give the fabrics a more spun-like character and handle.

The extra absorbency gained by bulking, particularly in synthetic yarns such as nylon and polyester, is not due to any change in property of the fibres. They still remain as unabsorbent as ever. But the air spaces in the yarns created by the bulking enable large quantities of moisture to be held in the yarns if necessary. These air spaces also give improved ventilation comfort and added warmth in the same manner as wool, as explained in chapter II.

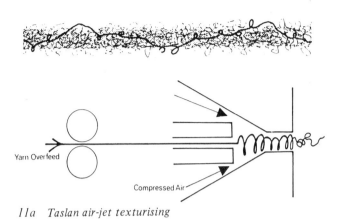

11a   Taslan air-jet texturising

Yarn Overfeed

Compressed Air

The early uses of 'stretch' yarns in fabrics were to obtain a close fit to certain parts of the body in garments such as ski trousers and 'trews', which still allowed the wearer freedom of movement. The limited elasticity of conventional woven fabrics makes this type of styling difficult. A simple knitted fabric would have the form-fitting stretch but could not be styled satisfactorily, although a combination of stretch yarn and a knitted structure simplified sizing problems in garments such as men's socks. Form-fitting stretch has obvious limitations, but the idea of stretch proved so attractive that it began to be used as a comfort factor in garments of normal type, enabling ease of fit to be obtained with economy of line. It was also claimed that an element of stretch in a fabric assisted in the shedding of unwanted creases and wrinkles. With this in mind stretch techniques were developed for natural fibres such as cotton and wool, so that fabrics possessing some stretch could be made and still have the handle and appearance of the natural fibre.

However, the development of the elastane synthetic fibre provided interesting possibilities in that elastane filaments can be used as the core of a yarn which can then be surrounded by staple fibres. This means that a stretch yarn or fabric can be produced in which the stretch element is completely covered and the handle and appearance of the fabric is that of the covering fibres. This eliminates the need for processes to be carried out on natural fibres, to give stretch properties, which might interfere with the handle or durability. The heat-setting properties of elastane fibres can be utilised in order to set the required amount of stretch, which is usually much less than the full capabilities of the core of the yarn. This is important where comfort-stretch is required because an excess of stretch would be undesirable on style grounds.

Stretch in woven fabrics

Amongst the several different processes developed to produce stretch properties in natural fibre woven fabrics there is a finish now termed 'piece goods stretch' by which 100% cotton and cotton blends, also 100% wool are shrunk without tension in a bath of sodium hydroxide solution, as normally used in cotton 'slack mercerising'. 100% wool fabrics are also given stretch properties by crimp interchange, ie weaving with a very tight warp so that the weft threads crimp themselves during the weaving process.

Another method is used to obtain stretch properties in woven polyester/wool and polyester/viscose cloths, making use of textured filament yarns, either in the warp or weft, with an intimate blend yarn in the other direction. In the weaving of these textured filament stretch fabrics, now often called 'mechanical stretch', the direction of stretch and the method used depends on whether the cloth is produced by a weaver used to dealing with staple spun yarns or one who is used to filament weaving. Staple weavers prefer to use a spun staple warp with the filament yarn in the weft, so creating *weft stretch*. To arrive at this elastic property the cloth is given a reduced sett (number of yarn threads within a specified area, eg per sq in. or cm) of warp threads in order to leave space between these threads, to allow for contraction. The fabric is woven extra wide, then reduced in width during scouring, heat setting at 190°C, dyeing and drying, producing a final closer set of threads. But this can be stretched out again, later returning to the heat-set width when released owing to its memory of the heat-set state. These fabrics show stretch percentages of 15% to 26% which is considered adequate for most outer-wear purposes, except for sportswear which needs varying amounts from 30% upwards, dependent on the activity.

With *warp stretch* the filament weavers have an advantage because they are more used to handling the textured polyester warp, with its inherent stretch potential. The blend yarn is in the weft and the stretch is lengthways. As there is the danger of accidental stretching taking place during rolling of the cloth, the clothing manufacturers need to lay up the warp stretch cloth on the cutting table more carefully than a rigid fabric or a weft stretch cloth, unrolling the fabric and letting it relax as far as possible before cutting (which is even more important when the fabrics contain elastane stretch yarns) after absolutely tension-free spreading.

The recent introduction of a bi-component polyester fibre, claimed to give a wool-like crimp, is being used to produce stretch properties in a fabric woven from spun yarns rather than filament, generally as an intimate blend with worsted or viscose, used in the warp or weft, or indeed both. In this new fibre the two polyester polymers are laid side by side on a 50/50 basis in the same way that wool fibres have their two components, ie a bi-lateral structure. According to the makers of the fibre, Rhone-Poulenc of France, it acquires a spontaneous three dimensional spiral crimp during drawing of the fibre, and its 'memory' can re-establish the effect during fabric finishing at a later stage. The outcome of this development is that it gives the fabric a stretch percentage of 18% to 25%, dependent on the proportion of bi-component polyester in the fabric's composition, whilst still keeping a natural handle and appearance. Trevira ESP yarn is a new stretch polyester.

However, despite these varied systems based on polyester fibres, there is no doubt that the majority of woven stretch fabrics for outerwear are being achieved through the use of Lycra or some other elastane yarn. These fibres are the synthetic equivalent of rubber, and are often used bare in 'power stretch' fabrics for foundation garments but in order to gain improved aesthetics and assist dye take-up, the yarn is more often covered or else core-spun to give it a sheath of another fibre, usually nylon. The elastane fibre disappears completely into the fabric's surface, whether it is gabardine, crepe or poplin.

Today these yarns are so fine a decitex that there is no way of detecting the Lycra without completely untwisting the yarn and stripping off the nylon covering, leaving the elastane almost as fine as a hair. Covered Lycra yarns can be combined with natural non-stretch yarns such as wool, cotton or linen during weaving or by yarn plying before weaving, so retaining the appearance and handle of the other fibres. The heat-setting properties of the fibre, which is mainly segmented polyurethane, can be utilised not only to set the required amount of stretch according to the type of garment for which it is required but also to heat-mould the shape, as in seamless bras, some of which are made in woven fabrics, although the great majority are in knitted fabrics or lace, many containing elastane yarns.

Elastane yarns have a very high stretch potential so that even a small percentage will give very adequate stretch for comfort purposes and the recovery factor is close to 100%. This is the really important point; many fabrics can be made to stretch but very few recover completely, so leaving a baggy stretched look to the knees, elbows or seat of the garment. Recovery cannot be stressed too strongly and all tests have shown that the elastane yarns give very good results in this respect. However, it is expensive and even 2%, which can give excellent stretch properties, can add substantially to the price of the finished cloth. Generally the elastane content is from 2 to 5% and the resultant stretch, which is largely controlled by the fabric's construction and finishing, can vary considerably even for the identical percentage of elastane, for the stretch is also dependent on the amount of tension placed on the elastane core during spinning.

There is no real technical ruling as to whether, from a garment maker's point of view, the stretch should be warpways or weftways. The fact is that for trousers stretch across the seat provides improved comfort, but so does downwards stretch. An important consideration for car drivers might be that when sitting for hours on end, the body's seat and waistline expands (also when flying) which tips the argument in favour of stretch across, which is also the best direction for the back of a jacket, although there are divided views about the best direction for sleeves. Downwards stretch helps the elbow to bend but stretch across the sleeves eases the front armhole when the arms are reaching forward. One textile researcher has found that the really important direction is the increased bias stretch which can be obtained through warp stretch or weft stretch.

Some pattern cutters and designers have found that there is a need to watch a technical point in cutting across and down, which concerns the direction of creases. Although, it is generally acknowledged that stretch fabrics oppose creases, if a strong yarn containing elastane is used across a weaker yarn, the strong yarn can crush the weaker one and so encourage creases rather than oppose them, which might apply to trousers stretching across. So this supports the preference for downwards stretch where the strong vertical yarns would oppose the accidental horizontal creases which normally develop across the front crutch, and at the back of the knees. In that case the pressing of vertical leg creases and the clean pressing of leg seams will be easier, not being opposed by strong horizontal stretch yarns.

Stretch in knitted fabrics

The percentage of stretch in a fabric should not be confused with the percentage of the stretch-imparting fibre within a fabric. Although 2% elastane fibre can help to produce 30% stretch in a woven fabric, which is easily sufficient for sportswear, the knitted fabrics intended for body-fitting swimwear need higher percentages. Leotards need even more because the fabrics may have to stretch as much as two and a half times in the warp direction ie 250%, although possibly only half that amount in the weft. This may require as much as 20% elastane.

The *average* stretch required for women's swimwear is 155% x 125% in warp and weft directions respectively, achieved through using 17% elastane. Inevitably the fabric manufacturers have to remember the cost of this fibre, only using a higher percentage for a specific reason, normally to provide the fabric with a greater 'spring-back' for a particular end-use. The stretch possibilities are also determined by the fabric's construction, with the elastane used as the recovery factor. But it does not follow that the higher the percentage of stretch then the higher the quality of fabric. In fact the degree of stretch has to be carefully engineered, since each end-use requires different characteristics. For example, competitive racing swimwear needs to be very light-weight; swimmers maintain that even a fractional decrease in swimwear weight can increase their speed, yet they need a closely fitting 'second skin garment'. This would need a fairly high percentage of the lowest possible decitex elastane.

Before the advent of elastane the swimwear industry was reasonably satisfied with 100% nylon tricot, which depended on the texturising of the fibre and the knit construction to provide two-way stretch. However, there is no doubt that the recovery has been considerably improved with the use of elastane and it helps to achieve a better fit and longer wear-life for the garment than would otherwise be possible. The types of fabrics now used for fashion swimwear are warp knit tricot (locknit), also single jersey, occasionally double jersey, often knitted from trilobal fibres in order to provide extra sheen for the fabrics, which are frequently printed. Surface textured beachwear fabrics include warp knitted stretch towelling and velours. Although there are problems with dyeing elastane fibres they are so well covered by other fibres that there is little trouble.

The counts of yarn commercially available for elastane range from 20 to 1120 denier, ie 22 to 1244 decitex, the latter for heavier corsetry fabrics where the elastane is unlikely to be so well covered; but the colours selected are usually pastels, quite easy to dye. The average decitex for swimwear is 44 but the 'power-set' fabrics for foundation garments, which are mainly Raschel knits, are more likely to contain 155 decitex. In this type of fabric the stretch is given as a modulus instead of a percentage, determined by laboratory tests in which a standard size strip of fabric is stretched 40% and the weight required to achieve this percentage is the fabric's modulus. For example, a light voile-type fabric using a 22 decitex *Lycra* with 33 decitex nylon yarn, resulting in a total 8% *Lycra* content, may produce a stretch modulus of 0.18 kg whereas for a heavier fabric using 155 decitex *Lycra* with 66 decitex nylon, resulting in 40% *Lycra* content, the stretch modulus is 0.87 kg. Another example is a heavy fabric also containing 40% *Lycra*, but in 1244 decitex, for which the modulus is 1.675 kg. Elastane is approximately half the weight of its equivalent yarn in natural rubber.

Measuring or sizing of yarns

Reference has already been made during this chapter to thickness, size and weight of yarns of various types and it must be obvious that there must be a method of measuring yarn size in order that the correct yarn can be selected, manufactured, used or identified.

There are two basic count systems for yarn sizing in textiles. In one, mainly for filaments, a fixed specified length of a particular yarn will have a certain weight, so for a coarser yarn of the same length the weight, ie the count, will *increase*. As a result the higher numbers relate to the heavier yarns in this Fixed Length or *Direct* system. For the other, the Fixed Weight system, the length, ie the count of yarn, will decrease for the heavier yarns, so termed the *Indirect* system.

There are two basic count systems for yarn sizing in textiles:

(a)	Fixed length (Direct)	Tex Count:	weight in grams of 1000 metres (staple)
		Decitex Count:	weight in grams of 10,000 metres of filament or filament yarns
		Denier Count:	weight in grams of 9000 metres of filament or filament yarns
(b	Fixed weight (Indirect)	Cotton Count:	number of hanks of 840 yd per lb (staple)
		Linen Count: (Linen Lea)	number of hanks of 300 yd per lb (staple)
		Woollen Count:	number of hanks of 256 yd per lb (staple)
		Worsted Count:	number of hanks of 560 yd per lb (staple)
		Metric Count: (Nm)	number of 1000 metre hanks per kg (staple) ie number of hanks of 496 yd per lb.

It seems unnecessarily complicated to have these varying hank lengths for the Indirect System but the different methods were evolved separately in somewhat isolated textile districts, each being appropriate for materials made in that area.

Normally the *Indirect System* is used for yarns made from staple fibre but the Tex System is an exception. This Direct System for staple yarns, agreed some years ago by the International Standards Organization, was intended to co-ordinate and replace the wide range of Indirect Systems. But it is not yet widely used.

The *Direct System* of Denier Count for synthetic filament sizes, first developed for silk, then adapted for synthetic filaments, is gradually being replaced by the Decitex System. When Tex is eventually used as the sole count method for staple fibre yarn and Decitex for filaments and filament yarns, the yarn measuring methods will be greatly simplified. But for the present the UK, the USA and Canada still use the Indirect Systems which means that when exporting yarn or fabrics to other parts of the world these textile companies have to convert their yarns into continental Metric Count (Nm) or else to Tex.

The strangest anomaly is that at present some fibres which are produced both in filament *and* spun form, such as silk, polyester and viscose, come under both the Direct and Indirect Systems, the former when in filament form and the latter when as staple. When Tex is universally used then all fibres and yarns will come under one or other of the Direct Systems and have the advantage of being international.

Sizing of sewing threads

Sewing threads provide a good illustration of international standardisation. Although they used to be sized by two different systems, both the fixed length system for synthetics and the fixed weight system for the natural fibres and blends of natural with synthetic, they have now become standardised to a *TICKET NUMBER*. Briefly this ticket system is based on the resultant thread count on the International Metric System *re-calculated* into 3 ply terms whatever the number of plies of yarn twisted together to form the thread. For instance, for a 4 fold thread quoted as 160/4 Nm, the resultant count is 40 Nm for the thread as a whole. This count is then re-calculated into 3 fold terms, which brings it to 120. The Ticket Number is therefore 120. This would also mean that Ticket No. 60, for example, could in fact be 60's/3, 40's/2 or 20's/1 but to the user, the size of the final thread is the same, ie in effect all are Ticket No. 60. The user does not need to know the count of the individual plies. The Ticket Number system is very simple, making it easy for a machinist to pick whatever size she needs from a stock of threads.

11b Comparative performance of fibres used for sewing threads (J & P Coats)

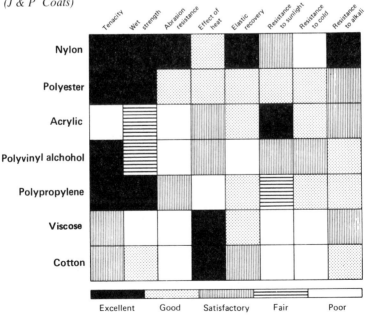

V Fabric structure

The textural function of any yarn can only be fully utilised by the appropriate fabric structure. For example, the stretch yarns just referred to in chapter IV cannot exhibit their properties unless special fabric construction settings are used which enable the necessary yarn stretch movement to take place.

The conversion of yarns into fabric is a major change of physical form. Yarns cannot be handled or used satisfactorily by themselves unless they are supported by being wound on to a bobbin or some other form of package. Fabric-making machines of all types must provide some form of support for the yarns until they have been put together into a fabric. Once the fabric has been made a new dimension has been created and fabric can be handled and used without support. Individual yarns may be quite limp and weak, but when a number of them have been combined into an appropriate structure a strong resilient fabric can be produced.

The fabric structure can be designated as a specific feature in itself prominent either in plainness, or in complexity of pattern. It can also be designed as a foundation for the display of particular fibre or yarn textures developed by finishing processes. Between these two extremes are many fabrics which combine some of both elements, and the scope of variety is increased by various forms of colour application which will be referred to in chapter VII.

The designing of appropriate structures is not necessarily an intricate task because many standard forms of fabric structures exist which produce satisfactory fabrics so long as certain principles are followed. Most of these constructions are based on particular types and sizes of yarn, and so long as the correct type of yarn is used fabric construction design is no more than routine, but, if for the sake of novelty unusual types of yarn, or unusual constructions, are used the designing of a fabric which is satisfactory in appearance, texture, and stability, calls for considerable and sometimes impossible ingenuity on the part of the designer. Very often novelty of appearance can only be obtained at the expense of stability and soundness of structure and many fabrics which are striking in appearance present the clothing manufacturer, and ultimately the user, with difficult problems.

Woven fabrics

Woven fabrics are commercially produced in length units, commonly called *pieces*, varying according to the weights and width of the fabric. Very heavy or special types of fabrics may be in pieces as short as 10 metres whilst light fabrics may be in pieces of 100 metres in length or more.

Fabric widths *see* Metrication and fabric measurement *page 118*

The width of woven fabric produced varies tremendously from 30 cm upwards. This excludes very narrow fabrics as ribbons, tapes, and braids which are made by a special section of the textile industry.

Certain types of fabric are associated with specific widths, for example:

Shirtings: dress fabrics	90 cm and 114 cm
Wools: tweeds: flannels	130—140 cm
Worsteds: other suitings	150 cm
Jersey dress fabrics	135—180 cm

At one time the textile industry was divided into separate districts in various parts of the country and each district manufactured a range of fabric types appropriate to its machinery and technical resources. This shows in the way certain textiles are referred to by the name of the district or part of the country, eg, Scottish tweeds, Lancashire cottons, Yorkshire woollens.

The former rigidity of the districts is being gradually broken by the growing common use of man-made fibres, which are not bound by tradition. At the same time metrication throughout the industrialised countries acts as a standardising medium. It is obviously more economical to weave the wider widths and to cut out the cloth in wider widths but many clothing companies oppose 150 cm for lighter fabrics because of their narrow cutting tables and other space problems.

An exception to standardisation is Harris tweed which, being hand woven, is still single width ie 72 cm. There is also a considerable variation in the knitted sector for reasons which are described later in this chapter.

Sometimes two or even three separate widths of fabric will be made in a wide loom and divided lengthways afterwards. This can be recognised by the fact that instead of having two complete selvedges a fabric will have one selvedge and a 'fringe' at the other side or even two 'fringes' if it was the middle of three.

It will be obvious that fabric widths should not be assumed or taken for granted and checking of width is essential where any large quantity of fabric is involved.

Fabric weights

The weights of woven fabrics also vary tremendously according to type. Weights are often expressed in grammes per running metre which means the weight of one metre length cut from the piece. The width dimension of the running metre depends on how wide the fabric is made. It is difficult to compare fabric weights if the widths are not reasonably similar and for this reason weight per square metre would be a more rational method because differences in width would not affect comparison. Fabric weight is an important influence on suitability, durability and cost, and should always be taken into account in any form of fabric evaluation.

The range of weights in woven fabric varies from as little as 15 gm per square metre for chiffon to 600 gm or more per square metre for heavy coating fabrics.

The lightest weight of fabric which can be satisfactorily made from any particular fibre depends on the strength of the fibre and its fine-spinning capabilities. As mentioned in chapter II the lightest practical weight of wool fabric is about 115 gm a square metre because of the low strength of wool. Stronger fibres such as silk, cotton, nylon, polyester can be made into much lighter fabrics, particularly when filaments are used. Ultra-light fabrics tend to be expensive because of the cost of producing and processing the very fine yarns. Medium weight fabrics are cheaper because they are produced from normal yarns and fabric structures. Heavy fabrics tend to be expensive because of the cost of the extra amount of raw material and possibly a more complicated structure. Selection of fabric weight should take into account intended garment use and frequency of wear. Light-weight materials are rarely satisfactory when given hard regular wear, because they do not possess the durability and recovery power of medium and heavy weights. As in many other cases weight is often a compromise between appearance, performance, and cost.

Woven fabric structures: weaves

In chapter I a simple woven fabric was described as being composed of two series of yarns (warp and weft) interlaced at right-angles. The weight, appearance, texture and stability of a fabric depends on the size, thickness, and composition of the yarns in combination with the fabric structure, ie the closeness of the yarns and frequency of interlacings, plus the effect of finishing processes.

The frequency of interlacings must conform to a pattern to form the *weave,* ie, the system of interlacings cannot be infinitely indiscriminate, it must form a 'repeat'. The size of repeat depends on the size and complexity of the pattern, varying from the small repeat of two warp and two weft yarns for plain weave to repeats containing a few thousand warp and weft yarns for a large figured pattern.

Diagram 12 shows the effect on the possible closeness of yarns in a fabric of different simple interlacing systems. At 'A' a series of warp yarns are shown side by side touching each other representing maximum closeness.

At 'B' a weft yarn is interlaced with the warp yarns in plain weave, or under 1 over 1 order. The diagram shows that to allow for the interlacings every alternate warp yarn must be 'dropped out' and only half the number can be used because of the frequency of interlacings. The yarns cannot move close to each other because of the interlacings between each pair and if the yarns were solid a wire-gauze effect would be visible, but the interlacings are tight and no lateral yarn movement is possible and a very stable fabric exists.

At 'C' the weft yarn interlaces over 2 under 2 and it can be seen immediately that more warp yarns can be used, in fact $66^2/_3\%$ can be used. More closeness can be achieved because each pair of yarns is touching and there are less interlacing interruptions but less tightness than at 'B'.

At 'D' with an over 3 under 3 interlacing 75% of the warp yarns can be used with corresponding less tightness of interlacing.

As the interlacings become less frequent the fact that greater numbers of yarns can be placed close together loses practical significance because they are not solid and fabric firmness will rapidly decline and lateral movement of yarns will become increasingly easier as the fabric loses stability.

Figured fabrics often contain large interlacings in the figured part but the looseness effect will be countered by having the ground interlacings much tighter to ensure a stabilising effect. Some figured fabrics and some novelty fabrics contain too many large interlacings which can be

12

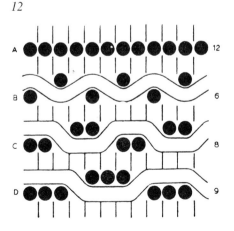

easily caught or frayed in wear, or which produce an overall loose effect and general lack of stability in the fabric.

The effect of yarn thickness and interlacing frequency on structural closeness mentioned above has a strong influence on the weaving process, and in fact maximum closeness is rarely attempted because of the chafing of yarns which would occur as they were interlaced. Furthermore, warp and weft do not interlace exactly alike as in diagram 12 because the warp yarns are under heavy tension and tend to lie straighter than the weft yarns which are not under such tension. Fabrics are therefore usually more extensible in the weft direction than in the warp. The difference is normally small and hardly noticeable except in wool fabrics where the elasticity of the yarns will show the difference. The extra stability of the warp direction is a convenience because most garment long dimensions run that way, and often waistbands and belts are cut in the warp direction for the extra stability offered.

The fact that yarns are not solid enables the final closing-up to be achieved by finishing processes and this can be enhanced by raising surface fibre from yarns, by causing felting and drawing together of yarns in wool fabrics, or by pressure processes which flatten the yarns and close up spaces. The success of finishing processes in this respect depends on the use of appropriate yarns and the correct spacing of the structure in the loom.

It must not be assumed, however, that the object should always be to produce a close dense fabric, because textural requirements often dictate otherwise. If the woven structure is deliberately made with spaces visible between yarns—as in a chiffon for example, then the possibility of the fabric being distorted by sideways slipping of yarns must be accepted in order to achieve the desired light filmy effect. The woven structure is not ideal for open textures; lace, or certain types of knitted structures are better.

It must not be assumed either that warp and weft yarns must be equal in thickness and spacing—they can vary in both respects, thus increasing the variety of woven fabrics.

Weave variety

There are three basic types of weave, namely, *plain, twill, satin*. The variations within each type and the combinations of types provide hundreds of different interlacing patterns so that only a few examples can be shown to illustrate.

Plain weave

This very simple interlacing system (13) cannot be widely varied and most of the variety in plain weave fabrics is produced by using different thicknesses, textures, and varying closeness of warp and weft yarns. Quite a few of the basic fabrics mentioned in chapter VIII are plain weave fabrics but they are individually different in appearance and texture.

Diagrams 14, 15, and 16 show three plain weave variations, rib, cord and hopsack respectively. The rib weave produces regular horizontal lines across the fabric; cord weave produces lines down the fabric, and hopsack is simply a plain weave doubled, ie, the yarns interlace in pairs.

13   *Plain weave*

14   *2/2 rib*

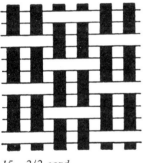

15   *2/2 cord*

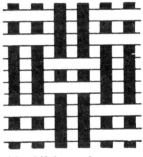

16   *2/2 hopsack*

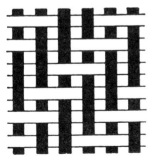

17   *2/2 twill*

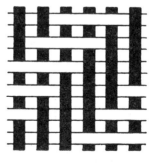

18   *3/3 twill*

This gives a coarser grain of appearance than plain weave but a softer fabric, because the interlacings are not as tight as plain weave. A simple combination weave on plain principles is the haircord weave shown at diagram 70, used in the cotton fabric of that name.

In the rib and cord weaves the 1 and 1 plain interlacing has been increased to 2 and 2 in warp and weft respectively, whilst in hopsack the interlacings are 2 and 2 in both directions. The interlacings could be increased further in size, as in 'D' in diagram 12, but increase brings looseness and instability and limits the practical use of many variations which are theoretically possible, so that the useful number of plain weave variations is quite small.

Twill weaves

Can be produced in a much greater numerical variety. These weaves all possess the twill characteristic which is the presence of diagonal lines across the fabric.

Two very simple twills are shown at diagrams 17 and 18, the 2 and 2 twill, and the 3 and 3. The twill effect is produced by the stepping one yarn space to the right of each successive weft yarn interlacings (warp interlacings, being equal, also move similarly). This movement enables yarns to be closed up effectively to make a compact but supple fabric, but as in the case of hopsack looseness begins to show if interlacings are increased much more than 3 yarns. The 2 and 2 weave is widely used for suiting fabrics and can be varied in several ways. A common variation of it is the herring-bone shown in diagram 19; this is produced by reversing twill direction every so many warp threads to produce a stripe effect which can be regular as in the diagram, or can be varied in a pattern of different stripe sizes.

Twill direction can be altered in weft direction in addition to the above and this produces a check effect as shown at diagram 20. The size of check can be as large as required.

This type of twill has equal warp and weft interlacings and thus gives 50% warp and weft on the face and the back of fabrics. Twills as shown at diagrams 21 and 22 give warp or weft surfaces according to the arrangement because the basic interlacings are not equal. Diagrams 21 and 22 show the 2 and 1 and the 3 and 1 warp twills, giving the fabric 2/3 and 3/4 warp on the surface respectively. These weaves can be used to give a solid hard-wearing warp surface, as in fabrics such as *jean* (2/1 twill) and *drill* (3/1 twill) with the appropriate construction. Or, they can be used as weft twills to present softer weft threads on the surface to be developed into a deep texture by finishing treatments or to display weft lustre as in some lining fabrics.

In the diagrams twill direction shows as 45° because thickness and spacing of warp and weft is equal. If, however, warp yarns are increased in closeness and weft yarns decreased the twill direction becomes steeper. This form of construction is used in *drill* (3/1 twill) and *gaberdine* (2/2 twill). Steepening of twill can be achieved by stepping interlacings two yarns vertically instead of one as in a *whipcord* (see chapter VIII). The line of true bias is 45° irrespective of the twill angle and the two directions should not be confused.

19   *2/2 twill, herringbone*

20   *2/2 twill, dice check*

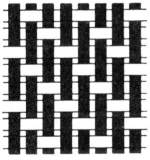

21   *2/1 warp, twill*

22   *3/1 warp, twill*

23   *3/2 1/2 twill, diagonal*

24   *5-thread, satin*

Twill weaves can be further varied by combining different twill sizes into a pattern. A simple diagonal of this type is shown at diagram 23.

These examples suffice to illustrate some of the variety possible with twill weaves and the use of colour (chapter VII) increases scope still further.

Satin weaves

Satin weaves are a group of structures designed to produce a smooth fabric surface without twill markings. The word *satin* creates a mental picture of a smooth lustrous fabric. Diagram 24 shows a 5-thread satin weave. It will be seen that the face of the fabric is predominantly warp and each warp yarn passes over four weft yarns and under one. The interlacings do not form a rigid twill line; the warp yarns are set almost twice as closely as the weft yarns so that as the surface closes up the single weft interlacings are hidden between the warp floats in each side of them. This gives the illusion of a solid unbroken surface if the structure is correctly set, but creates a one-sided fabric in that the reverse side is coarser in texture, and not smooth. Larger weaves give a smoother surface by enabling the weft interlacings to be hidden more efficiently but tend to produce loose fabrics unless the setting is very fine. Diagram 25 shows the 8-thread version where the basic interlacing is 7 and 1.

This is only used in more expensive fine fabrics because it would produce a very loose structure in a cheaper setting.

These weaves are used extensively with filament yarns to obtain maximum lustre and smoothness. The long 'floats' of the interlacings expose the filaments to damage in making-up and wear. Satins are not very durable if subjected to much abrasion, unless made from very strong synthetic fibres, and cheap satins, which usually lack closeness, are subject to yarn slippage and 'cracking' of fabric.

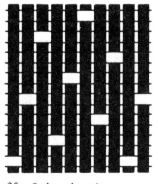

25   8-thread, satin

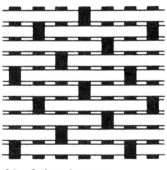

26   5-thread, sateen

94

The *sateen* weave produces a weft-faced fabric by reversing the satin interlacings and by having the weft yarns set more closely together than the warp. Diagram 26 shows a 5-thread sateen structure. This weave is often used in cotton fabrics where lustre is obtained by special finishing processes and could be regarded as a cheaper version of the satin.

The three basic types of weave can be used either individually or in combination so that almost limitless variety in woven fabrics is possible when the other variety factors of yarn types and use of colour are taken into account, but yarn thickness and texture combined with yarn spacing and frequency of interlacing are the significant factors of woven fabric stability.

Knitted fabrics

These are of two basic types; *weft-knitted* and *warp-knitted*.

Weft-knitted fabrics

These are made on machines in which the yarn forms horizontal rows of loops across the fabric, ie in a weft direction. These machines are of two general types:

1 Machines which produce flat fabrics.
2 Machines which produce circular fabrics.

Each vertical row of loops in a fabric is made by one needle and the horizontal distance between needles is known as the gauge of the machine. This does not mean that a machine of a certain gauge can only produce one type of fabric, because the stitch density of a fabric (ie, the number of wales and courses per square cm) can be varied by using different yarn sizes and different feeding tensions, but it would be true to say that the loom can produce a wider variety of different structure types – from point of view of range of yarn thicknesses and closeness settings—than the knitting machine.

Each type of machine can produce either pieces of fabric, which are cut and sewn to make garments in the same manner as woven fabrics, or shaped garment parts which can be put together without waste. This facility of fashioning is an advantage which the weft-knitting machine has over the loom. Circular machines are faster in production than flat machines, particularly on simple types of fabric, because many yarn 'feeds' can be used in rapid succession giving a production rate many times faster than a loom. Circular machines can vary in size from small machines 10-20 cm in diameter, used for making socks, to large machines 76 cm or even more in diameter making tubular pieces which are later cut lengthways and opened out. Knitted piece-goods vary in width but in general they are much wider than woven piece-goods, being up to 170 cm wide or more.

Fabric weights also vary, but ultra light-weight fabrics made on the weft-knitting principle are very unstable and are seldom made to be used alone. Medium and heavy weights can be made in reasonably stable constructions of the *double jersey type*. The term *jersey* is rather vague and applies to almost any knitted structure, but in general *single jersey* implies an ordinary plain weft-knitted structure made on a machine having one set of needles and the term *double jersey* meaning a more complex fabric knitted on a machine having two sets of needles.

Weft-knitted structures

Diagram 27 shows the *face* side of plain knitting, and it will be noticed that the long sides of the loops form series of interlocking 'V's in vertical rows giving a fairly smooth surface when the structure is compact.

Diagram 28 shows the *back* of plain knitting where the tops of the loops form an indented regular pattern which is less smooth than the face side.

A short study of this structure will reveal that it could not be as close and firm as a plain woven fabric because where the loops interlock there are four yarn thicknesses in each wale if the fabric is at maximum closeness, but between these points there are only two yarn thicknesses, ie, the long sides of the loop. This is necessary to have a loop formation at all, but it creates alternate areas of non-rigidity which allow the structure to be distorted by tension to a much greater degree than a tightly interlaced woven fabric.

Variety in weft-knitted structures is achieved by the use of different stitches and compound structures which together with the use of colour give a wide range of fabrics. Diagrams of a few basic stitch variations are shown, to give some idea of the way in which different patterns and constructions are created.

27   *Knitted fabric, face side*   28   *Plain knit, reverse side*

Courses

Wales

Needles 1   2   3   4

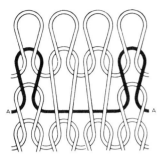

29   *Float stitch*

30   *Tuck stitch*

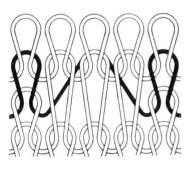

31   *Accordion stitch*

32   *Inlaid effect*

The *float stitch* shown in diagram 29 is a way whereby colour can be made to show intermittently in the face of the fabric.

The diagram shows that needles 2 and 3 did not take the coloured yarn A, but kept and extended their original loops and the coloured yarn *floats* at the back. The float effect can be made to extend for more wales, but long floats would make loose stitches at the back of the fabric, which could be inconvenient. Frequent floats give some reduction of width-ways extension because straight lines of yarn are being created by the floats. The traditional Fair Isle patterns are produced by this method.

The *tuck stitch* is shown in diagram 30. It can be seen that needles 2 and 3 have kept the loop of coloured yarn A when they rose to make the next row (B). This stitch can be used in colour designs to transfer a colour to the back of the fabric and it can also be used to give a gathered effect in the fabric by prolonging the tuck for more than one course. Tuck stitch designs are used to give ladder resist mesh effects in ladies' stockings.

97

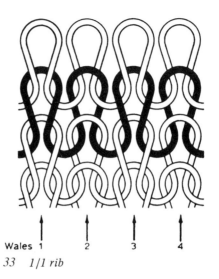

Wales 1   2   3   4

33   1/1 rib

In each of the above stitches it is undesirable to have too long a float on the back, but if it is required for a colour to be in the back of the fabric for any great distance looseness of float can be reduced by the *accordion stitch*, which is a combination of float and tuck as shown in diagram 31. By the use of this type of stitch patterned single Jersey fabrics can be made.

Inlaid effects   These introduce an extra yarn horizontally which does not knit but is tucked and floated alternately. If it tucks and floats on alternate needles as in diagram 32 the inlaid yarn has a width stabilising effect on the fabric, and if it is a thick or a fancy yarn it creates a fabric appearance similar to a woven fabric, using the back of the fabric as the face. Fleecy back fabrics are made by allowing the inlaid yarns to float for two or three wales between tucks and then the fibres are raised from these yarns to form the fleece effect.

All the above effects can be obtained on machines using a single set of needles. The use of a double set of needles enables more complex structures to be made which can produce greater variety of stitch and colour effect and more compact and stable fabrics.

Rib structure   In this structure the loops in some wales knit to the face of the fabric and others knit to the back. This can only be done by a machine having two sets of needles and the size of the ribs can be varied as required.

Diagram 33 shows 1/1 rib, ie alternate wales knitting to face and back, wales 1 and 3 show the loop sides on the face as normal plain knit whilst 2 and 4 are the opposite, or 'purl'. In this fabric wales 1 and 3 would tend to draw together on the face of the fabric and wales 2 and 4 draw together on the back, creating a double fabric effect, and the width

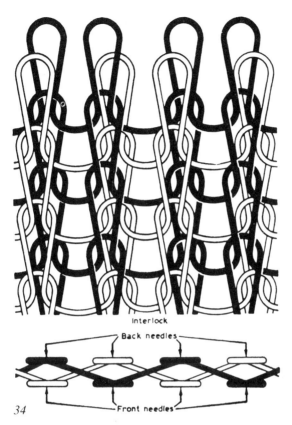

Interlock

Back needles

34 Front needles

of a 1/1 rib fabric would be about half that of a similar plain knit fabric but it would have great elasticity widthways. This structure has equal loop tension each side and does not tend to curl when cut, and it does not ladder or run easily.

Interlock This is a double 1/1 rib fabric as shown in diagram 34. Two yarns are used which cross each other and knit alternately on face and back needles. The interchange of rib prevents the fabric from contracting and gives a smooth compact appearance each side. This structure is used for cotton underwear and for double jersey outerwear in wool and other types of yarn.

Patterned double jersey These are a more complex form of double fabric where two or more colours are used to form a fancy pattern on the face by varied needle selection on the face, but instead of yarns floating on the back when not required to show on the face, they are knitted on the back needles and can thus interchange from face to back as required. The back of the fabric does not have to be a reverse of the face, although it can be made so on certain types of machines if a reversible fabric is required.

Warp-knitted fabrics

These are made on a completely different system of interlocking loops. It was seen in the case of weft-knitting that the name was derived from the fact that courses of loops are formed horizontally by a row of needles. The warp-knitting machine has a row of needles but the yarn is fed to the needles in the form of warp yarns—at least one warp yarn per needle—and each needle makes a lengthwise chain of loops in each yarn vertically. Each yarn passes through an eye in a guide bar which can move sideways each way and the loops are caused to interlock with their neighbours on each side by reciprocating movements of the guide bar.

Diagram 35 shows the simplest form of warp-knit structure with one warp yarn per needle and one guide bar. If the path of yarn A is traced it will be seen that the guide bar presented the yarn to needles 2 and 3 alternately in succeeding courses. In this way the vertical chains of loops are connected sideways and a fabric is formed.

This form of fabric is not very stable and does not produce straight wales because the loops stay inclined, so that it is seldom used. The vast majority of warp-knitted fabrics are produced by using two or more warp yarns per needle and these fabrics have much better stability and density and the loops form straight wales.

Warp-knitting machines are capable of very high speed of production because a complete course is formed by simultaneous needle movement across the full width of the fabric. Yarns are fed to every needle simultaneously by a small guide bar movement, so no time is wasted by a feeder

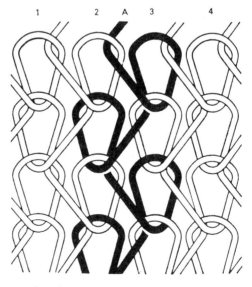

35   Simple warp-knit

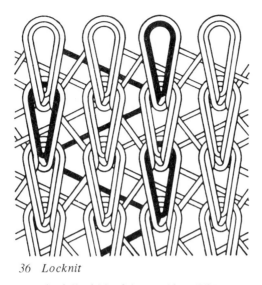

36   Locknit

travelling across the full width of the machine. Widths up to six metres are possible and the wider width does not involve sacrifices of speed as it would in woven fabric and to some extent in weft-knitted fabric. Speeds of over 1000 courses a minute can be obtained, and on a wide fabric this would mean a production of nearly two square metres of fabric a minute, which is many times faster than a loom. Needle gauge, varying from 8 to 16 per cm does not affect speed.

Warp-knitting favours the production of fine fabrics and is particularly suited to filament yarns; nylon, polyester, viscose rayon and cellulose acetate and triacetate are all used; some staple fibre yarns are also used but to a very much smaller extent than filament yarns.

Fine compact fabrics with a stability equal to that of woven fabrics can be produced in a wide range of stitch and colour patterns. Net, cellular and lace type fabrics can also be produced as well as pile fabrics. Most warp-knit structures are very complex, almost impossible to unravel and completely ladder-proof. Mention of this latter property usually provokes the question 'why aren't ladies' stockings made this way?' The answer is that they can be and they are, to a small extent, but as they have to be made with a seam and they lack sheerness they are not likely to be in great demand, unless prevailing tastes change.

Locknit   Is probably the most widely used form of warp knitting used for lingerie fabrics. Diagram 36 shows the face side of the fabric and it will be seen that the wales consist of vertical double loops, although in an actual fabric only one loop is seen, the other is hidden behind it.

This fabric uses two guide bars, one of which moves only one needle space whilst the other moves two needle spaces in the opposite

37 Dress fabric

direction. These crossing 'laps' form the back of the fabric and the straight wales form the face.

By this use of this construction very light open fabrics can be made from fine monofilament nylon or polyester yarns without the thread slipping, which would occur if an open woven structure was used. This enables a comfortable reasonably stable ventilated fabric to be made from non-absorbent synthetic fibres, so that it is almost the standard lingerie fabric construction.

By the use of coloured yarns threaded in various orders in the guide bars and by more complicated lapping movements, pattern effects such as stripes, checks and all-over designs can be produced.

Very stable shirting and dress fabrics can be produced by allowing one guide bar to make laps of 3 or 4 needle spaces whilst the other makes a one-needle movement. The long laps introduce an almost horizontal yarn effect which produces a very compact and stable fabric. A diagram of the back of the fabric is shown at 37. And the technical back is often used as the face side for shirting fabrics and printed dress fabrics because it gives a more matt surface than the face —which consists of vertical wales and loops.

Open work and mesh or net effects can be produced by leaving out threads in the guide bars in a set sequence, so that adjacent wales are not always connected and can form open effects, although each needle must receive at least one thread in each knitting course. Cellular fabrics for underwear and sportswear can be made by this method, as can curtain nets and 'angel lace' trimmings. These latter are narrow fabric strips made originally in a series across the full width of the machine, each strip connected to the next by an acetate yarn which is later dissolved out by acetone, thus leaving the strips separate.

38a Marquisette net

Milanese fabrics are very complex fabrics made on a special type of machine with two guide bars, but each warp thread traverses right across the fabric, both sets moving in opposite directions. This produces very compact stable fabric which looks like a plain weft-knitted fabric on the face but shows the crossing laps on the back in the form of diagonal crosses instead of the purl loops.

Marquisette curtain nets can be made on warp knitting machines by a laying-in technique whereby one bar makes vertical rows of loops and the other 'lays-in' yarns which interlace with the vertical rows of loops but do not actually knit. Diagram 38a shows a typical construction.

Yarns can also be laid in with the knitting process of *Raschel* machines which are generally of coarser gauge than the other warp knitting machines, constructed with several variations, usually having two sets of needles and multiple guide bars for complicated patterns. Plush and pile fabrics can also be made on special types of Raschel machines.

One Raschel variation is used for 'weft insertion' fabrics where a spun yarn is laid through the fabric continuously in the weft direction, passing through the knitted loops but not through the needles, to provide a fuller handle than the more standard warp knits in 100% synthetic filament fibres. The fabric's stability is also controlled in this weft or 'course' direction by the tension of the laid-in yarn. Most of these

103

fabrics are used for interlinings, with viscose spun yarns within the nylon or polyester warp knit base.

Another Raschel development is the use of laid-in yarns in the *warp* direction, different from weft insertions. These laid-in yarns are usually a spun staple blend of polyester with wool or viscose, similar to the 'intimate' blend yarns used in weaving. By a complex knitting pattern these fabrics are given the same face construction as barathea or twill weaves, with the polyester warp knit loops holding in the spun yarns and making a firm fabric back. They can be made just as rigid as a woven cloth or allowed a degree of 'give' if preferred by the customer. They are given the same finish as woven fabrics, but avoiding any tension in the knitted construction, which is always advisable with knitted textiles. Normally it would be difficult to use these spun yarns through the needles because broken fibre ends caused by friction, however minis-cule, would tend to clog the delicate mechanism of the latch or compound needles used in Raschel machines. Yet as a laid-in yarn, being moved by the guide bars but not touched by the needles, it is not subjected to the same friction, and the needles are left clear.

Men's suitings have been produced by transfer printing more standard types of fine gauge polyester warp knits by using traditional pattern designs and colourings to print Prince of Wales checks, herringbones, houndstooth patterns, but the slightly glassy look of the 100% synthetic filaments has proved a drawback. Yet transfer printed designs for women's dresses, blouses, lingerie and overalls have proved very successful, using either polyester or nylon, although they tend to be a little stiffer than the soft, fine single jerseys with which they compete.

As with weaving, warp knitting needs long production runs because the warp yarns have to be wound onto a 'beam' in the first place,

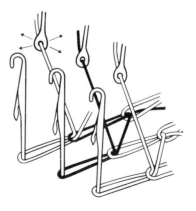

38b   Movement of yarn guides in warp knitting

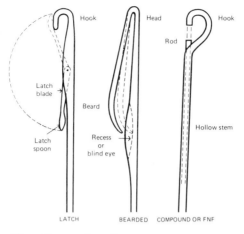

Hook

Head

Hook

Rod

Latch
blade

Beard

Latch
spoon

Recess
or
blind eye

Hollow stem

LATCH

BEARDED

COMPOUND OR FNF

38c Types of needles

arranged in the correct order for threading through the eyes of the guide bars of the knitting machine, before knitting can start. This has to be carefully planned when several different types of fibre, even several different deniers, are being used in one fabric to obtain a pattern. A series of these beams are arranged across the machine to the width being knitted, not necessarily the full width, then hand threaded literally through hundreds of eyes. This warping and threading is one of the fundamental practical differences between warp knitting and weft knitting. As a result warp knitted fabrics have to be made in quantity whereas a weft knitting machine can be set up quickly and the pattern more easily changed for comparatively short production runs. Such versatility enables weft knitters to show greater variety and novelty for a wide range of fabrics. But the warp knitters compete by means of technical innovation and price.

Lace

Laces are produced in wide all-over patterns for dresses and blouses—and of course wedding dress trains—or in narrow widths for trimmings, sometimes with scalloped edges. Although lace making is perhaps the most complicated of all textile constructions, associated with luxury and delicacy throughout the ages and still a thriving 'cottage industry' in many parts of Europe, from France and Belgium to Greece, Crete, Malta and Turkey, it is available at all prices, some of the least expensive being lace curtaining. Synthetic fibres are used extensively in the manufacture of modern washable laces and these can be heat-set to give them the required stability. But the treatment tends to reduce their draping properties. Stabilising treatments for cellulosic laces, originally starch, are now the same type of resins as for woven fabrics.

Machine made lace is generally named after the machine on which it is made. Leavers lace, fine and intricate in construction, is made on the Leavers machine and the same applies to Nottingham, Schiffli and Raschel laces, but strictly speaking Leavers, Nottingham and Schiffli are embroidery machines with the design developed on a previously constructed net background. Yet Raschel is a knitting machine which can develop background net and design at the same time and is used for a great variety of lace trimmings, with separation of the narrow fabrics achieved by special linking arrangements. Intricate figure effects can be obtained by complicated warp knit lapping movements and 'laying-in' of figuring yarns on a basic net ground. Nottingham laces have large designs of coarser yarns, widely used for table cloths, but when fashion dictates that dresses should be made in this type of lace, the shrinkage is often a serious matter, having to be carefully controlled.

The correct lace definitions specify that 'all-over' laces should be 90 cm wide or more, some today being as wide as 4 metres. A 'galoon' is any lace up to 45 cm wide, with both edges scalloped. 'Edging' is the same as galoon but with one edge straight and the other scalloped. 'Insertions' have both edges straight. Wide widths are often split up into these narrower widths by the removal of draw threads arranged at calculated intervals. 'Flouncings' take the form of wide edgings, generally more than 30 cm wide, with one edge scalloped and the lace design similar to the more expensive all-overs.

Handmade laces are likely to be named after the town or area with which they are associated historically eg Chantilly, Valenciennes, Cluny, Alençon, Venetian Point, Maltese, Honiton, etc. Technically they are bobbin, needle point or pillow lace and can be made by crocheting, knitting, tatting or embroidery. The very expensive Guipure lace is in reality an embroidery, and 'broderie anglaise' speaks for itself. In modern factory-made copies some of these patterns are made by 'burnt out' designs using acetate yarns for a base fabric which are later dissolved with acetone, leaving an open embroidered or lace-like pattern such as Guipure. The same technique is used for dress fabrics not necessarily classed as lace.

Each lace has a certain characteristic by which it can be recognised, perhaps sometimes only by experts. Alençon lace usually has fine flower designs outlined by heavy threads, often with one edge scalloped, whilst Chantilly is similar except that the motifs are usually delicate tree branch or vine motifs, probably originating from wedding traditions, and dots are often included within the design. Valenciennes or Val lace, frequently used for narrow edgings, has diamond or round-mesh backgrounds mostly with simple flower designs and a picot edge. Cluny lace is coarser than these three and is not made on a net background but has open spaces within the pattern. Torchon is even heavier and coarser, whilst Filet lace has a square mesh construction with the squares filled in to make the design.

Pile fabrics

These are a special type of fabric having a dense upright fibrous surface obtained by a special form of construction which permits pile yarns to be completely cut through, whilst ground yarns, which are not cut, form the basis of fabric strength and pile support.

Diagram 39 shows the method of construction of velvet. The pile warp A is thicker than the ground warp B, and is on a separate beam. The weft W interlaces with both ground warp and pile warp for a few yarns and then the pile warp only is lifted. A wire blade is inserted instead of a weft yarn and when this is beaten into the cloth the pile yarns form loops around it in a row across the fabric. Normal weft is inserted for a few picks and then another wire. After a few wires have been woven in they are pulled out one by one as weaving proceeds and a small knife at the end of the wire cuts the loops and forms tufts and the cut ends form the pile —which is trimmed by cropping in the finishing

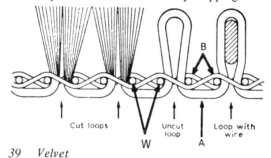

39   Velvet

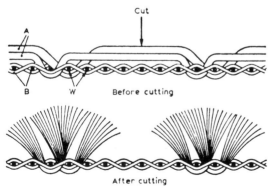

40   Corduroy

processes. The diagram shows the pile as vertical but in fact pile fabrics are 'one-way' because in a plain velvet the pile leans in one direction and gives a different shade effect according to the direction of view along the warp.

The loops can be left uncut if desired, or combinations of cut and uncut loops or loops of different heights can be used. Wilton carpets are made on a similar principle to velvet.

Corduroy fabrics are weft-pile and diagram 40 shows a typical section. It can be seen that the pile weft A forms long floats whilst the ground weft B interlaces more tightly with the warp W. These floats form stripes down the fabric and in the finishing process special knives cut down the cords and sever the float threads leaving the ground intact. The cut ends are raised up forming the traditional cords of pile.

Knitted pile fabrics can be made either by weft-knitting or by Raschel machines. In weft-knitting the pile and ground yarns are fed into the needles and a special mechanism makes the pile yarns form large loops on the back of the fabric. These loops, when cut, form the pile and the back of the fabric becomes the pile face. Diagram 41 shows a typical construction. In the Raschel machine instead of a double needle bed, one bed is replaced by pile points around which the pile yarn is lapped when pile loops are required, in a rather similar manner to the formation of the pile loop in velvet.

Pile fabrics such as plush, velvet, velveteen and corduroy have long been used for furnishing and clothing use. This type of fabric has also been often used to make artificial fur fabrics with colour markings either printed on or as part of the construction. At one time these fabrics were easy to distinguish from real fur because of the uniform height of the pile, but simulated fur fabrics are now made which have the 'guard hair' effect of the natural skin and varying pile density, giving a much more realistic effect.

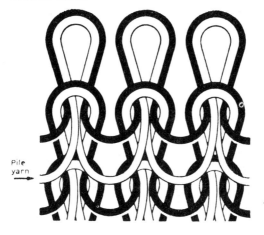

Pile
yarn

41 *Knitted pile fabric*

It is usual for the pile yarn to be made from a fibre with good handling and appearance properties and silk, mohair and wool are the traditional pile materials, and each of these fibres possesses very good recovery (ie from crushing). The ground yarns can be a completely different fibre, cotton being frequently used for cheapness as well as strength, although obviously if cotton is used it might impair the drape and crease resistance of the fabric unless the pile is heavy enough to dominate the fabric. Man-made fibres, both regenerated and synthetic, are also used and none has the recovery and handle properties of the natural fibres mentioned above, but the cheapness of rayon and the durability of the synthetics, and in particular the good handling properties of acrylic and modacrylic fibres, provide an interesting range of materials at varying weights and prices.

The term *nap* is often confused with *pile* in describing the fibrous surface of a fabric, but it is now accepted that *pile* refers to the actual cutting of yarns whereas *nap* fibres are raised from the yarn—without severing them — during finishing processes, and the raising process is referred to in chapter VI.

Tufted fabrics

Pile fabrics as described above are more difficult and expensive to produce than ordinary fabrics because of the more elaborate construction and special machine arrangements. This is particularly the case in heavy structures such as carpets, where the object is to produce a dense pile surface which is the actual wearing surface as well as the medium for displaying design and colour. Machine-made carpets are an attempt to copy the pile effect produced by hand-knotting individual tufts—a slow and very expensive method. A method similar to that used for velvet is used for Wilton carpets but the expense of this method and its limitations in design and colour have led to modified methods, such as Axminster, in which the horizontal rows of pile tufts are prepared and strung together in a long chain of carriers which present each row for insertion at the appropriate time. The pattern is built up line by line and there is no colour restriction, and several carpets can be made in succession by storing each carrier with sufficient pile yarns. Production by this method is still slow and cumbersome and special looms are necessary.

The technique of tufting was developed in the USA during the 1950s as a means of producing carpet pile or loop structures quickly and cheaply using man-made fibre yarns instead of the conventional wool yarns. The idea of pushing tufts of material through a base fabric was not in itself new but had previously been confined to candlewick designs and home-made rugs, and the tufting machine extended this principle to produce a solid pile on a ground fabric by operating a row of needles each fed with a pile yarn so that a complete row of tufts could be

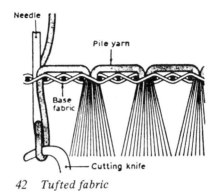

42   Tufted fabric

inserted by one strike of the needles. This enabled a pile fabric to be produced very quickly but did not give a secure anchorage for the pile tufts, so that some form of back treatment was necessary to secure them. The most common way of doing this is to impregnate the back of the fabric with a rubber latex or a plastic compound which holds the tufts and gives a nonslip backing (42).

At first it was only possible to produce plain carpets or very simple design effects, and some very poor structures were produced in the early days of this new type of manufacture. The speed of production and the relative cheapness of the method eventually caused a change in attitude to carpets as a form of floor covering, in that the use of carpet extended and did not merely consist of replacing conventional carpets by cheaper tufted carpets. Advanced tufting techniques can now produce a wide range of tuft and colour patterns.

The use of the tufting technique to produce pile type fabrics would seem to be a logical development calling only for a lighter type of machine. But the problem of securing the tufts remained and could not be solved in the same way as carpets because of the necessity for suppleness and softness. Efficient methods of fabric bonding (referred to later in this chapter) provided the answer initially but more recently a different construction method has enabled a firmly anchored pile to be produced. This construction is a variation of the sew-knit method referred to later.

The tufting method enables fleecy pile fabrics to be made quickly and cheaply to be used as warm linings, and these are usually made from acrylic fibres tufted into a cotton fabric, some very realistic-looking sheep-skin effects can be produced.

Non-wovens

If staple fibres can be converted directly into a fabric, expensive and involved production stages such as spinning and conversion of yarns into fabric can be by-passed. The idea has therefore always been attractive because of the time and trouble saved, and the web-like sheet of opened-out fibres produced by the carding process suggests a fabric, but the necessity for fibre cohesion restricted the formation of fabrics from fibres to felt because the natural felting property of wool provided the necessary bonding element.

Felt has long been made in this way, by building up webs of fibres into sheets of the required thickness and then by heat, moisture, pressure, and milling, causing the fibres to felt together into a fabric. It was also known that a certain proportion of fibres other than wool, eg, cotton, could be incorporated for economy but only wool possessed the property of felting alone, and that there was a limit to the proportion of non-felting fibres which could be mixed with wool.

Another attractive aspect of the idea of making fabrics directly from fibres was that it might provide a means of making very cheap disposable fabrics from waste fibres unsuitable for normal spinning. This last consideration provides a link with the paper-making industry because the manufacture of paper involves the use of very short fibres, and many types of disposable 'textile-paper' products are now in common use, such as handkerchief tissues and towels.

Much research work was carried out during the 1930s, and the inevitable shortages of conventional materials produced by the Second World War stimulated developments to such an extent that commercial production of non-woven fabrics followed not long after the end of the war.

Today one of the principal fibres used for non-wovens is polyester, particularly suitable for clothing interlinings, sometimes on its own, or else combined with other fibres, according to the manufacturer's own ideas of how to produce the best fabric for a particular purpose. These fibres have to be carefully mixed — different types and sometimes different deniers — usually short staple lengths, both crimped and straight, which are made to cohere by using chemical 'binders', then dried to leave a fairly strong fabric. Non-wovens can be left plain or coated with adhesives for fusing at a later stage in the clothing factories to garment parts such as collars, cuffs, front openings and jacket fronts, to reinforce and stabilise areas which would otherwise be limp or might stretch during wearing, washing and cleaning. Sometimes non-wovens are 'needled through' to a woven scrim if they have to serve as outer fabrics requiring extra strength and wearing properties.

There is considerable expertise in the blending of fibres for non-wovens, in the way they are laid into a web and then given properties they may not have had on their own, using very individual formulation for the chemical binders and a variety of ways in which they are applied to the web, either by saturation or spraying, sometimes intermittently by

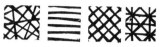

42a   Direction of fibre laying in random, parallel, cross and composites

printing. For instance, standard viscose has very good moisture absorbency but is normally weak when wet, losing nearly half its dry strength, and its wet crease recovery is also low. But a suitable binder can counteract both these deficiencies, to improve the washability of viscose non-wovens. Alternatively the viscose fibres can be mixed with stronger fibres like polyester or nylon. The binder serves the double purpose of holding the web fibres together and giving the finished fabric suitable properties for its particular end-use, making the fabric resistant to washing or dry cleaning, showerproof, flame-resistant, etc, dependent on the chemical mixed in with the binder. In modern fusibles and other interlinings made by the non-woven process, cross linking agents are often added to the binders, then cured at a high temperature after the drying-off process.

But first the mixed fibres have to be carded and combed into a web or batt, with the fibres either random-laid or parallel-laid. Then several layers of webs are combined, sometimes at an angle, to get the fibres laid in several directions, to give better strength and at the same time to provide a certain amount of stretch in one, two or three directions. Fully cross-laid fabrics often contain 15 to 16 webs whilst parallel-laid consist of 4 upwards.

An alternative method of compacting the webs for clothing interlinings without binders makes use of the thermoplastic properties of the fibres within the web. The development was originally started by ICI Fibres in the early 1970s, using a bi-component fibre, usually formed as a core with the outer layer having a lower melting temperature. When the web containing these fibres is heated to a temperature above the melting point of the outer layer but below that of the inner core, the points where the fibres cross each other become fused together, or spot welded, and when cooled remain in a combined state. The heating is sometimes applied by heated rollers with hot spikes, radiant heat or hot air, often with the addition of steam. Fabrics made this way from ICI's *Heterofil* polyester bi-component fibre have now been used for sew-in interlinings resembling a light and lofty felt, sometimes to provide extra warmth for a garment. The main advantage is the excellent washability without risk of disintegration.

Other methods of heat bonding have been achieved by mixing a certain proportion of low melt temperature fibres into the fibre web eg acrylic or polyethylene with polyester, or undrawn polyester (not heat-set) with standard polyester. Nylon 66 can be mixed with nylon 6, the latter having a lower softening temperature. The resultant heat-bonded non-woven needs little if any binder; its main attraction is the soft and lofty handle. Several interlining suppliers claim to produce non-wovens by this method, which avoids the messy mixing and application of binders, at the same time producing a softer handling fabric.

Another system using heat to secure the loose fibres into a fabric is termed 'spun-bonded'. Molten polyester polymer is extruded and allowed to fall in an evenly spread web of hundreds of filaments onto a moving belt which takes them in a hot state through a bonding unit where pressure is applied to fuse the fibres together, then cooled. Du Pont has produced several fabrics by this method, the first for a range of interlinings under the brand name *Reemay* (polyester), another *Typar* (polypropylene) which includes waistbandings amongst its end uses, whilst *Tyvek* (polyethylene) is best known for clean-air and hospital clothing. A small percentage of binder is often applied to spun-bonded fabrics but the filaments have greater strength than the short staple fibres used in the other system, where the fibres are only from 3 to 7 cm long. Spun-bonded fabrics also have greater pliability and can be constantly flexed without damage, but their draping properties are limited. However, 'spun-laced' non-wovens under the brand name *Sontara*, also produced by Du Pont, are softer and loftier, being extruded as finer polyester filaments and laced by water jets to form the web. As interlinings, the white is exceptionally clean and clear. Both spun-bonded and spun-laced fabrics can be embossed, permanently pleated or given an open mesh pattern.

Non-woven interlinings can be made resistant to washing as well as dry cleaning, but not necessarily the two together. Because so many different types are made care should be taken to select the correct quality, with appropriate properties. For clothing purposes non-wovens generally consist of dry fibres laid into a web whereas the wet-laid techniques derived from paper making have their uses in the truly disposable market. The fibres are made into a slurry by means of a water-based acrylic or other emulsion, with the water then drained off to leave the web, which can be perforated into an open mesh pattern by blowing air through a metal mesh drum on which the slurry is formed, as seen, for instance, in some tea bags. Self binding viscose fibres were developed specially for wet-laid non-wovens.

Amongst other variations of non-wovens a flocked pile can be applied by coating the non-woven with adhesive, then half curing it to a tacky state so that loose short fibres can be directed towards the fabric by an electrostatic charge, making them perpendicular before reaching the fabric surface. In some electrostatic systems the loose fibres are drawn upwards to a tacky fabric passing overhead. After final adhesive curing the flock fibres can be brushed to produce a nap and regularise the pile, some even being cropped. These non-wovens are used for velour type gift cases, wall coverings, flock transfers and similar products.

Needle loom fabrics

The needling process used when non-wovens need to be strengthened carries a selection of the top fibres vertically through to the underside or vice versa, without threads. The needling machine holds several rows of barbed needles right across the width of fabric, driving them down into the fibre layers, then withdrawing before driving down again, continuously, whilst the fabric moves on a conveyor belt. In this way the fabric is strengthened without spoiling its softness and pliability. Where scrim is used, either polyester or nylon, it is sometimes laid between two layers of non-woven, at other times only on the underside. The addition of scrim is essential for some industrial purposes and defence warfare protective clothing, to make the fabric stronger and more stable. The needle loom process has been used for a long time to manufacture cheap felt-like materials from vegetable fibres like jute waste, to serve as carpet underfelts. The same principle is used in making blankets and car rugs, using waste wool or acrylic fibres.

Sew-knit fabrics

The different methods of fabric construction already mentioned in this chapter demonstrate that stability, drape, handle, variety of texture and appearance, speed and economy of production, cannot be ideally combined in any one method.

Woven fabrics are perhaps better than other construction methods in all the above-mentioned properties except speed and economy. The necessity for interlacing warp and weft methodically, and usually one weft yarn at a time, imposes a speed restriction.

Knitted fabrics can be produced very quickly in simple structures but these lack stability and are difficult to handle. Complex knitted structures are more stable but tend to be expensive or limited in texture and variety.

Webs of fibres can be made quickly, but lack cohesion, and chemical bonding can seriously reduce softness and drape flexibility.

The sew-knit technique attempts to combine production advantages in various ways. The technique is illustrated diagrammatically in diagram 43. *Malimo* and *Arachne* fabrics are made in this manner.

It can be seen that the weft is merely laid across the warp without being interlaced, and it will be appreciated that this can be done very quickly since no complicated interlacing control movements are necessary. Warp and weft are seen to be firmly bound together by a simple arrangement of warp-knit stitches. In this way two structures—neither of which would be satisfactory alone—are quickly combined into a stable fabric with good handle and drape. Thickness, spacing and texture of warp and weft can be varied so that differing weights and

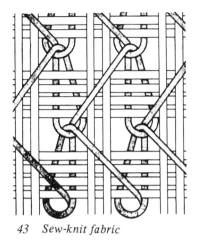

43   Sew-knit fabric

textures of fabric can be produced, although it would appear that variety is somewhat restricted, but production is fantastically quick, well over a hundred metres an hour being possible.

This sew-knit technique can also be used to stabilise a fibre web, or can be used to produce loop or cut pile on one or both sides of a base fabric — this technique resembles tufting, already referred to, but it produces locked loops or pile, whereas ordinary tufting does not.

These processes have not made as much progress as expected partly because traditional basic fabrics are being manufactured more cheaply by the developing countries and there has been little need for the sew-knits substitutes as a result. The sew-knits are mostly restricted to domestic furnishing fabrics.

Lamination and bonding

The cost of producing complex fabric structures has already been mentioned as a stimulant to development of cheaper and quicker processes.

In a simple woven structure extra weight and thickness of fabric can only be obtained by the use of thick yarns, and this very soon leads to a very coarse fabric appearance which is not always desirable for clothing purposes. The only way in which weight and warmth can be increased and a reasonably fine appearance maintained is by the use of the double-cloth. This is quite literally two fabrics woven together one on top of the other, with two warps and two wefts and with sufficient interchange of yarns between them to bind securely the two fabrics together as one. In this way a heavy fabric can be made with an entirely different appearance on face and back, but both the face and back fabric have a single-fabric appearance and do not look as clumsy as would a single fabric of the same weight as the double-cloth.

This was a traditional method of producing heavy coating fabrics and a similar method was adopted for producing heavyweight suiting fabrics with a fine appearance; these were known as *double-plains* because they were made by weaving two plain weave fabrics together and obtaining the face design effect by interchanging the face and back fabrics. Diagram 44 shows a typical section of a double cloth fabric.

The production of double cloth structures is difficult and expensive, based on the erroneous idea that fabric warmth is entirely a matter of weight. One of the important warmth factors of a textile material is the amount of air which can be trapped in the texture of the material, and this would seem to be more important than sheer weight.

Some years ago when it became possible to make plastic foam, ie, synthetic plastic material with small air cells created by gas bubbles, the idea of combining a fabric with a sheet of this foam was tried. It was found that the foam increased the thickness and warmth of the fabric but did not increase the weight to any great extent.

It was found that a thin layer of foam could be used to bond two fabrics together, by the use of heat, forming a triple laminate with the foam inside or, by using a very thin sheet of foam which virtually disappeared, being used entirely as an adhesive to fix the fabrics together.

Fabric laminates are not in themselves new—Mackintosh produced his now famous rubber and fabric laminate in 1823—but until fairly recently they were only of limited clothing use because the method of lamination detracted from the handle and drape of the fabrics concerned. Special adhesives have now been developed which enable fabrics to be durably bonded without any noticeable effect on handle and drape, and these are used perhaps more than the foam method mentioned above.

Furthermore, now that wide webs of adhesive filaments are being produced by the manufacturers of non-woven fabrics, originally intended for fusing facings and hems of garments without the need for an interlining 'base cloth', this gossamer sheet of adhesive fibres is laid between the two layers of fabric, all three fed from rollers, pressed together and passed through heated ovens to cure the cross-linking agents in the adhesive, so making a very soft and supple composite fabric, which can be washed or dry cleaned according to the properties of the individual fabrics which have been laminated. As to whether the mini-layer of foam, a synthetic adhesive or the adhesive web is used depends on the end-use and the weights of the fabrics being bonded.

Bonding of fabrics now offers a cheap and easy method of improving the stability of fabrics such as single jersey by bonding two together.

44   *Double cloth*   ● Face warp   ▬ Face weft
                       ○ Back warp   ═ Back weft

Loose open weave novelty fabrics can be stabilised by bonding them to a light warp-knitted or plain woven fabric. Lace fabrics can be attractively backed and stabilised by bonding; rough prickly materials can be bonded to a soft comfortable lining. Linings and backings of various types can be bonded to face fabrics, simplifying making up and enabling reversible styles to be produced.

Considerable savings are made in the garment manufacturing costs compared with methods which use a separate lining, involving additional cutting and stitching. The more stable character of the laminate assists cutters and machinists in handling these firmer fabrics, which also do not fray. Strictly speaking the cut edges would not need to be overlooked but traditionally raw edges are expected to be finished in some manner despite the fact that it may be unnecessary from a performance point of view.

It is not claimed that bonding will solve every fabric problem but without doubt it has simplified and made cheaper many problems of fabric use and combination. It is certainly cheaper to bond two fabrics together than to knit or weave a double structure, and where previously an unstable fabric was difficult and costly to make up and questionably durable in wear, bonding would seem to offer an effective solution.

Lamination and bonding

The best known modern waterproof laminate is *Goretex*, a three-fabric composite with a waterproof but porous membrane bonded between outer fabric and lining. The membrane is micro-porous polytetrafluerethylene (PTFE) in which porosity is achieved by mechanical methods. However, there are now various homogenous membranes (in polyesterether) which are sheets of film where water vapour permeability is provided by chemical reactions instead of micro-pores. The water vapour passes through by a diffusion process; the thinner the membrane the higher the diffusion coefficient. The face fabric still needs to have a hydrophobic finish for rainproofing but the membrane will stop heavy rain and wind. With these homogenous membranes there are no micro-pores to become blocked by salt (sea air) or adhesives, but on the other hand the outward passage of water vapour is slower so they should be as thin as possible, preferably 10 microns.

Akzo/Enka's membrane *Sympatex* is well known as a thin homogenous film which is available in several forms. One is for bonding to the back of a face fabric, another for bonding to the lining. A third is to form a 3-layer composite and the fourth for lamination to a knitted or nonwoven carrier, to serve as a loose sew-in layer between outer cloth and lining. Kufner, normally supplying interlinings, now produce another under the name *Kufner Climate Membranes*. A further membrane, *Porelle IV*, launched in 1992, is 12 microns thick yet still soft.

117

Metrication and fabric measurement

Generally the change from Imperial measurements to metric in Britain during the 1970s did not cause much difficulty for clothing manufacturers as far as fabrics were concerned. Many had been importing from the continent of Europe where the fabric suppliers had quoted widths in centimetres for many years, only converting to inches and yards when dealing with Britain and the USA. So gradually the British clothing manufacturers had become used to metric widths and lengths; they were in any case using Centigrade temperatures for fusing many years before official metrication.

Once Britain 'went metric' it was expected that everyone would use 'gm per square metre' as the standard weight unit and indeed for lightweight fabrics and those up to 115 cm (45 in.) widths this has proved to be the case. But for suitings and coatings where the long held tradition had been a weight 'per running yard' even when the width varied from 54 to 60 in., so that no accurate comparison could be made this way, the Yorkshire mills still voted to keep their running length and merely adjusted it to running metre. Occasionally these mills quote weight per square metre at the same time but generally they leave the customer to make the simple calculation.

Widths of worsted and blend suitings which used to vary from 56 to 60 in. have now become standardised at 150 cm surprisingly well, so that weights per running metre now provide a good comparison one to another, although there is no immediate comparison possible between these suitings and the heaviest in the 115 cm widths, which would be similar types of cloth, eg linen-type suitings, which would be quoted at weight per square metre. However, many of the woollen dress fabrics which used to be 54 in. wide have now joined the worsted suitings at 150 cm, which helps the situation. The knitted fabric widths are, however, very difficult to standardise and suppliers try to avoid quoting any weights at all! When weight is quoted it is likely to be per square metre, but with true knitwear fabrics it would be the 'yield' per kilo of yarn.

Metric widths and approximate imperial equivalents
5 cm = approximately 2 in.

cm	in.	cm	in.
90	35-36	150	59-60
100	39-40	160	63
120	47-48	170	66-67
130	51-52	180	70-71
140	55-56	200	78-79

The finished width of a woven fabric is dependent on the degree of contraction of the fabric after it leaves the loom. Contraction is caused by the various fabric construction factors, all predictable, and the width in the loom must be in accordance. A range of different woven fabrics required to finish at the same width would vary, perhaps quite considerably, in their loom widths. They could also vary considerably in yarn thickness and spacing of yarns in warp and weft. This is quite practicable providing suitable looms are available, and it is not necessary to use the full width of a loom if it is not required.

In a circular knitting machine the whole circumference must be used every time and the gauge of the needles is also fixed. The effects of these restrictions are, firstly, that the range of fabrics which can be knitted in any one machine cannot be as varied in weight and construction as a range which could be woven on a loom. Secondly, the range of fabrics will vary in the amount they contract during finishing to give a properly balanced structure, so that they will vary considerably in finished width, between approximately 135 cm and 185 cm. Once a fabric specification has been decided, however, it can be produced consistently in the same width, subject to agreed manufacturing tolerances, and a metric width can be conveniently expressed.

The use of grams for expression of weight will produce a much greater change of relationship between Imperial and Metric figures than in linear measurement, because of the much greater difference between the 'ounce' and the 'gram' (1 ounce = 28.35 grams). For example: a fabric weight of 1 oz per square yard becomes approximately 34 grams per square metre (33.9).

Fabric weights can only be expressed accurately when the measurement is made in scientifically controlled conditions. For normal purposes weights are approximate and subject to variations within certain manufacturing tolerances. These can vary from $\pm 2^1/_2\%$ upwards according to the weight and character of the fabric. However, to express even approximate weights of fabrics in ounces it is often necessary to use fractions of an ounce to convey significant differences between fabrics, particularly in lightweight fabrics. The metric system is therefore convenient in that the use of a small weight unit such as the gram enables very small significant weight differences to be expressed in whole numbers. The effect of percentage tolerances can also be more conveniently calculated and expressed in grams than in fractions of an ounce.

There appear to be no plans yet for the USA to 'go metric' so that European textile suppliers exporting to the USA will still have to deal with Imperial measures for the foreseeable future.

VI Finishing processes

This heading covers all the processes to which fabrics are submitted after being constructed, and in certain circumstances the application of colour can also be included, but this will be dealt with separately in chapter VII.

The work of the finisher can be summarised under the following general headings:

1 Preparatory processes Thorough cleansing of the fabric by removing dirt, any remaining natural impurities, manufacturing additives such as size or lubricants no longer needed. Bleaching where necessary, either as a basis for further colour application or for whiteness.

2 Development processes Treatments which produce the required appearance, texture and handle of the fabric.

3 Performance processes Treatments which aim at the improvement of fabric performance.

4 Presentation processes Final neatening by pressing, folding, rolling, etc., as necessary.

At their simplest, finishing operations are similar to the domestic processes of washing, drying and ironing, except that the finisher handles large pieces of fabric.

At their most complex, finishing operations completely transform a dingy unattractive material into a beautifully handling fabric glowing with colour.

The above headings are an over-simplification in many respects, but this chapter will deal only with development and performance processes because these are the most interesting and spectacular, although the other more mundane processes are equally important for many fabrics.

The finishing processes are the culmination of a planned sequence of manufacturing operations. The finisher may appear to be playing the most important part in the final appearance, handle and texture of many fabrics and it may seem that he actually makes the fabric. In a sense he does but only because earlier manufacturing processes were designed with that view, and certainly the finisher must do his work carefully otherwise a fabric may be irreparably spoilt, but his main task is to develop the fabric as required by the manufacturer or designer.

In view of the tremendous number of processes and the variety of process sequences included in the above headings, it is not surprising that finishers are usually specialists dealing with the finishing only of a particular range of fabric types, although some large textile manufacturers and some small but specialised manufacturers have their own finishing department.

Development processes

Properties of appearance and handle can be considered and described separately simply by imagining that sight and touch are exercised separately. The properties of texture are rather more difficult to describe because they represent the combined effects of fibres, yarns, fabric structure and finishing processes on both sight and touch, so that terms used to describe texture can have an affinity with appearance and handle.

The following pairs of terms describe appearance, handle and texture properties and they are obvious opposites, representing extremes with a range of varying degrees of effect in between. Neither extreme is in itself good or bad, and whilst more than one pair in the same category can apply to one fabric it does not follow that the same extremes must apply in each case, eg, a fabric may, under 'appearance', have the two pairs of terms, 'clear—fibrous' and 'lustrous—matt', applicable to it. A clear finished fabric can be either lustrous or matt depending on its construction, it does not have to be lustrous.

Fabric construction, appearance, texture and handle are so varied that it is difficult to cover all possibilities in a few brief expressions, but the following will serve as a guide to the basic principles of the many routines of finishing processes devoted to the development of appearance, texture and handle.

Appearance Clear—fibrous; fine—coarse; lustrous—matt; plain —patterned; smooth—uneven.

Handle Soft—crisp; flexible—stiff; full—compact.

Texture Close—open; light—heavy; loose—firm; flat—raised; uniform—varied.

Clarity of appearance

This property is necessary in many fabrics to display colour, structure, pattern, or merely to present a smooth plain appearance and uniform texture.

A clear finished fabric should not have any fibre ends protruding from its surface if it is to be perfect. Chapter IV made it clear that the only yarns which can fulfil this requirement are filament yarns where the length continuity of the individual fibres will ensure that no fibre ends exist to protrude—unless filaments are broken. However, it may not be practicable or desirable to use filament yarns, which leave

121

staple fibres in either carded or combed yarn form. Combed yarns would be preferable since the straightening action of combing produces a tidier fibre arrangement than carding with fewer fibre ends protruding, but carded yarns may have to be used for economic reasons —they are cheaper than combed yarns, or, for textural reasons—they give a fuller handle than combed yarns.

The finisher must first ensure that the preparatory processes do not disturb the fibres in the yarns if he is to produce any degree of clear finish, otherwise he is creating extra work for himself and causing extra loss of fibre which may affect the handle of the fabric.

Fabrics made from celluosic fibres like cotton, which burn easily, can have their surface fibres removed by singeing, which consists of running the fabric at open width through the tips of gas flames, or in close proximity to a very hot metal plate. The protruding fibres are burnt off very quickly without the body of the fabric being affected and this provides a very quick method for clearing the surface of cotton fabrics, even those made from carded yarns.

Animal fibres and other types which do not burn well enough for the singeing treatment to be effective can be cleared by *cropping*. The surface fibres are raised by a gentle brushing action and then the fabric is run beneath rotary spiral cutting blades, rather like the blades of a lawn-mower. This machine can be very finely set to crop fibres level with the surface of the fabric. Obviously, the closer the cut the more even and uniform must the fabric be, otherwise it would be damaged by the blades. Fabrics made from combed wool yarns, ie, worsted fabrics, are flat and uniform in texture and can be cropped very close and clean. Fabrics made from carded wool yarns, ie, woollen fabrics, are more full and less uniform in texture and therefore cannot be cropped as closely as worsteds.

Final smoothing of appearance or flattening of texture can be achieved by physical pressure, referred to later in this chapter under *Smoothness*.

The durability of a clear appearance depends on, firstly, the type of yarns used, and secondly on the structure of the fabric and the finishing techniques used.

Abrasion will disturb surface fibres and will impair clarity of surface. Smooth yarns of filament or combed type will resist this action better than carded yarns, since the latter are usually made from short staple fibres which are relatively easily disturbed. Long floats or a coarse structure will expose fibres to a greater degree of abrasion than a tight structure. Fine filaments can be broken in this way, causing a roughing of the surface in satin type fabrics; certain forms of cheap lining are susceptible to this form of damage.

If the yarns are made from staple fibres the firmness of twist in the yarns is a contributive factor to clarity of appearance. The firmer the twist, ie, the more turns per inch, the closer the fibres are packed in the yarn and the more securely they are held, so that when protruding fibres have been cleared, and if the structure is fairly close without long floats or loose stitches, the fabric will not be easily disturbed by abrasion or flexing, to the extent of lifting further fibre ends out of the surface. However, hard twist produces a hard or crisp handle and unless this particular factor is desirable normal twist yarns are used, and the finisher must produce as clear a surface as possible, and he cannot prevent the possibility of wear and abrasion impairing the surface clarity.

The development of surface fibre—nap fabrics

In the development of surface fibre, or *nap*, the art of the finisher reaches perhaps its highest level because in the treatment of fabrics to produce this effect the finisher brings about a complete transformation of the fabric in appearance and handle, and in perhaps no other form of finishing treatment is the borderline between success and failure so narrow.

The terms *nap* and *pile* are often indiscriminately used to describe surface fibre, but it is now accepted that nap refers only to surface fibres obtained by raising or brushing the surface of a fabric, and that the surface fibres are attached by one end to the yarns comprising the fabric. Pile fabrics are described in chapter V as being of special structure which allows the complete cutting through of pile yarns.

The traditional fibre for napped fabrics is of course wool, but other types of fibre can be so treated. Cotton winceyette and flannelette, brushed rayon, brushed nylon, all have a raised fibre surface produced by appropriate fabric construction and finishing treatments.

Wool is perhaps the most versatile fibre in this form of finishing treatment, firstly because it is a natural fibre for this form of presentation. Wool fibres being crimpy and resilient do not readily lie down and behave in a docile manner, in fact for this reason the production of clear finished compact worsted fabrics tends to be expensive because the properties required are completely against the natural tendencies of the wool fibre, and need more selective qualities and more complicated yarn and fabric production processes than woollen fabrics.

The *woollen* form of wool yarn, ie, carded only, is the most common type of yarn used for this type of fabric because the haphazard fibre arrangement lends itself to surface fibre development.

The raising process consists of systematically brushing or plucking the fabric surface with either fine wire teeth or the spines of teasels. The thistle-like head of the teasel was the traditional medium for nap production on woollen fabrics in the West of England and the West Riding of Yorkshire. It is still used for this purpose, but most raising is done by machines fitted with wire-covered rollers, although stricter control is necessary because of the more drastic action of the wire teeth as compared with the gentle action of teasel spines.

The fabric is passed, at open width, in close proximity to rollers or drums covered with fine wire teeth, or teasel heads. Fibre ends are plucked out of the surface yarns and the fabric structure is usually so arranged that a surface of mainly weft yarns is presented for the plucking action. If fibre ends are being plucked out of the weft yarns it is obvious that the strength of the weft will decrease as more fibre ends are raised. This weakening action must be allowed for in the construction and the finisher must be extremely careful to avoid over-raising or over-weakening of the weft beyond the point intended by the fabric designer, or else a 'tender' fabric results which will not be durable in wear because of weakness in the weft direction.

The fibre composition of the weft is extremely important because the length and density of the nap to be developed depends entirely on it. The raising process may need to be repeated several times in order to develop length or density of surface fibre, and in between the fibres may be cropped to trim them to an even length. The nap fibres may also be brushed or laid in one direction to give smoothness and lustre; this is the *dress-face* finish which is imparted to traditional napped clothing fabrics such as *doeskin* and *broadcloth*. These fabrics have a fine dense short nap so that fine wool qualities are needed to make them. Coarser quality wools and hairs such as mohair, alpaca and llama are used to give longer lustrous 'fleecy' types of nap.

The finisher is quite often required to consolidate the fabric structure before the raising process by deliberate *milling*. In this process the fabric is pounded and squeezed repeatedly in warm soapy water to cause the wool fibres to mat together, and this action is started during the preparatory processes. It was mentioned in the case of clear finished fabrics that the finisher had to ensure that the preparatory processes did not disturb the yarns. However, in the case of *milling* the finisher needs to disturb the yarns and sets about doing it. Felting of the fibres causes the fabric to shrink in length and width and to become denser and thicker. The tangling of the wool fibres strengthens the fabric and enables it to withstand severe raising if necessary without becoming too 'tender'. Felting tends to reduce the softness and suppleness of the fabric, so its effect is confined to the heavier type of fabrics such as overcoatings. Dress and suiting fabrics are not heavily felted because they must remain soft and supple for drape and handle properties.

Nap fabrics which have received any form of dress-face finish are one-way fabrics. This fact is obvious if the fingertips are brushed gently on the fabric surface in the warp direction; the fibre points will be felt as the finger tips go one way and in the other direction the surface will feel smooth. In the weft direction no appreciable difference will be noticed either way. If the fabric is examined with a magnifying glass the nap

45 'Nap' fabric weave

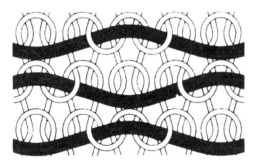

46 Knitted 'nap' fabric

47 Brushed nylon fabric

fibres can be seen to be lying in one direction and this is always in the warp direction. It is a useful indication of fabric grain if no selvedge is visible. Many fabrics are lightly napped and the fibres are not laid in one direction, and in some heavy coating fabrics such as *melton* and *pilot* coatings the nap is deliberately flattened and made non-directional.

The raising process can be carried out on cotton and rayon staple fibre fabrics to give a warmer softer handle to fabrics made from these fibres and to produce a cheaper napped fabric than would be possible with wool. The use of *Sarille* is particularly appropriate in this connection because it enables the warmer handling properties of this modified form of rayon to be utilised.

Another form of napped fabric which is now very common is the brushed nylon type of fabric. This is in fact a warp-knitted structure made from nylon filament yarns. As it comes from the machine it is rather loose and unstable, but when it is raised the long laps of filament yarn which form the technical back of the fabric are plucked into a mass of loops, and this draws the structure together and makes it more compact as the loops tangle with each other. The success of this type of fabric depends on the high strength of nylon, in that the filaments are not broken by the raising but are plucked into loops. If the raised surface of this type of fabric is examined under magnification the mass of tiny loops can be clearly seen.

Typical structures for woven, knitted and brushed nylon, nap fabrics are shown at diagrams 45, 46 and 47.

In the woven fabric a 2/1 weft twill has been shown, and the weft is obviously thicker than the warp and would also be more softly twisted. This gives 2/3 of the weft on the surface and provides a structure for a good dense nap.

In the knitted fabric the inlaid technique is used and the long floats on the technical back of the fabric are of thicker softer yarn than the body of the fabric to provide the nap basis. Fleecy-back cotton underwear is made on this basis.

The warp-knitted brushed nylon structure has been described above.

The development of smoothness and lustre

Smoothness and lustre are to some extent connected with clarity of appearance, referred to earlier in this chapter, but since clarity of surface and lustre are by no means always connected, the use of physical pressure to obtain smoothness and lustre is better dealt with separately.

The basic physical methods of obtaining smoothness and lustre by pressure were developed many years ago for cotton fabrics. This goes back to last century, before the era of man-made fibres, when the only really smooth lustrous material was silk which was scarce and expensive, and linen which, again, was more expensive than cotton.

48   *Normal fabric*

49   *Calendered fabric*

Cotton is not normally lustrous but it can easily be given a clear surface by singeing. This still leaves a fabric surface which is by no means flat, particularly in ordinary quality plain weave fabrics, because of the round shape of the yarns and the interlacings of warp and weft at right-angles to each other. Diagram 48 shows a section of such a fabric, and it can easily be seen that whilst the fabric may be quite regular it is not flat.

A flat compact surface can be obtained by physically flattening the fabric surface by passing the fabric between rollers under pressure. The yarns are squashed into a flattened elliptical shape and this closes-up the fabric, making it flat and compact as shown in diagram 49.

The calender machines can have several rollers, some of which can be heated and varied in speed, so that in addition to pressure a polishing action can be exerted to increase lustre.

To improve the flatness and compactness of cotton fabrics the practice of adding starch or other filling substances was adopted. These compounds filled in the small spaces between the yarns, enabling a very smooth surface with a distinct polish or lustre to be produced.

These finishes, as described for cotton fabrics, were not permanent because on washing the cotton fibres would swell, and gradually the flattening action of the calender would be removed and domestic ironing could not replace it. Furthermore, the filling material would be removed by washing so that the fabric surface would gradually become rougher. Sometimes a deliberate excess of filling would be used to give a better appearance of fullness and compactness as a cheaper alternative to setting the yarns closely on the loom, and when the filling had washed out or had been lost by flexing and abrasion, the fabric would have a very open appearance and would become very thin and limp in handle.

A good simple test of the durability and amount of filling in a cotton fabric is rapidly to flex a small portion between finger and thumb of each hand and then to look at the fabric with a strong light behind it to see if any difference is noticeable between the flexed portion and the surrounding fabric. If a large amount of the filling has been used a roughening of the surface will be seen and spaces between the yarns will become visible against the light.

Lustre is produced by regularity of light reflection from a surface and a flat surface would seem to be the most logical way of achieving this. In chapter IV it was seen that when staple fibres are twisted into a

127

yarn they incline in the twist direction, so that in a yarn of regular twist the fibres would be parallel slanting across the yarn. Many years ago, Schreiner, a German technician, reasoned that if all the fibres in the warp and weft yarns of a fabric could be arranged absolutely parallel, lustre would be produced because of regularity of light reflection. It is impossible to produce this condition by spinning, so Schreiner simulated this by a special calender which instead of having a smooth roller had an engraved roller which embossed very fine slanting lines, 200 or more to 25 mm, on the fabric surface. The Schreiner calender in this way produces a subdued silky sheen on cotton fabrics, the fine slanting lines are visible on the fabric surface under magnification and it can be seen how they simulate the slanting fibres in the yarns.

This type of finish is also not permanent to washing because the swelling of fibres gradually removes the line effect.

The *moiré*, or *watered* effect on silk was a pressure effect obtained by passing two similar fabrics through pressure rollers with their faces in contact; ribbed or taffeta type fabrics were usually used, and as their features never accurately coincided a *pressure pattern* was produced which gave a shimmering wavy effect without any visible repeat.

When thermoplastic fibres are used the pressure effects referred to above can be made permanent by the use of heat, which enables the softened fibres to be flattened and the deformation is not removed by washing.

Since the mention of thermoplastic fibres quite clearly implies man-made fibres which can be produced in highly lustrous filament form, it may seem superfluous to use pressure methods. Whilst lustre can be produced in these materials without pressure some fabrics are flattened and glazed by this method, particularly plain weave materials, which even in filament yarns are not highly lustrous to the degree that a satin would be, and pressure improves them in this respect. The Schreiner finish has been found to improve the opacity of *delustred* nylon materials, presumably by causing light to be reflected from the surface instead of passing through.

Since thermoplastic fibres are sensitive to the softening effect of heat care must be taken to prevent the accidental or unwanted imposition of 'pressure effects', such as glazing or flattening during finishing, and in garment making-up by excessive use of heat and pressure, because once imposed these cannot be removed.

Permanency of pressure effects in cellulosic fibres, such as cotton and viscose rayon, can be obtained by the use of synthetic resins, referred to later in this chapter. It will be appreciated that if smoothness and lustre are obtained by pressure, and that if it is necessary to use some form of filling added to the fabric to enhance the pressure effect, or to make it more durable, then these fabrics will be stiff in handle in some degree. If the finish is durable the properties of handle will remain reasonably constant, but if it isn't the fabric will become fuller and more limp in handle as the finish wears off or washes out.

Where the lustre is produced entirely by the yarn and fabric structure, as in a filament silk satin for example, properties of handle and appearance will remain constant so long as the fabric surface is not damaged by wear and abrasion.

The chemical process of *mercerisation* was developed in the 1890s as a means of giving permanent lustre to cotton. The cotton fibre is shaped like a flat twisted ribbon and is not lustrous in its normal form. Treatment by caustic soda in the mercerising process causes the fibre to swell and become more cylindrical and in the latter form its surface becomes permanently lustrous.

This process can be applied to either yarn or fabric, and provides an enduring lustre which can be enhanced by pressure but which is not entirely dependent on it. This process is usually carried out on cotton fabrics made from better quality cotton and from combed yarns. In this way a smooth lustrous fabric surface can be produced, smooth and lustrous both from cleanliness and lack of protruding fibres and from smoothness and regularity of fibre surface.

Unevenness of surface appearance

The *unevenness* of a fabric surface can be deliberate and not necessarily irregular, the term is being used as a general description of a fabric surface which is not intended to be smooth and level, so that pressure processes—other than final smartening pressing—are not used.

An obvious source of deliberate unevenness as an effect is the use of different thicknesses of yarn, or the use of deliberately uneven (ie, fancy) yarns, or yarns with differing twist.

A further, or an additional source of unevenness is the use of a definite weave, or stitch pattern.

If both sources of effect are used together very uneven and varied fabric surface appearance can be achieved. The heat and moisture processes applied by the finisher are often responsible for the successful development of uneven fabric surface because the final effect is produced by the differing shrinkage, or reaction of the yarns to heat and moisture, in combination with the weave or knit pattern.

Crepe effects

The term *crepe* refers to a fabric which has a crinkled surface and a fairly crisp handle. The degree and depth of crinkle and the crispness of handle vary according to the construction of the fabric and the type of fibres used in the yarns. The traditional method of producing crepe fabrics requires the use of very hard twisted yarns (referred to in chapter IV) and it is this fact which produces the crisp handle of many crepe fabrics.

As explained in chapter IV, these hard twist yarns exhibit a tendency to kink, or snarl, unless held at tension or unless the yarn is set by the use of heat and moisture. The yarns are set after twisting to render them inert and easy to use in weaving or knitting. When the fabrics come in contact with heat and moisture during finishing the set previously imposed on them is released and they at once try to contract and kink. They are prevented from doing this freely by the fabric structure but the strains imposed by the contracting yarns cause the fabric surface to be distorted into a crinkled form, the depth of the distortion depends on the closeness of construction and the weave or knitted structure. If the structure is close and tight the amount of crinkle will be fine and limited, but if the structure allows much movement by virtue of open stitches or long floats, a very deep crinkle effect can be obtained.

This method of creping is only possible with fibres which swell when wet because this produces the reaction mentioned above. Silk, wool and viscose rayon are the commonly used crepe fibres and most crepe dress fabrics originated as silk materials, crepe-de-chine and georgette being the two perhaps best known examples. There is not a large range of cotton crepe fabrics, but hard twist is used in cotton fabrics of the voile type which are crisp in handle.

Man-made fibres such as cellulose acetate, triacetate, nylon and polyester do not respond to normal creping treatments because they are not absorbent and do not swell when wet. As they are all thermoplastic they can be given a crinkled appearance either by the use of a fancy crepe weave, or knit, or they can be embossed in a crepe pattern by heat and an engraved roller. Heat alone can be also used with synthetic fibres using different types of yarn such as plain and textured which react differently, and the difference in heat contraction produces a crinkled surface, usually in combination with a suitable structure.

Viscose fibre fabrics can also be given a crepe appearance by a combined embossing and resin treatment. This results in a stable crease-resistant fabric using ordinary yarns, the resin (referred to later in this chapter) holds the embossed effect in the fabric where otherwise it would be only temporary.

When the crepe effect has been obtained by the traditional hard twist method control of shrinkage is very difficult and it is often impossible to allow the fabrics to relax completely. The most common form of crepe fabric is produced by using hard-twist weft and ordinary warp and considerable width shrinkage takes place during finishing. It may be necessary to hold the fabric out in width to prevent it contracting too much, and it can be temporarily set in this position by drying it whilst under tension. Unfortunately this set can be released, perhaps inadvertently, later on when the fabric is being made-up, or when it is in use, and it will then contract further trying to reach its natural equilibrium. Crepe fabrics of this type should always be tested for sensitivity before use so that heat and moisture treatments can be controlled or even entirely eliminated.

Crepe fabrics made from synthetic fibres, either by embossing or by the use of different yarns, will have been adequately heat-set in treatment so that, providing the normal heat-sensitivity precautions in respect of thermoplastic fibres are observed, trouble in the form of unwanted shrinkage rarely occurs. Similarly resin-embossed viscose rayon fabrics are not troublesome in this respect.

Examination of the yarns will soon reveal whether the effect is due to very hard twist or not.

Piqué, blister, and matelasse effects

These effects are produced by raising part of the fabric surface in the form of a set pattern which produces a three-dimensional or embossed effect.

Piqué and cord effects are perhaps the most simple forms and demand only the use of a special weave structure which throws a regular series of long floats on to the back of the fabric in the weft direction interspersed with weft yarns which interlace more tightly and produce the face effect.

During hot wet finishing treatments the long floats are free to contract and in doing so they cause the face effect to rise up because it is interlaced too closely to shrink as much. The risen face effect can be enhanced by padding it with extra yarns which lie between the face and the long floats in the back. Diagram 50 shows the basic principle of this form of construction.

More exaggerated raised effects are obtained by using yarns which have a high degree of contraction for the back floats. Very hard twisted crepe-type yarns are used for this purpose, or wool yarns which contract easily in hot moist conditions. More recently unset synthetic fibres have been used which contract when heated producing a similar effect .

The traditional crinkled *seersucker* effect in cotton is produced entirely by different tensions of warp yarns. Two warp beams are used and the warp yarns in the fabric are supplied alternately from each in stripe form. One beam is heavily tensioned and the other comparatively

50   Cord weave

lightly so that in finishing the tight yarns contract in their stripes leaving the looser yarns to form a puckered stripe in between.

These structural methods are rather complicated and expensive to produce and as the final surface effect resembles that of an embossed fabric it is logical that the production of direct embossed effects should be resorted to as a quicker and cheaper expedient.

Very little of this nature was practicable until thermoplastic fibres and synthetic resins became widely used because it is of little use to emboss a fabric if the effect cannot be held. Natural fibres such as cotton and wool become slightly plastic when under the influence of heat and moisture and in this condition can have pressure effects imposed on them, but only temporarily.

Durable embossed effects can be produced on cotton by the use of synthetic resins and in this way piqué, cord and more elaborate embossed effects can be imposed much more cheaply than by conventional structural methods. There is a tendency, however, for this type of fabric to become rather papery in handle, due to the effect of the resin, and if the embossing is fairly deep there is a risk of the fabric having a very low tear resistance. This is particularly the case if a light weight fabric is used to produce a cheap embossed style because the resin diminishes the flexibility of the fibres making them more rigid and brittle.

Embossed effects of the plisse type, which resemble a fine seersucker, or waffle effect can be imposed on synthetic fibres such as nylon by the use of heat, and the result is permanent.

This type of effect can be produced chemically on cotton by the use of caustic soda which causes the fabric to crinkle into plisse effect as if it had been embossed. The resultant fabric handles more softly than a resin impregnated fabric and is more absorbent.

It will be seen that the finisher plays an important part in the development of emboss type effects. If they are produced by the use of a special structure the finisher must develop the appearance taking care that the face of the fabric is clear and crisp in effect without any unwanted surface fibres disturbed from the face yarns and that the shrinkage is regular and controlled. If the effect is produced by heat emboss, resin or chemically, the finisher is entirely responsible for the effect itself, because the fabric is merely raw material to be manipulated.

Development of fabric handle

Enough information has been given in this chapter to demonstrate that appearance, texture and handle are closely related and that finishing processes rarely have an effect on just one of these properties and the finisher cannot deal with the properties separately.

The handle of a fabric is to some extent dictated, or at least indicated, by the fibres, the type and composition of the yarns, and the fabric structure. In dealing with a fabric the finisher must be prepared to cause the minimum of disturbance to the fabric appearance and handle or he must be prepared to carry out an extensive change of these properties depending on requirements.

These considerations govern the choice and type of preparatory treatments because the work begins with these, and although they have not been described in any detail their importance was mentioned at the beginning of this chapter and though their effects are not spectacular they are part of the pattern of treatment and must fit in with the later treatments.

If a fabric is required to be *soft* but *compact* in handle, the finisher must be careful to remove all impurities and any manufacturing additives without disturbing the yarns and he must close up the fabric adequately again without undue disturbance of fibre from the yarns. The surface cleaning techniques have been referred to earlier this chapter and these work in conjunction with the preparatory processes.

If *fullness* of handle is required the finisher adjusts his preparatory processes accordingly to 'burst' the yarns in order to release fibres to provide the requisite fullness. The fibre content and construction of yarns and fabric will or should have been designed to assist the finisher in this. Raising and milling process, particularly in the case of wool, complete the 'fulling' of the fabric but as mentioned earlier the finisher must take care not to over-process in these particular effects because they are irreversible.

Crispness of handle can be produced by specific types of yarn and fabric structure. Raw silk yarns, ie with the natural gum coating, are quite crisp in handle so that if the gum is deliberately not removed in finishing either wholly, or in part, the full softness of silk is not apparent. Hard twist yarns, or monofilament yarns in combination with a fairly tight fabric structure also produce a crisp effect. Additives such as resins and filling and weighting materials assist in producing crispness and stiffness of handle.

If *stiffness* exists in a fabric in an undesirable degree the fabric can be rendered softer and more flexible by a variety of mechanical and chemical methods. It can be passed through a flexing machine which rapidly flexes it all over and makes it more supple. The finisher's control of drying processes is a valuable contribution in this respect because incorrect drying can produce an objectionable harshness in handle. Chemical softening agents, which are usually compounds of oils, fats and waxes are also used.

Performance processes
These are processes which aim at improvement of some specific aspect

of fabric performance. They cannot be completely separated from development processes because in some instances they precede them and inevitably they have some effect on appearance and handle and their use can lead to some modification of the finishing routine. It must not be assumed that some form of performance process is carried out on every fabric during finishing as a routine. The following groups of processes will be dealt with briefly.

1 The use of synthetic resins.
2 Processes controlling dimensional stability.
3 Processes conferring particular performance properties.

The use of synthetic resins

Frequent reference has been made during development process description to the use of synthetic resin. This illustrates the difficulty of completely separating different types of finishing treatments and indeed it indicates the undesirability of such separation—except for initial study and explanation. Resin treatments are now very widely used and enter into finishing treatments for many purposes so that it was felt advisable to deal with them as a group under the heading of performance but not confined entirely to this function.

The dictionary definition of natural resin is an 'adhesive substance secreted by and exuding from plants especially fir and pine' or it can be a similar substance obtained by the chemical treatment of various vegetable products. There is also mineral resin obtained from asphalt or bitumen. The synthetic resins are similarly varied in character.

Crease resistance

Intensive development of viscose rayon in staple fibre form started about the middle 1920s. One discouraging feature, however, was the limpness in handle and almost total lack of crease resistance of fabrics made from rayon staple. The creasing tendency of the natural cellulosic fibres such as cotton and flax was already, of course, well known but the handling properties of these two fibres were better. It was realised that rayon staple fabrics could not make much headway unless some 'body' and 'crease resistance' could give them an advantage. The initial development of synthetic resin to achieve this objective, which was accepted commercially during the 1930s, was therefore considered a very important step forward.

The form of application consisted of two stages:

1 The resin-forming chemicals were made into a water-based solution and the fabric was impregnated with this liquid.
2 The fabric was then heated in a chamber at about 150° C for a few

134

minutes. The heat caused the resin components to combine, inside the fibre, into an insoluble resin. The fabric would then be thoroughly washed to remove any resin which had formed on the surface of the fabric. This chemical reaction is termed 'curing' of resin.

The presence of the resin inside the fibres gave 'body' without too much stiffness of handle—although this latter property varied according to the type and efficiency of the process. It also gave a good measure of crease resistance, so much so that fabrics made from rayon staple fibre became a practical proposition. At the same time the resin treatment was found to be suitable for crease resisting cotton and linen. However, the property of crease resistance is only a comparative term. Many people incorrectly assume it means crease-proof, which was never intended to be the case.

It was also found that the presence of the resin made the rayon fabrics more resistant to shrinkage although it could not eliminate completely a small amount of progressive shrinkage during wash after wash, which is a problem with viscose rayon. The reduction of shrinkage was a very valuable side effect of the crease resistance because rayon fabrics are not amenable to the processing normally used to make cotton fabrics shrink resistant on washing. Blending the viscose with synthetic fibres such as polyester made a further improvement and eventually a special resin treatment resulted in highly washable fabrics of this type, able to compete with the polyester/cottons in performance. The introduction of synthetic fibres and the widening knowledge of synthetic compounds in general increased the scope and variety of resin finishes, leading to the use of bi-functional reactants during the mid 1960s, loosely termed cross-linking agents, which in turn led to permanent press. Often they are mistakenly referred to as resins, which is incorrect because such compounds are incapable of being formed into a resinous product. But the reaction with cellulose is permanent and the finish usually outlasts the garment, unlike a resin, which gradually washes out. Extensive R & D is devoted to this area in various countries, with numerous patented processes.

Durable glaze and emboss effects

One of the earliest expansions of resin use was in the production of durable smooth surfaces, and the fixing of embossing in fabrics such as cotton and rayon. For glazing processes the fabric would be resin-treated on the surface and then calendered and polished and the resin surface cured by heat. It was found necessary to limit the penetration of resin into the fabric because it tended to make the fabric hard and brittle. This was done by filling the back of the fabric temporarily with a starch preparation. This would prevent the resin from going too deeply into the fabric and after treatment of the surface the starch filling could be removed.

Various types of resin can be used for this coating technique, some of them being of the thermoplastic type. This means that care in heat treatments, or pressing is necessary to avoid permanent damage to the effect. Some effects are sensitive to moisture spots—combined with heat — and dull patches can be produced if heat and moisture are inadvertently used in combination. It is advisable to test a fabric for this sensitivity if it appears to have had a resin face-finish.

Coated and impregnated fabrics

The coating of fabrics with rubber, oil compounds and various plastic substances has been carried out for a wide variety of purposes such as water proofing, easy cleaning, imitation leather effects, etc. It was perhaps inevitable that the more durable resin materials should be used for these purposes to replace rubber and oil compounds which have disadvantages in respect of durability. The impregnation of fabrics for stiffening purposes, improvement of transparency, and various forms of proofing, protection and glazing effects also provides scope for resin treatments which have in general better stability and durability than the traditional methods and the ability of resins to be combined with attractive colours provides additional variety of appearance. The use of fine strong synthetic fibres enables strong lightweight coated fabrics to be made which are flexible and durable, quite an improvement on the older type stiff heavy materials which were limited in colour variety. Many of these coating or impregnation resins are thermoplastic in nature and in consequence are sensitive to heat although otherwise durable, so that again testing is desirable before use to determine this and to avoid damage in making up. The thermoplastic nature of these materials has been utilised in the adaptation of welding techniques for seams instead of conventional sewing.

The coating most widely used is polyurethane, which can be dry cleaned or washed whereas fabrics with PVC coatings can be washed but only dry cleaned with cold solvents. These coatings are generally impermeable to air and water vapour unless provided with microperforations; otherwise they can be uncomfortable to wear for long periods. However, research in the late 1980s produced more comfortable fabrics which are effectively waterproof (pages 62 and 149).

Easy-care and durable press effects

The easy-care properties of garments made from synthetic fibres such as nylon presented a serious challenge to the conventional natural fibres and the older established man-made fibres such as viscose rayon.

Admittedly these easy-care properties are conditional upon certain controls of temperature and method of handling in washing and drying but even so they represented a convenience which virtually revolutionised the attitude of the consumer towards textile materials and soon became normal requirements. Drip-dry properties; easy ironing; permanent retention of shapes, creases, pleats, are the most important manifestations of easy care and it became obvious that if cotton and viscose rayon were to compete successfully they must acquire these properties in some degree.

The use of synthetic resins to produce permanent glaze and emboss effects was one of the first steps. Crease resist resins based on urea formaldehyde were used for several years, the fabric being described as 'minimum iron', but they were not very efficient in preventing wet creasing during washing. In this physical process a small particle of resin was absorbed by the fibre being treated and then during 'curing' in an oven it expanded, locking itself into the fibre—at least in theory. In practice a proportion tended to wash out at every laundering and in consequence the performance results were very limited, apart from the stiffening effect such products had on the treated fabrics. Eventually the discovery of bi-functional reactants which work by chemical action, cross-linking the molecules with the cellulosic fibre itself meant new levels of performance were possible, for the effect was permanent and could not wash out.

The successful use of these cross-linking agents led to a more specialised system of crease, pleat and shape retention in cotton and rayon garments known as *durable press* finishes. There are two different methods of processing, using the same chemicals but arranging the curing at different stages of garment manufacture. To appreciate the difference one must understand that when a cotton fabric is resin treated for crease resistance, as described at the beginning of this section on resins, the treatment takes place during finishing and the fabric is processed in a flat state. The presence of the resin inside the fibres helps to keep the fabric in this flat state and this is the origin of the fabric's crease resistance, in that it is trying to remain flat. When the maker-up (clothing manufacturer) uses this fabric for garments he has to 'fight' the finish to some extent because the fabric has to be shaped into garment form and naturally resists this in the same way and for the same reason that it resists accidental creasing.

This seems absurd when examined but it was accepted for want of a better alternative. However, the 'shape set' finishes differ from ordinary crease-resist treatments in that the actual heat curing and formation of the resin is deferred until after the garment has been made and shaped. This is achieved by impregnating the fabric with a reactive resin/catalyst system (cross-linking agents) but then, instead of heat-curing, the fabric is merely dried so that the resin chemicals do not combine. The fabric is then made up into garments and offers no resistance to shaping. The garment is completely shaped and pressed into pleats or creases as necessary and then it goes into a curing oven where it is treated at 150° C or thereabouts for a controlled time period and the resin is caused to form in the shaped pressed garment. The resin now assists the garment to keep its shape —whether creased or flat—even during and after washing and its resistance to change in shape can be fully utilised.

This system, generally known as *post-cure*, was developed and patented during the early 1960s by an American company—Koratron — then licensed in many countries under their own description of Delayed Cure, which can quite legally be defined as Permanent Press, not merely *durable press*. Initially the fabrics approved under licence were polyester/cellulosic blends but in the late 1970s Koratron extended their Delayed Cure to treat 100% wool, and blends with polyester with either 65%, 45% or 30% wool. This treatment does not degrade the fibre but in fact strengthens it through the coating action of anti-felting chemicals. Like all fabrics being used for this system, the dyestuffs must be carefully selected to be fast to sublimation through heat, and fast to washing. Resin can also be used in the treatment of wool solely for anti-shrinking, but this will be referred to later.

The second form of durable press finish is one in which the impregnated fabric is partially or completely cured in the flat state and the garments are subsequently shaped in special 'hot head' presses. These presses can be raised to and controlled at much higher temperatures, such as 180°C, than the normal steam operated 'Hoffman' type of press in which 120°C is the top effective temperature. In the case of partially cured fabric, the curing is completed in the hot head press whereas for completely cured fabric the higher temperature has to break down the previously imposed finishing set and re-impose it in garment shape.

This type of process is known as *pre-cure* and whilst it is not considered as efficient as the *post-cure* process it is less expensive to install and more flexible because there is no problem of storing impregnated fabrics, as in post-cure, which have a limited shelf life. However, the easiest and simplest durable press of all consists of pressing at high temperature of 100% polyester or blend fabrics with high polyester content, using the thermoplastic properties of the polyester to 'memorise' the crease or pleat it has been given in the press. The durability of the crease is usually in direct proportion to the percentage of polyester in the cloth. However, polyester is not the only thermoplastic fibre which can be durably pleated, for triacetate has the same properties, used for attractively pleated skirts and dresses. Nylon can be pleated by heat-setting and the blended mixture of triacetate and nylon, under the name *Tricelon*, is another suitable fibre.

All these durable press processes are intended to be machine wash-

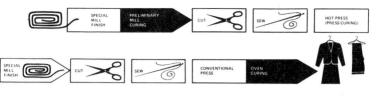

50a   Pre-cure (above) and post-cure durable press systems

able providing the specified laundering temperatures are observed. It also follows that there is no difficulty with dry cleaning.

Effect on tear strength and abrasion resistance

It was found initially that resin actually increased the strength and abrasion resistance of a rayon fabric up to a certain proportion of resin. If the resin was increased in quantity beyond this point it began to have a weakening effect. Cotton and linen fabrics were found to be weakened to some extent by the addition of resin, the amount of weakening increasing as the amount of resin increased.

With cotton and linen fabrics therefore the use of resin is a compromise between the amount of crease-resist, etc, desirable as against reduction in tear strength and abrasion resistance. Resin-treated cotton fabrics can be very low in tear-resistance and this caused the failure of many embossed fabrics of the lightweight type and is responsible for many disappointments in the wear durability of garments, fraying of cuffs, collars and edges. In the case of the durable-press finishes just referred to, stringent specifications are laid down by the proprietors of the processes as to the minimum weight of fabrics to be used and the suitability and compatibility of associated trimmings and even zips and sewing threads, and it is an express condition of the licence that the specifications shall be strictly observed. This is a sensible precaution to prevent unsuitable materials being used either deliberately or through ignorance. Fabrics containing 50% cotton 50% polyester fibre have been found to resist the weakening action of the curing process much better than 100% cotton because the polyester content is unaffected by the resin and is 'heat-set' by the curing process. The use of this blend in durable-press garments is widening considerably because it enables lighter weight fabrics to be used than is practicable with all-cotton.

Chlorine sensitivity

Certain resins used were found to be chlorine retentive, ie, if chlorine bleach was used in washing liquids it was stored up by the resin. This could cause discolouration of the fabric and loss of strength when ironing heat was applied. If a chlorine-retentive resin is used, the garment should carry a label warning against the use of chlorine bleaches, but types of resin exist which do not give great trouble in this respect.

Processes controlling dimensional stability

Fabrics are usually made to 'finish' at certain specific dimensions—in width particularly, and it is the responsibility of the finisher to ensure that fabrics are reasonably correct in dimensions when finishing treatments are completed. This presupposes that the fabric has been designed correctly and that it will behave predictably during finishing treatments, and that the finisher has merely to ensure that the fabric is treated correctly. Circumstances are seldom so straightforward and fabrics do not always behave as the designer expects for a variety of reasons, and separate pieces of fabric which have been identically constructed as far as humanly possible will frequently behave differently in finishing so that the finisher has to be constantly prepared to adjust dimensions in order to obtain uniform results even in a number of pieces of the same type.

If a fabric shows a tendency to finish narrower than the intended width the finisher can either allow it to finish narrow or he can pull it out to its intended width. The consequence of the latter course is that unless he can stabilise the fabric at this width there is a risk that it will contract or shrink sometime later on, either during making-up or in wear. The same considerations apply to length; some contraction is normally allowed for in costing but if the actual contraction is much more the finisher can pull the fabric out to its correct (calculated) length with the same stipulations as for width. The decision deliberately to adjust width and length is usually taken at the request of and in consultation with the fabric manufacturer.

The finisher is under no obligation to present a fabric which is completely and reliably stable in dimensions under all reasonable conditions of making-up or use unless such stability is accepted as a normal consequence of his processing.

The consumer, or the fabric user, cannot therefore expect that dimensional stability will be a normal fabric property in every case. With many types of fabric it is an extra which must be requested by the fabric manufacturer and which adds to the cost as compared with a normal fabric. In some instances ideal dimensional stability cannot be reasonably expected unless certain stipulations of future fabric treatment are made. This is one of the many sound reasons put forward in support of a sensible and comprehensible system of fabric and garment labelling to guide consumers in respect of correct treatments and to give information on the type of fabric behaviour which can be expected.

Dimensional stability is concerned with both *shrinkage* and *elongation*. Of the two perhaps shrinkage has caused more trouble in the past but with the increased use of synthetic fibres, knitted structures, and deliberately stretchable fabrics, elongation, or perhaps to be more precise, elongation without complete recovery has become an additional problem, quite as inconvenient as shrinkage.

Setting of fabrics

The use of heat, moisture and physical pressure to set fabrics either in a flat state or in a crease or pleat is well known from point of view of pressing, a process carried out during garment making and as part of garment finishing either just after making, or after cleaning during garment use.

It is also well known that natural fibres such as cotton and linen, and older man-made fibres such as viscose rayon can only be temporarily set by pressing in their ordinary state and that they lack resistance to ordinary or accidental wear creasing. For these reasons the use of resins, referred to earlier in this chapter, to confer some easy-care properties has expanded considerably. Silk and wool can be temporarily set and their superior natural resilience and crease resistance to the above-mentioned cellulosic fibres makes them a better wear proposition but even so deliberate creases and pleats have a limited life and need frequent renewal, although the shape retention property of these two fibres is good providing suitable fabric structure and correct make-up methods have been used.

Permanent set wool

The temporary set of wool under normal conditions is due to the ability of the wool fibre to regain its unstressed state, ie, a fibre which has been bent into a crease is able eventually to straighten itself.

The Commonwealth Scientific and Industrial Research Organisation in Australia has developed a process for permanent setting of wool in creases and pleats. The process consists of impregnating the area to be creased with a solution of a chemical compound. When the crease is pressed—under controlled conditions—the chemical compound inside the wool fibres locks them in their creased position and prevents them from exercising their normal recovery powers. The process is being marketed by the International Wool Secretariat and it is claimed that durable creases and pleats in garments can be ensured.

Another IWS permanent set process called *Lintrak* can be applied to a trouser crease from a hand applicator or a machine resembling a sewing machine. After pressing and finishing in the normal way the garment is turned inside out to expose the inside of the crease and a thin layer of resin is applied in the groove of the crease. When pressed again the resin is cured, leaving a crease which is fast to washing and dry cleaning.

Stretching and relaxation

The finisher and the clothing manufacturer can command and control much more severe conditions of heat, moisture and pressure than the domestic user. This makes it possible for the finisher to set fabrics in a stretched condition if circumstances demand this action, and the more stretchable a fabric is under hot moist conditions the more latitude the the finisher has in this respect. Cotton and linen are not appreciably more stretchable when hot and moist than when dry, but viscose rayon, silk and wool can be stretched considerably if required to. If a fabric is dried whilst being held in a stretched state it will be temporarily set in that state, but if later it is treated at or near the temperature at which it was set it will lose its temporary set and will begin to relax in an effort to reach normal equilibrium. This relaxation can occur in pressing, washing, drying or even in wear conditions and the most common result observed is shrinkage, or distortion of garment shape caused by uneven shrinkage. Obviously there will be a greater likelihood of shrinkage in this way in stretchable fabrics and for this reason the finisher must take care when processing stretchable fabrics made from wool, silk and rayon not to set them in a greatly stretched state. The clothing manufacturer should also test every piece of knitted fabric since the relaxation shrinkage may vary even within a finishing batch of apparently identical fabric.

Synthetic fibres such as nylon and polyester can be set by heat and moisture, or by dry heat, in a permanent manner, ie, unless the fabric is again subjected to the setting temperature and conditions. Modern setting is done at temperatures well above boiling point, which of course demands strict process control, to avoid the risk of accidental release of set. As a further safeguard washing and drying temperatures for synthetic fibre fabrics must be kept well below boiling. The main reason for this is that at or near boiling temperature unwanted creases can be accidentally set in these fabrics. The main set would not be disturbed but the appearance of a fabric can be completely spoilt by the imposition of creases which resist all attempts to remove by ironing.

The stabilisation of dimensions of fabrics made from synthetic fibres by heat setting is an important part of finishing and usually takes place in preparatory processes and temperature control has to be carefully observed by the finisher as well as careful handling to avoid accidental heat creasing as referred to above. Without this stabilisation synthetic fibres can shrink up to 20% or even more at boiling temperatures and this fact is used to obtain special relaxed effects in fabrics usually in conjunction with stabilised yarns. This has been referred to in methods of texturing and in obtaining 'blister' and crepe effects on fabrics.

There is a serious problem for clothing manufacturers when fabrics have not been correctly stabilised because shrinkage will occur during fusing, pleating or transfer printing, all of which are processes carried out at high temperatures varying from 150°-210°C. The real problem is that the shrinkage occurs only at the parts which are processed in this way, leaving surrounding areas unshrunk. There is also the risk of shade change if dyestuffs are not suitable for high temperature processing. This means that clothing manufacturers ought to test every fabric for dry heat shrinkage unless their suppliers can provide a guarantee of finishing standards.

Heat setting is usually sufficient to control the stability of synthetic fibre fabrics insofar as shrinkage is concerned. This is a convenience particularly where textured forms of synthetic fibres are used in knitwear in uses which were formerly exclusive to wool in that the garments can be washed without fear of the felting shrinkage to which wool knitwear is susceptible.

The acrylic fibres were the first synthetic fibres to be exploited in this particular use and it was found that the washing properties of garments in relation to shrinkage were much superior to wool. However, trouble was, and to some extent still is, experienced in stretching and some garments particularly the heavy knitted styles very quickly became shapeless through excessive stretching which could not be recovered. Part of the trouble was found to be caused by using machine settings which were inappropriate for the types of yarn and so produced structures which were too easily distorted. Improvements in manufacturing techniques have undoubtedly helped but great care is still necessary in the washing of this type of garment because of the sensitivity of the material to stretching when in a warm moist condition and treatment and care labels are a necessity.

In general then, synthetic fibre materials can be reasonably stabilised so long as subsequent treatments involving the use of heat and moisture are controlled and that where necessary certain handling precautions are observed.

Control of shrinkage

The shrinkage of fabrics on washing is a problem which existed long before man-made fibres and certain traditional attitudes to textile materials are a direct consequence of the shrinkage problem.

Broadly speaking, the cellulosic natural fibres, cotton and flax were, or are, considered to be good washing fibres whilst wool and silk, and animal natural fibres are not. Shrinkage is not the only factor in this because the superior resistance to heat and washing processes in general of the cellulosic fibres is also significant and it must not be supposed that shrinkage is not, and has never been, a problem in these fibres either.

Cotton fabrics

The cheapness and versatility of cotton has meant that the fibre has for a very long time been used in a wide and varied range of fabrics which needed regular washing and the shrinkage which inevitably followed was a difficult problem. Many ideas were tried to overcome it but without a great deal of success until the principles of Controlled Compressive Shrinkage treatments were discovered during the 1930s.

In a cotton fabric there are two types of shrinkage:

1 Relaxation shrinkage As the name implies this shrinkage is caused by relaxing of tensions imposed in fabric manufacture and finishing. The warmth and moisture of washing processes provide ideal relaxation conditions. As cotton is not a very extensible fibre relaxation shrinkage is not great and in itself is not a problem.

2 Washing shrinkage This is a much more troublesome shrinkage. Fabrics have been observed to shrink as much as 17% in extreme conditions. This shrinkage is caused by physical adjustments in the fabric brought about by swelling of the fibres when wet. When the interlaced yarns of a woven fabric swell, room to accommodate this swelling must be found. This room is most commonly provided by the weft yarns being compressed closer together by the warp yarns which interlace with them. This compressing action takes place over a number of washes until equilibrium is reached and the fabric will not shrink any further. This was the reason why pre-washing of fabric was never a success as a shrinkage treatment because one wash is never sufficient and in any case it left the fabric second-hand looking and without the smart mill finish. Width-way shrinkage is not normally a problem except in special fabric types such as crepe; most shrinkage is in length because the initial tension on the warp yarns usually spaces the weft yarns sufficiently for compression room to be available. There is no actual contraction of individual cotton fibres. Diagram 51 shows the principles of compression.

At 'A', before washing, the warp yarn can be seen to be separating the weft yarns partly by tension and partly by its thickness.

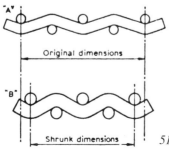

51   *Compression shrinkage*

144

At 'B', during washing, the swollen yarns have readjusted themselves; the warp yarn now curves more deeply and touches the weft yarns more closely and to accommodate this extra contact it has squeezed the weft yarns more closely together thus producing shrinkage.

Controlled Compressive Shrinkage treatments work by compressing fabrics the amount they actually shrink so that the yarns are in their shrunk position before the fabric is used, and this can be done without spoiling the finished appearance of the fabric. Different types of fabrics have differing shrinkage potential so that testing of fabric for shrinkage is an essential part of treatment. When the series of tests reveals the shrinkage potential of the fabrics, the processing equipment is then set to compress the fabric to zero shrinkage, with a deliberate margin of plus or minus 1% which prevents any risk of over-treatment. Practice shows that subsequent shrinkage or regain of 1 cm in a metre causes no inconvenience. Over-compression must be avoided because it may wrinkle the fabric's surface and, during making-up and after washing, an over-compressed fabric will certainly elongate. The Sanforized treatment, the earliest patented process, is in use under licence in most textile-producing countries. Rigmel is a similar system, another early process.

The use of resin to inhibit shrinkage of rayon, cotton and blends has been mentioned earlier, and it is thought that the coating of resin on the cellulosic fibre reduces swelling and thus inhibits fabric shrinkage. But these resins tend to reduce the fabric's strength so that another process has been developed, combined with Controlled Compressive Shrinkage, under the name *Sanfor-Set*, which—by the use of liquid ammonia—changes the molecular structure of the cellulosic fibres to reduce their shrinkage potential and improve the crease recovery.

Wool fabrics

Like cotton, wool fabrics are subject to two forms of shrinkage:

1 Relaxation shrinkage It was seen that because cotton is not very stretchable it has no great relaxation potential. Wool is quite different; it has considerable powers of extension and recovery so that tensions are accumulated during manufacture and finishing. When all processes are completed the wool fibres if left alone will try to creep back to their unstressed length. They may be prevented from doing this by temporary set, but if and when the set is released by heat and moisture contraction will begin. As with cotton, tension in the warp direction is the greater in woven fabrics so greater relaxation contraction takes place in that direction. Because of the stretching capacity of wool, and because relaxation shrinkage is completely independent of washing it presents a great problem in wool fabric use. Many people are aware that wool shrinks when washed but relaxation is a complete mystery when it happens without washing contact. Heat and moisture produced in pressing or even in wear can produce relaxation shrinkage.

As far as woven fabrics are concerned deliberate relaxation processes such as *London shrinking* are the means of either removing this form of shrinkage or reducing it to negligible proportions. The principle of this process is moistening of the fabric and then drying without tension. As this can be rather slow there are quite a few speeded up versions involving the use of heat and steam. The sponging of fabrics as practised by tailors and dressmakers on short lengths by using a damp cloth and hot iron, is a form of relaxation treatment. On long lengths, or pieces of fabric this effect can be duplicated by blowing steam through the fabric as it is tightly wound on a perforated roller. Relaxation processes are not a normal routine of finishing so that it is unsafe to assume that a fabric has been relaxed. Many clothing manufacturers have installed shrinkage machines and treat all their wool fabrics themselves irrespective of whether relaxation was part of fabric treatment or not. This is to avoid shrinkage and distortion occurring during making-up when pressing operations are used.

Knitted wool fabrics are also subject to relaxation shrinkage, but it is an area shrinkage and not as directional as in woven fabric. Because of the greater elasticity of the knitted structure control of dimensional stability of knitted fabrics is more difficult. Great attention must be paid to the correct balance of the fabric structure as it leaves the machine so that the structure is correctly compacted and if this is done the finisher can produce a relaxed fabric. The same considerations apply to fashioned garments and care must be taken to prevent undue stretching when they are finally boarded and pressed.

2 Milling or felting shrinkage This is completely separate from and independent of relaxation. Because of the well-known difficulties in washing, many wool fabrics are not intended to be washed but even so some degree of felting can take place.

Felting is produced by the combined effect of heat, moisture, and movement on a mass of wool fibres. Heat and moisture make the fibres

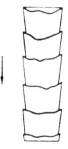

52 *Wool fibre scales*

swollen and soft and flexible. In this condition they readily move when the mass is agitated. A dominant characteristic of the wool fibre is the scaly surface which varies according to quality. Soft fine wools are covered with scales and the scale tips project giving a serrated edge to the fibre. Diagram 52 shows the effect of this. It will be seen that the tips project in the same direction and this has a ratchet effect, ie, it allows movement in one direction only — as shown by the arrow. Movement in the opposite direction is prevented by the protruding scale tips and the fibres catch and tangle with each other as they attempt to move back. This one-way movement causes a mass of fibres to gradually become denser as felting proceeds with a consequent reduction in volume. Felting is progressive and shrinkage will occur as long as felting conditions operate so that pre-shrinking, as for cotton, is completely ineffective.

Felting shrinkage can be deliberately provoked to produce felt as a fabric; or a fabric can be deliberately felted by milling to close up the structure and make it more dense, but in each case the process must be stopped when the required degree of effect is reached. Tailors use the felting property of wool to shape garments and to reduce fullness at appropriate points in a garment. Where heat, moisture and movement are produced by the body felting can occur in garments in the actual area affected.

The common sense washing instructions for wool, ie, lukewarm water, mild soap, minimum of rubbing and squeezing, are designed to minimise felting and to delay its onset.

Anti-felting treatments for wool have been in existence for many years but they were not widely used because the earlier forms of treatment were not uniformly reliable and tended to reduce the softness of wool handle. This latter feature was important because most of the wool garments which needed to be washed also needed to be soft in handle, eg, baby wool garments.

The desirability of easy-care properties in wool stimulated research in this direction and treatments now exist which claim complete machine-washability for certain types of wool garments, such as underwear and casual wear, in knitted structures.

The basic principle of these treatments consists of modifying the surface scale structure to allow two-way fibre movement. Two main methods are used:

1 To attack the surface of the fibre chemically causing the projecting tips to be 'eaten away' thus producing a rounded edge which does not inhibit two-way movement. Diagram 53 shows the effect of this.

2 To coat the fibre with a thin film which fills in the space between scale tips and fibre body and again produces a rounded edge. Diagram 54 shows the principles of this method.

147

53   Scale tips chemically removed   *54   Scale tips filled in*

The earliest form of chemical treatment used simple methods of releasing chlorine gas which attacks the wool fibre surface producing the required effect on the scale structure. These simple methods which could be applied to fibre, yarn, or fabric, were cheap and easy to apply but very difficult to control to give uniform treatment and to avoid over-treatment which gives a harsh handle to the wool.

New processes have now been developed which enable chlorine to be efficiently controlled but they are not as simple or as cheap as the early processes.

In addition treatments using other chemical compounds, easier to control than chlorine, have been developed and these processes are more expensive than the early chlorine methods but again the effectiveness of control means less risk of damage to handle.

The earliest forms of the coating method used resin which, whilst efficient in preventing felting, completely spoilt the handle of the wool. However, development of this type of method went on, particularly in the United States of America, and improved forms of synthetic resins were used to produce treatments which are much more acceptable in handle. Certain resin treatments produce a spot-welding effect, ie, where fibres cross each other the resin coating of each merges fixing the fibres together at that point. This is claimed to reduce fibre movement and assist felting resistance but resin treatments in general have been criticised for the tendency to produce a rather 'firm' handling wool fabric although later forms of treatment are acknowledged to be improved in this respect.

Anti-shrink treatments for wool

The form of treatment used in the production of Woolmark knitted wool garments promoted by the International Wool Secretariat, is a combination of both chlorine and coating treatments.

The wool fibres are first given a chlorine treatment and then a very fine synthetic polymer coating. It is claimed that this treatment does not affect softness and that the polymer coating gives increased strength and abrasion resistance in addition to such an inhibition of felting shrinkage that full machine washability is practicable.

The base process was developed by wool research organisations linked with the International Wool Secretariat, but similar processes are being developed by individual firms.

These processes, being fibre treatments, can be applied during preparation of the wool for spinning, to the yarn after spinning, to the fabric, or even to knitted garments. They are not, therefore, strictly finishing treatments and it must be emphasised that they do not prevent *relaxation* shrinkage, so that measures to achieve fabric stability in this respect still have to be taken. For example: a fabric may be knitted from a yarn which has been treated quite efficiently with an anti-felting process. If the structure is not knitted compactly enough; ie, correct gauge, loop size and tension, etc, relaxation in wear could still occur causing shrinkage, which would probably be misinterpreted as a failure of the anti-felting treatment.

Full machine washability is claimed for knitted wool garments bearing the 'machine wash' label. If this claim can be fully and consistently justified, it will represent a marked advance in 'easy-care' wool treatment and will bring the washable wool suit ideal nearer to realisation.

Waterproofing and water-repellency treatments

Certain types of garment fabrics need to have resistance to penetration by water. There is a distinct difference in degree between the terms *waterproof* and *water-repellent* which should be clearly understood.

Waterproof is, or should be, quite definite in meaning that a fabric is *proof* against penetration by water without any qualification of conditions. This term is therefore applied to fabrics which have been given an occlusive coating of rubber, oil-compound or solid plastic substance. This means that all spaces between yarns have been completely blocked and as a result the fabrics are also impermeable to air, and wear discomfort can be caused by the ensuing lack of ventilation of body heat and moisture. This type of fabric was used mostly for uniform-type garments where performance under severe conditions was perhaps more important than comfort but the increased use of decorative plastic coatings such as PVC (polyvinyl chloride) which enables bright colours to be used, has given this type of fabric a fashion value not wholly concerned with waterproof performance.

Water-repellent treatments were originally developed to give some measure of protection whilst leaving the fabric with sufficient air permeability to be comfortable in wear. These were developed for use with natural fibres such as cotton and wool which are absorbent and normally allow penetration by drops of water which will cling to and be absorbed by the fabric surface.

Early forms of treatment consisted of impregnation of the fabric with a solution of water-repellent substances which would prevent the drops of water from clinging to the fabric so that under ideal circumstances the drops of water remain spherical and tend to roll off the fabric when it is in movement—as it would be in wear. If the drops are prevented from clinging to the surface they cannot remain long enough to pass through the spaces between the yarns and a very close textured fabric with small spaces would assist this tendency; cotton is ideally suited to this form of fine construction and the gaberdine fabric is a standard form of rainwear. Wool fabrics are more difficult to treat because the ideal smooth surface to prevent clinging of drops is more difficult to achieve with this fibre.

Early forms of treatment were simple to apply, but tended to give rather a stiff handle to fabrics, which was a serious disadvantage for wool fabrics, and in addition the effectiveness deteriorated with wear and was not fast to washing or cleaning.

Improved treatments were developed using compounds of fats, waxes and oils, which gave a softer handle and were suitable for wool fabrics and more durable to washing and cleaning. These treatments often involve fairly high temperature curing and some of them incorporate resin formation.

The use of nylon or polyester microfibres woven with many filaments packed closely together has resulted in non-absorbent *shower-proof* fabrics – water vapour porous – for sportswear and anoraks. To make them *rainproof* they must be given a water repellent finish. There are also synthetic *waterproof* membranes for bonding to outer fabrics, which are water vapour porous (page 117)

The formation of *silicone* compounds fixed to the fibre surface proved to be an important development in durable water repelling treatments and these are suitable for synthetic fibres also. The early forms of treatment needed a heat curing process to form the silicone compound but later developments were able to dispense with this so that treatment for actual garments became possible.

These processes are reasonably fast to washing and cleaning so that attractive colours and fabric textures can be used which would otherwise be impracticable. They have little effect on handle because only a small percentage of silicone chemical is required.

Stain-repellency and soil-release

Research into water-repellent compounds, suitable for use in fabric treatments, carried out in the United States some years ago revealed that certain compounds containing fluorine gave repellency to both water and oil. From this discovery modern stain-repellent treatments have evolved combining silicone and fluorine compounds which prevent both water and oily or greasy substances clinging to the fabric.

This stain repellency, in effect, makes the fabric both hydrophobic and oleophobic, ie water opposing and oil opposing. Another type of anti-stain processing is Soil Release finish, generally applied to polyester/ cotton workwear fabrics, which enables stains and grease marks to be more easily washed out of a fabric so that they do not become set in. Basically it makes the fabric more amenable to water and less attractive to oily substances. There are two methods of achieving this objective and they appear at first sight to oppose each other, but in fact both theories are logical. One process concentrates on making the fabric more oleophobic so that it opposes the oil in the first place and the alternative system, used more frequently, has a hydrophilic effect (the opposite of hydrophobic) on the polyester fibres, virtually making them welcome the water and permit its cleansing effects. This nullifies polyester's natural tendency to oppose water. The process also acts as anti-stat finish, which prevents the attraction of soil particles to the fabric's structure. Opinions vary as to the durability of these soil release finishes, but most agree that they last from 25 to 40 household washings or 20 commercial launderings.

Anti-static treatments

Static electricity is created when two dissimilar substances are rubbed together and then separated, causing negatively charged electrons to be removed from one surface and attached to the other. The surface from which the electrons are removed becomes positively charged and the surface to which they are attached becomes negatively charged. In list 54a, textile fibres are arranged in such an order that any one of them rubbed against another *below* it on the list will become positively charged, and if rubbed against another *above* it, will become negatively charged. The further apart they are on the list, the greater the charge generated. Human and animal skin occupies a position near to cotton and viscose rayon.

Positive end
Polyurethane
Nylon
Wool
Silk
Viscose rayon
Cotton
Acetate
Polypropylene
Polyester
Acrylic
PVC
Teflon
Negative end

54a Fibre static charge order

For example, it has been found that a person with leather-soled shoes walking on an acrylic carpet will accumulate a positive charge because the acrylic fibre will attract electrons (negative components of an atom) yet when walking on a nylon carpet will obtain a negative charge because the nylon will lose electrons. A person wearing an acrylic or PVC garment could produce a fairly strong charge which will show sparks when the fabric is removed from the skin. Equally two fabrics worn together, eg an acrylic sweater over a wool or nylon dress, when separated could produce the same result.

Natural fibres generate less electrostatic charge than synthetics because they absorb moisture, which is a conductor. Synthetic fibres, being non-absorbent, tend to store static charges. The human body is a conductor but can act as a capacitator (storage facility) if insulated from earth by non-conducting footwear. Quite high charges can be built up and shocks felt when the charge is earthed. These charges generally occur in hot dry weather when there is little moisture in the air or in centrally heated premises which can produce the same conditions.

There are problems in obtaining a really durable anti-stat process for synthetic fibres. As they are normally hydrophobic the aim of the anti-stat finish is to make them hydrophilic, to provide some degree of moisture absorption, which helps to conduct away the static charge. ICI's *Permalose TG* provides this finish for polyester and blend fabrics. There are other fabric finishes for anti-stat nylon and acrylic. A more permanent method is to introduce anti-stat components during polymerisation in order to provide hydrophilic properties and this has achieved excellent anti-stat results for nylon lingerie in Du Pont's *Antron* and Monsanto's *Ultron*. A very effective anti-stat is provided by carbon black blended into PVC or polyester/cotton fabrics but the speckled black colour is not popular.

Flame-resist treatments

The fact that the majority of textile fibres are flammable in some degree is frequently and sometimes tragically made apparent. The necessity for some form of treatment which would reduce flammability risk in fabrics has been on record since the seventeenth century at least, and the earliest concern in this respect was directed to safety measures in theatres where large areas of fabric were in use as curtains, hangings and scenery in close proximity to hot lights.

Regulations controlling the use of fabrics, from the point of view of fire risk in public buildings and places of entertainment, have been in existence for many years. In the 1960s the Home Office issued a similar statutory regulation to control the manufacture of children's nightwear. This was replaced by the Nightwear (Safety) Regulations 1985 which introduced more stringent flammability performance requirements for all nightwear garments, whether for babies, children or adults. These regulations affect fabric producers and suppliers, importers of garments, also wholesalers and retailers, including mail-order outlets.

A new feature is that positive labelling is now specified whereas in the previous regulations only warning labels had been employed. The new type of label presents a basic 'safety scale' while not implying that any product is actually safe. The flammability test now used is British Standard 5438 Test 2 where the fabric is held vertically and lighted at the bottom edge.

During work at the Shirley Institute, an authority on flame retardance, it was found that carelessly selected printed patterns, embroidered motifs, sewing threads, zip tapes and narrow fabric trimmings all presented flammability hazards in a garment. Quilted fabrics tended to spread the flame horizontally more than other constructions. The effect of fabric structure on flammability is the subject of current research at the Institute.

Untreated cotton, viscose and acrylic products burn readily with rapid flame spread. Nylon, polyester and elastane are examples of fibres which are difficult to ignite, being slow burning, and melting with dripping. Wool and silk tend to resist flame, burning only feebly. Modacrylic, chlorofibre (PVC) and FR polyester, do not sustain burning once the ignition source is removed, so that these two can be considered flame retardant. It has been found that blends of cellulose with synthetic fibres usually burn fiercely owing to the cellulose scaffolding of the relatively safe synthetic. However, a finishing treatment for polyester/cotton is now available.

Many processes have been developed for use on cotton and viscose rayon to provide good flame resistance which will withstand repeated washing. Many of these processes use a compound of phosphorous rejoicing in the name of *tetrakishydroxymethyl-phosphonium-chloride*, or THPC. This compound provides efficient flame protection when used in conjunction with a heat-cured resin. There have been, and still are, many snags in process development such as hardness of fabric handle, lowering of tear strength, adverse effect on pale colours, lowering of efficiency after many washes, and general expense.

Although wool has natural anti-flame properties, the urban riots of the 1980s resulted in a recommendation that police uniforms should be made with Zirpro treated wool, to reduce the hazards of petrol bombs. This is a simple and inexpensive process development by the IWS to improve the natural flame retardant properties of wool. It can be applied at any stage of processing from fibre to fabric, during or after dyeing. There is no problem with washing or dry cleaning afterwards.

An inherently flame retardant (FR) polyester fibre used for nightwear in addition to heavier fabrics for bedding and furnishings is *Trevira CS* developed by the West German fibre producer Hoechst. This is 100% polyester modified at the extrusion stage to have permanent flame retardance. The fibre is available as staple fibre from which fine yarns can be spun, or filament. FR polyester, being thermoplastic, melts away from flames, making it difficult for combustion to take place. On removal from the heat source it is self-extinguishing, as are molten drips. With the presence of larger flames the phosphorous FR component prevents the melting drips from burning further.

A special treatment for cellulosic fabrics – principally cotton – is *Proban*, claimed to be a durable flame-retardant finish for woven, knitted or terry fabrics, in addition to bedlinens and hospital curtains. *Proban*'s small molecules penetrate the fibre and ammonia gas cross-links with the *Proban* trapped within the fibre. There is a quality control scheme operated by the licensors Albright & Wilson which involves checking every finished batch for flammability, including tests after washing. Before the *Proban* labels may be used for nightwear the garment must pass BS 5438 Test 2.

Comparisons of fibre flammability are inexact because of the effects of fabric structure, surface finish and garment design on garment flammability. An accepted method of assessing the propensity of fibres to accept flame is LOI (Limiting Oxygen Index) which determines the minimum oxygen concentration for fibre ignition in a specified atmosphere and temperature. As air normally contains 21% oxygen, fibres with LOI above that figure would not burn in a normal atmosphere. Cotton and viscose have LOI of 20%, nylon and polyester are rated at 22%, wool at 27%, whilst acrylic has only 19% LOI.

When a high degree of fire resistance and protection was needed, fabrics of asbestos or glass fibre used to be worn. Asbestos is completely fireproof but is a danger to health. Glass melts only at extremely high temperatures. Fabrics specially developed for US combat forces are made from *Nomex*, which serves as protective clothing where exceptionally high temperature flames might be encountered. This is an aramid fibre, very much lighter than glass fibre, which does not melt but starts to char at 378°C. For protection against naked flames *Nomex* fabric is coated with aluminium foil. The heat insulating properties of a fabric are equally important, depending on fibre and fabric construction. Another aramid fibre equally flame resistant is *Keviar*, which has exceptional strength. A small amount (5%) is sometimes blended with *Nomex* to form an extra strong *Nomex* III protective fabric.

Two recently developed flame retardant fibres are carbonised or oxidised. *Firotex* is viscose partially carbonised at high temperature to form a carbonaceous, heat stabilised fabric. Air oxidised acrylic fibres used for *Panotex* have similar properties, not igniting in a naked flame. There is no melting, dripping or flaming debris, after-glow or noxious fumes and smoke. There is, however, a loss of abrasion resistance which can be counteracted by blending with approximately 10% aramid fibre. Several fabric weights are produced, flexible enough to be worn over normal uniforms. The fibres can also be knitted into pullovers and balaclavas for extra protection. Surface coatings can be applied to *Panotex*— aluminium, stainless steel or one intended for protection against burning petrol and napalm, also nuclear flash for a very short while. This is likely to be in the region of 10,000°C.

VII The application of colour

It would be quite true to say that the colour of a textile fabric is the first property which is noticed and frequently is the first factor governing fabric choice. Any person selecting a fabric or a garment will either have a definite colour in mind or will be initially attracted by a colour and will investigate further from the point of attraction.

The importance of colour in textiles has been recognised for thousands of years and ancient writings contain frequent references to colour in fabrics.

Colour is applied to textile materials in the form of *dyestuffs* which can be used in two basic forms of process.

1 *Dyeing* In its simplest form consists of the immersion of the textile fabric material in a solution of the dyestuff in water. When the temperature is raised sufficiently the dyestuff passes from the solution into the textile material and colours it uniformly.

2 *Printing* Various colours are applied to a fabric surface in the form of a set pattern which shows clearly on one side of the fabric only.

Dyeing

Dyeing is a complex specialised science which deals with the application of an ever-widening range of dyestuffs to an ever-widening range of fibres, and the very simple definition given above suffices merely to convey the basic idea of the dyestuff being in all-over contact with the textile material, and is not intended to be a precise and comprehensive technical definition of dyeing.

Until 1856 the dyestuffs used on textiles were all obtained from natural sources, animal, vegetable and mineral. This does not mean that they were either simple to obtain or easy to apply, some of the ancient dyes such as tyrian purple—obtained from a species of shell-fish, and indigo and woad —obtained from plants, needed complicated application techniques because they were not simple water-soluble substances. Preparation of these colours was a lengthy operation to make them soluble, carried out in a vat, hence the origin of the term *vat dye*, which describes a very fast type of dye which is resistant to washing and exposure to light. These old colours were very rich and fast and were prized for that but they were expensive because of the difficulties in obtaining and applying them.

155

In 1856 a British chemist, W. H. Perkin, discovered the first synthetic dye when he produced a brilliant mauve dyestuff from coal tar. This discovery was an accident because Perkin was at the time trying to synthesise quinine but it opened a whole new field of activity. Dyeing became a science and once the chemistry of it was understood other synthetic dyes followed very quickly so that by the end of the nineteenth century the natural dyes were almost completely superseded by synthetic dyes.

There were several very good reasons for this. Synthetic dyes provided a wider, clearer and brighter range of colours. This can be seen if a range of authentic historical costumes is examined and it will be noticed that, with a few exceptions, the colours are dull compared with the vivid range commonly available now. Synthetic dyes could be made pure and constant in colour value. Natural dyes varied greatly in quality and lack of precise chemical knowledge in applying them made it difficult to produce constant matching colour tones, they also contained impurities which hindered operations, and once the chemists could isolate and prepare the pure colouring, preparation became simpler and quicker; instead of days to prepare a vat, it could be done in hours. Synthetic dyes were also cheaper than natural dyes particularly in terms of time and trouble.

Very few natural dyes are used nowadays and then only for aesthetic, artistic or traditional reasons; they have no advantage to offer for general use.

Dyeing is complicated for two main reasons:

1   It is not sufficient merely to apply colour to a textile fabric; it must stay in the fabric and not fade quickly when exposed to light; it must not bleed or run out of the fabric if it is washed; it must not rub off on to the wearer. These are some of the main considerations but they can be summed up by saying that colour fastness to various agencies is desirable. No dye is *absolutely* fast, to all circumstances in all its colour range. Broadly speaking the easier a dye is to apply the less fast it is otherwise the complex vat procedures would have no point. Fastness and cost requirements vary according to circumstances of use so that a wide range of dyestuffs is necessary to cover all requirements.

2   The various natural and man-made fibres vary in their affinity, or capacity to take dyestuffs. This is because the fibres differ in physical and chemical composition. The theories explaining the attachment of dyestuffs to fibres are controversial and complex but the practical consequence is that different types of dyes have been developed to suit particular types of fibres and whilst there is some overlapping it is true to say that no one type of dye is universally suitable for all fibres.

The science of dyeing was complicated by the introduction of non-absorbent man-made fibres. Cellulose acetate was the first of this type and it was found that this fibre would not accept cotton dyes even though it was made from cellulose, and a special range of dyestuffs was created for it. The even less absorbent synthetic fibres created further problems in dyeing, some of which have been solved by modification in dyestuffs, dyeing processes, and the fibres themselves.

These facts together with fastness and cost requirements influence the selection of dyestuffs and the method of application. Dyeing is not just a method of staining a textile fibre with a colour solution; it can be a highly complex operation involving strict control of time, temperature and chemical processes but the ultimate object is to colour the textile material to the best degree of colour and fastness that the fibre or fibres, the selected dyestuff and process of application will know, taking cost into consideration.

The application of dyestuffs to fabrics

In chapter I a table outlining the sequence of textile fabric production is given. This shows that dyeing can take place at any one of three stages:

1   The fibres can be dyed before or during preparation for spinning.
2   The yarn can be dyed after spinning but before fabric construction.
3   The fabric can be dyed after construction, during finishing processes.

Dyeing of fibres

If the fibres are dyed whilst they are in a loose state the dye solution has more chance of reaching all the surface of every fibre than when they have been twisted into yarns or when yarns have been woven or knitted together into a fabric structure. Fibres can be dyed either before any preparation of spinning has been carried out at all, or during preparation when the fibres have been carded into a sliver, or after combing processes, but certainly before the fibres have been twisted firmly together.

This method gives three advantages. Firstly it gives better penetration of dyestuffs into the fibres; secondly, it enables mixtures of colours to be produced by dyeing separate batches of different colours and then blending the batches together during spinning processes; thirdly, if a large quantity of fibres is to be dyed one colour it enables a more even colour to be obtained over the whole consignment.

Not all dyestuffs penetrate fibres easily and if the fibres have been made into a fabric before dyeing, and if the fabric is fairly dense, there is always a risk that fibres beneath the surface of the fabric will not have been so heavily coloured as the surface fibres. When the surface fibres have been worn away the lighter coloured fibres become visible, particularly in cuffs and edges of garments and around button holes. Dark coloured garments usually show this effect quite plainly and the colour change can spoil the garment appearance completely. Dyeing of fibres obviates this risk and produces a fabric which will not change colour by reason of wear, so that although wear takes place it is not as obvious.

The manufacture of fabrics from yarns which contain a mixture of different colours is an essential part of colour application because it enables subtle blends of colour to be combined with texture in a way that no solid colour could emulate. Tweed fabrics use this method of colouring in a striking way which is entirely in keeping with their traditional texture and appearance.

There is a limit to the amount of material which can be dyed at any one time, the actual amount depending on the capacity of the dyeing vessel. Where large quantities of fabric of one colour have to be produced it necessitates the dyeing of separate batches of material which should match each other exactly. This can be difficult because although dyestuffs can be made quite uniform in quality slight variations in processing and in the textile material can produce visibly different tones of colour in successive batches.

If the batches are fibres they can be thoroughly blended with each other during preparation and spinning and colour variations become dispersed.

Wool and hairs are the main natural fibres dyed at the fibre stage. Cotton and flax are never dyed as fibre and silk, of course, is a filament and is prepared directly as yarn.

Man-made fibres can be dyed in staple fibre form and they can also be spun-dyed, ie, colour introduced into the actual spinning liquid so that coloured filaments are produced.

In general the practice of fibre dyeing is reserved for better-quality and more expensive fabrics because it is more expensive and troublesome in fabric production than dyeing at a later stage. The dyeing of fibres commits the material to colour a long time before it will reach the consumer as a garment, and the textile manufacturer must predict a year or more ahead the colours likely to be in demand. This is no idle prediction because capital must be spent to pay for the fibres to be dyed. It would be useless to wait until colour demands were confirmed because there would then be insufficient time to make the fabric and the garments.

The prudent manufacturer therefore does not attempt to run a huge stock of fibre-dyed colours but tends to concentrate on a limited range of safe colours. The practical consequence of this is that the range of fibre-dyed styles offered in any one quality by a manufacturer will not be wide.

There are also processing hazards, such as the necessity to keep light and dark coloured blends well away from each other to avoid contamination; the problem of disposal of surplus or unsold coloured material and the care which must always be taken to avoid incorrect colours, or incorrect yarn sizes finding their way into fabrics. In view of the difficulties mentioned above it is usual for fibre dyeing to be carried out on better qualities only, particularly in the case of worsted wool fabrics.

However, as an exception to this general rule the practice of fibre dyeing in the medium or low-class woollen trade must be referred to. This trade uses re-manufactured wool which can vary somewhat in colour — depending on the degree of grading and the origin of the fibres. In order to minimise these differences the material may be fibre dyed because this is the most effective way of giving evenness of appearance to a mixture of various quality wool fibres.

This method does, without question, offer the most versatile method of fabric colouring obtainable by dyeing because any number of colours can be used in whatever degree of mixture or combination required. Reference has already been made to mixtures of colours and the fact that subtle blends of colours can be produced by this method of colouring. This in itself creates a whole range of colour possibilities which are closed if dyeing takes place at a later stage. Colours can be blended intimately or they can be introduced in flecks or a relatively coarse mix to give a bolder effect and perhaps to enhance the use of fancy yarn. In fact any of the colouring possibilities, which are referred to later when other dyeing stages are being described, can be achieved by fibre dyeing in a much more varied combination of colour effects.

The versatility offered must be balanced against the expense and inconveniences in manufacture which have already been mentioned.

Dyeing of yarns

The dyeing of yarn, ie, after the single yarn has been produced by the spinning machine, removes some of the processing inconveniences mentioned in connection with fibre dyeing. This is achieved to some extent at the loss of penetration, because the fibres have been twisted, but it is rarely noticeable. There is some loss of versatility also because the yarn is dyed a solid colour and the type of complicated mixture obtainable with fibre dyeing is impossible. However, colours can be combined by folding different coloured yarns together and producing coloured twist effects and this is again a traditional form of colour effect used in some tweeds and suitings. Different colours of yarns, either in solid form or in twist form, can be arranged in stripe or check patterns and wide versatility of effect is possible apart from the restriction mentioned above relating to degree of colour combination.

Differences in colour between batches cannot be easily dispersed as in the case of fibres and great care must be taken to avoid these showing in the fabric in the form of unwanted stripes down the fabric, if the fault is in the warp, or as bars of different colour if the fault is in the weft, or if the fabric is weft knitted.

The time factor mentioned in fibre dyeing is still a disadvantage and leads to rather restricted colour ranges. A complication is stocking and the precautions necessary to avoid incorrect colour selection, as mentioned for fibre dyeing, make this method of colouring only slightly less expensive than fibre dyeing so that it is mainly used for better-quality fabrics. Yarns made from all types of natural and man-made fibres are dyed and for some fibres this is the earliest colouring stage.

Dyeing of fabrics

This is the cheapest and perhaps the most common form of colour application by dyeing. In its simplest form *piece dyeing* as it is called produces solid colour fabrics but, as will be seen later, this need not necessarily always be so.

If fabric is dyed there is the possibility that the dye will not be able to reach all the fibres, particularly if the fabric is thick or is very firmly constructed. This method is considerably cheaper than the two already mentioned because it involves no complications of stocking or processing different colours. Furthermore, it enables a manufacturer to offer a much wider selection of colours to his customers because he is not obliged to commit fabric to colour until the pattern of demand shows. The fabric can be held in stock in the undyed state and sent to be dyed when colour preferences are known because this procedure does not involve great delay; dyeing can be done in a few weeks. Manufacturers frequently offer a piece dye range of twenty or more colours.

This method does have disadvantages: where different batches are to be dyed it is impossible to guarantee an exact match of all the pieces. This can be inconvenient for a clothing manufacturer because if he intends to cut a large number of garments out as one operation by laying up layers of fabric, great care must be taken to ensure that garment parts match each other in colour and pieces must therefore be matched for colour before cutting begins.

In addition there is always the possibility of colour variation within a piece—due usually to processing irregularities. A piece of fabric can vary in colour from one end to another, or it can vary across the width. Again this means inspection if faulty garments are to be avoided.

However, in spite of the disadvantages the cheapness and convenience of piece dyeing makes it an attractive proposition.

Cross dyeing

So far, the three stages at which textile materials can be dyed have been described in simple terms, ie, assuming that one type of fibre only is being used. This makes it easier to describe general principles and effects

160

but it is necessary now to consider the application of colour to blends or mixtures of different fibres.

Earlier in this chapter when dyeing was being described it was stated that one of the complications was the fact that fibres differ in their affinity to dyes. If a fabric contains fibre types which have not the same affinity for dyes a procedure known as *cross dyeing* must be adopted. In brief this means that more than one dyestuff must be used in order to colour a mixture, or blend, of fibres which possess different dye affinities.

Cross dyeing can be concerned with three different combinations of colour application:

1   A mixture or blend of fibres may be required to be dyed into a solid colour. The fibre types in the fabric which differ in affinity must be dyed separately and matched to produce the required solid colour.
2   In a fabric containing a mixture of different fibres it may be required to dye one type only, leaving the other type undyed or 'reserved'.
3   Different types of fibres in a fabric may need to be dyed completely different colours.

It will be noticed that, given the appropriate circumstances of use of different fibres, it is possible to produce by piece-dye methods colour effects which at a casual glance would seem to be the product of more expensive fibre or yarn dye processes. This enables the colouring versatility of the latter method to be effectively combined with the convenience and cheapness of piece dyeing.

For example by blending together, before spinning, two fibre types of different dye affinity (such as wool and viscose rayon staple) a plain white fabric would be produced. This fabric could then be coloured, by cross dye methods, in any one of the three ways mentioned above so that from the same basic fabric a solid colour range could be produced; a further range could be produced with the wool only dyed and the rayon left white as a colour/white mixture effect, or the wool and the rayon could be dyed different colours to produce a range of two-colour mixture effects.

If, to take another example, a woven fabric was made using yarns of both viscose rayon and cellulose acetate in combination in both warp and weft a plain white fabric would be produced which could be dyed into a range of two-colour checks by dyeing the viscose and acetate separately.

Selection of dye colours for cross dyeing is not a simple matter because differences in dye affinity for fibres are not consistent throughout the colour range of every particular dye. It does not follow that any two colours can be dyed or any two different fibres so that the dyer must take care to avoid unsuitable dye combinations.

Differential dyeing

Reference has been made in chapter III to the way in which man-made fibre characteristics can be altered for specific purposes. The dye affinity of nylon, polyester and acrylic fibres can be varied during manufacture so that tone effects, and even different colour effects, can be 'piece-dyed' into synthetic fibre fabrics.

The advantage of this technique is that the fabric is completely synthetic fibre in composition and will therefore be consistent in all aspects of performance, irrespective of colour or tone proportions.

In ordinary cross dyeing a range of colour effects produced by using various proportions of fibres which differ widely in their basic properties (such as wool and rayon) could result in a range of fabrics which would vary considerably in handle, performance and durability.

In view of the different methods of colouring available it follows that the fibre composition of a fabric cannot be assumed. Any examination of fabric arrived at identifying the fibre or fibres used must include examination of colours separately to determine whether the different colours are produced on one type of fibre only by conventional fibre or yarn colouring methods, whether cross dyeing of different fibres has been carried out, or whether different types of the same fibre have been used. Chemical modification of natural fibres, such as wool and cotton, to give differences in dye affinity is also possible but these techniques are not common.

Colour and weave effects

The appearance of a plain colour applied to a woven fabric will vary according to the weave and texture of the fabric. In a simple weave and smooth-textured fabric the colour will be flat, even and plain unless the fabric is made from lustrous yarns, or has been given lustrous finish. In a bold or fancy weave the three-dimensional effect and the different light reflection of warp and weft will add interest and depth to even a plain dyed fabric.

If colour is combined with the interlacings by the use of differently coloured warp and weft yarns textural interest can be increased and a visual effect produced which does not resemble either the weave itself or the order of colouring.

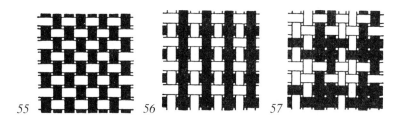

55   56   57

The three diagrams show how the appearance of a plain weave fabric can be changed by the use of colour.

In diagram 55 the plain weave has been coloured black in the warp and white in the weft. The plain interlacing mixes these colours evenly and would give a grey colour from a distance which would become coarser in grain as the eye began to perceive the actual interlacings. When two colours are used in this way the combination of them appears to vary as the fabric is moved or draped because of different direction of warp and weft. When lustrous coloured yarns are used in this way a shimmering variable effect is seen known as *shot* effect.

In diagram 56 the dark and light colours are still evenly divided between warp and weft but they are now used in alternate yarns in warp and weft. This is seen to produce fine vertical hairline stripes of colour and the weave interlacings cannot be perceived as a separate factor and no horizontal colour effect is seen even though the weft yarns are coloured alternately dark and light.

In diagram 57 the same two colours are used in warp and weft in the same proportions but now in pairs. This creates a totally different colour effect in the form of a small neat check which again dominates the weave and gives no indication of the order of colouring.

The standard forms of weave and colour effect are hairline, check, and birdseye effects which are produced by simple weaves and orders of colour. More elaborate effects can be produced by combining more than one type of weave and colour effect in stripe or block check form; by the use of more than two colours, or by using coloured twist yarns.

Limitations of colour use in fabrics

The number of colours which can be used in a fabric depends on the type of machine being used and the type of fabric construction. No machine will allow unlimited variation in pattern size and number of colours, so that where colour is being woven or knitted into a fabric in the form of yarns of different colours which are being fed singly into the fabric in the form of weft yarn, or as a knitting feed, the number of colours which can be efficiently handled is limited to six or seven in the case of woven fabrics and about three in the case of knitted fabrics. Where part of the fabric is fed in the form of a warp, ie, in a parallel series and not individually, the number of different colours is theoretically limited only by the number of yarns in the warp but in practice a repeat of pattern is desirable both to balance with the repeat of weft colouring and to make the production of the warp sensible and economical. Extra colours can be added, in the form of vertical stripes, into certain weft-knitted structures in the form of embroidery plating as, for example, in certain types of men's socks.

To present large areas of pattern in numerous colours calls for a complex mechanism and a complicated fabric structure in order to display the colours where required and then to conceal them where not. This can only be done either by allowing colours not required on the face to float loosely on the back of the fabric with the consequent risk of damage by catching the loose yarns in use, or by using a complex double-cloth structure where yarns not required on the face can be absorbed into the back structure. The latter type of fabric is expensive to make and tends to be heavy in that the double structure adds to the weight. With the advent of bonding techniques the loose back of a fabric is no longer a great risk because a lightweight fabric can be bonded to it to make it smooth and secure.

Hand techniques as used in tapestry and carpets where the different colours are inserted only in the place where they are required to show in the form of stitches or knots, fixed to a groundwork of woven yarns, enable a much wider number of colours to be used because the problem of disposing of colour not required on the face does not exist. However, these fabrics are impracticable for general use because they are very expensive and limited in production. Many ingenious machines have been invented in attempts to apply the colour versatility of hand techniques to the speed of machine production. None has succeeded completely but techniques of producing chenille and patent Axminster carpets by machine have enabled designs to be used involving the use of thirty or forty colours, and very large repeats.

Printing

The application of colours in the form of a pattern to a fabric surface might seem to be a logical solution to the problem, discussed above, of combining colours, design and fabric because of the freedom it gives in the use of a number of colours, and in the use of shape and line without the complication of having to embody these into a practical and sensible fabric structure.

However, the art of printing is very old and it developed as a separate art form when fabric manufacturing methods were simple and complex patterns could not be produced. Next came techniques of adding ornamentation by hand to a simple fabric base as in hand-knitted carpets, tapestry and embroidery. The art of weaving complicated designs was perfected by Jacquard who invented his remarkable engine very early in the nineteenth century and by this time machine printing was established.

There are three ways whereby colour can be applied in the form of a design, namely, by the *block* method, the *stencil* method, or the *transfer* method.

164

Block method

In its simplest form a design is traced on the hard smooth block surface and the block is then cut away leaving the design standing in relief. The block is then smeared with colour and then stamped on to the fabric transferring the design as cut in the block. Each separate colour in the pattern will require a separate block. A disadvantage of this method is that if a large area of colour is required it will tend to be patchy and uneven because of the impossibility of holding a uniform layer of dye on a large flat surface.

An improvement of the above method is to cut the design *into* the block instead of leaving it in relief so that the engraved parts form a reservoir of dyestuff and the smooth parts of the block are wiped clean. In this way large even areas of colour can be applied.

Hand block printing is still carried out to a small extent but it is very slow and expensive and limited to exclusive designs usually printed on relatively small quantities of expensive fabrics.

Modern roller machine printing is a development of the engraved block method.

Stencil method

A design shape is cut out of a piece of thin, hard, non-absorbent material and when this is placed on a fabric and the colour brushed or sprayed in, the cut out portion allows the colour to pass through to the fabric in the design shape. A separate stencil for each colour is necessary. The design potential of the stencil is limited to simple masses of colour because if line shapes are desired the necessity for *ties* in the stencil—to prevent the inside of the shape from falling out—imposes an unacceptable rigidity. For example if a simple 'O' line shape is required it is obvious that the centre would fall out if a stencil was cut to shape so that ties must be left as shown in diagram 58 and this spoils the continuity. *Screen* printing is a development of the stencil method. A fine mesh 'screen' made of silk, man-made fibre or fine metal wire is

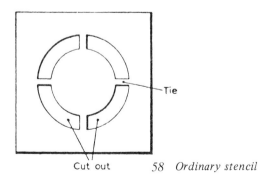

Cut out   58   *Ordinary stencil*

used. A portion of design, relevant to one colour, is marked on the screen and then the screen is *stopped*, by applying lacquer compound to the portion of the screen where colour is *not* required leaving the screen open where colour is required. Colour can therefore be transferred through the screen to a fabric underneath. The continuity of the screen removes the necessity for ties and the fineness of the mesh allows fine line registration. A separate screen for each colour is necessary.

Form of dyestuffs used for printing

Conventional dyestuffs, as opposed to paints or pigments, are mostly used for printing. Earlier in this chapter it was stated that the normal simple method of dyestuff application to textiles consists of a solution of dyestuff in water, and that the textile material is coloured by absorbing the dyestuff from the solution.

If a drop of coloured solution is placed on the surface of an absorbent textile material it will quickly spread into an irregular shape according to the strength of capillary attraction of the fibres in that area. Obviously then if a clear cut pattern of several different colours is required the dyestuff cannot be applied in a simple solution. To hold the colours in position a thick dye paste is made, using various thickening agents which prevent colour migration, and the paste holds the dyestuff until it has been fixed by finishing processes after printing and then the unwanted paste ingredients can be removed.

Machine roller printing

The idea of transforming an engraved block into a roller which could be operated by a machine was developed during the latter part of the eighteenth century. This eventually transformed the slow costly hand block process into cheap mass production which revolutionised the cotton print industry.

The principles of the roller printing machine are shown at diagram 59. The design is engraved on to a set of copper-surfaced rollers, the number depending on the number of colours in the design. Twelve or even more colours can be used but the number is usually much smaller. The rollers are situated in sequence round the circumference of a large pressure cylinder: the diagram shows *one* roller assembly only for simplicity. The pressure cylinder surface is padded and is protected from staining by dyestuffs being pressed through the printed fabric.

The pressure of the print rollers drives the fabric and cylinder and as the print rollers revolve dyestuff paste is applied to them by the furnishing roller which picks up the paste from the trough. A long sharp knife, the 'doctor knife' scrapes excess paste from the print roller leaving it only in the engraved parts so that as the roller presses against the fabric the paste in the engraved part is transferred to the fabric

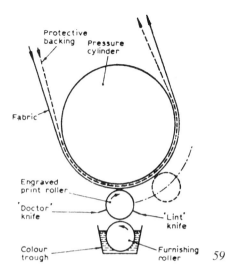

Protective
backing   Pressure
           cylinder

Fabric

Engraved
print roller

'Doctor'
knife   'Lint'
                         knife

Colour   Furnishing   59
trough   roller

surface. A 'lint' knife removes any loose fibres which the print roller
might have picked up from the fabric and which would clog the roller if
allowed to accumulate.

The separate colour rollers work independently but they must be
synchronised so that the design fits together. The paste holds the colour
and enables several colours to be printed close to each other without
blotching or running together.

Once the printing machine has been set up hundreds of metres per
hour can be printed. The colour combinations can also be changed as
required for different runs of material. Large quantities of print are
essential for the economic operation of this type of machine because the
initial cost of engraving the rollers is very high. The process is therefore
suitable for medium and low-priced prints which are not exclusive in
design and quality of fabric and is ideal for mass-production of standard
types of print.

Screen printing

For this method of printing a series of screens is prepared as described
earlier, and each screen forms the base of a rectangular tray which
covers the width of the fabric.

The fabric to be printed is laid on a long table and the screens move
on rails fixed to the table outside the fabric edges. When a screen is in
position colour paste is pressed through it by a squeegee roller. The
screen is moved along one repeat exactly and the process repeated. The
different colour screens follow on in succession until the whole table
length of fabric has been printed. The process as described above is
much slower than machine roller printing but it is much better suited to

the production of small quantities and more exclusive designs because the preparation of screens is not as costly as the engraving of copper rollers.

The screen process can cope effectively with long design repeats, or large motifs which would be utterly uneconomic for rollers (the usual length limit for rollers is about 46 cm). In addition, delicate stipple and colour mingling effects can be produced. Photo-chemical methods of screen preparation which reduce screen preparation time, are extensively used.

The screens were at one time entirely hand-operated as described above, but machines are now used for most routine printing. These are of two types: *Flat* screen, and *Rotary* screen.

On the flat machine the screens are positioned side by side over a long table. Colour supply and squeegee movement are mechanically operated and the fabric is temporarily fixed by adhesive to a conveyor belt to ensure the essential accuracy of intermittent movement in relation to the screens. In this machine the fabric must pause during printing and then move exactly one screen space.

In the rotary machine the screens are fixed side by side over a long table. The fabric, fixed to a conveyor belt, moves continuously. The rotary screens print by contract as they revolve in synchronisation with the fabric movement, colour feed and squeegee operation takes place inside the rotary screen cylinder.

These machines are obviously expensive, but they are very much quicker and require less space and labour than hand operation.

Finishing processes

In the case of both roller and screen printing the dyes have been applied in the form of a thick paste as previously described.

After printing, the fabric is steamed in an enclosed chamber and this causes the dye to pass from the paste to the fabric surface and it becomes fixed to the fibres. When this has happened the surplus paste, and any dye which has not entered the fabric, can be washed away and the fabric is then dried smooth and flat and any necessary stabilising of dimensions or surface glazing carried out.

Special printing methods

So far the simple or direct forms of colour application have been described, ie, the application of a colour pattern to a white ground. Many print styles show a white pattern on a coloured ground, or a coloured pattern on a different coloured ground.

These styles can be printed in a simple manner but it is not always the most efficient or the most economical way to produce them and it is often more convenient to combine printing and dyeing.

168

For example if a small spot or sprig design is required on a coloured ground this will be frequently done by the *discharge method*. The fabric is dyed to the ground shade first and then printed with the necessary design using a *discharge paste*. This is a chemical compound which removes the ground colour and either leaves the design showing white or a different colour dye can be incorporated into the paste and developed in place of the ground colour. This gives a cleaner result than would be possible by printing a large area of ground colour around a small design.

Resist printing

Another variation of method is *resist printing*, whereby the fabric is printed with a compound which prevents the absorption of dye. After printing the fabric is dyed and the treated part stays undyed and the ground takes the colour. This is a development of older handicraft methods such as *Batik* printing where a pattern was applied to the fabric with wax which prevented absorption and which could be removed after dyeing leaving an undyed design on a coloured ground. Another handicraft method of a similar type is the *tie-and-dye* where the fabric is knotted or tied tightly at various selected points so that certain areas are constricted. This prevents complete penetration of dye and an irregular combination of undyed and partially dyed shapes on a coloured ground is formed.

Reference has already been made to the fact that certain dyestuffs are not easy to apply to textile fibres. For example *mordant* dyes have no direct affinity for textile fibres unless the appropriate mordant is present. In simple terms the mordant acts as an intermediary between the dyestuff and the fibre, or again, *azoic* dyes are formed by coupling or joining together two substances, in the form of solutions, whilst they are in the fibre. Neither component will by itself colour the fibre.

Dyestuffs of the above types can be used to produce *dyed style* prints. The design is printed with a paste containing either a mordant or one of the azoic coupling compounds. The printed fabric is then dyed in a mordant dye, or in a solution of the other azoic coupling compound, with the result that the colour only appears on the portion which was printed. The design need not necessarily be simply one colour in an undyed ground because different mordants can produce different colours from the same dyestuff.

Flock printing

Interesting textured effects can be produced by *flock printing*. The fabric is printed with a design in an adhesive substance and whilst this is still tacky short fibres are blown on to the fabric surface and they adhere to the adhesive forming a pile type pattern. This technique has been used extensively in the manufacture of expensive wallpapers to give a fabric effect on a paper base. It was not used a great deal on fabrics except for very small spot designs because of the unpleasant hardness of handle produced by the adhesive if it was used on a large scale. However, improved adhesives are now available which allow a more supple drape to be obtained, and the use of man-made fibre flock which can be made accurately and uniform in dimensions, and the use of electrostatic methods of flock control, have made this technique a much more practical proposition.

Chemical printing

These methods can be used to produce puckered effects or to simulate open-work or embroidery by printing either chemicals which cause the fabric to pucker in the printed parts, or chemicals which dissolve or destroy selected parts of the fabric leaving deliberate holes.

Transfer printing

This process, originally called *Sublistatic* when developed by a company of that name in France in the mid 1960s, consists of first printing a coloured design on paper and then transferring the design from the paper to a fabric by heat and pressure. The process is now termed heat transfer printing or simply transfer printing. The novelty of the system is that a fabric, or a garment, can be completely printed in many different colours, in one operation, without any further colour fixing or finishing treatment. Previously transfers had been confined to small motifs, labels, trademarks, appliqué guide lines etc.

The transfer printing process uses 'disperse' dyes. These dyes are known to 'sublime': ie, at a sufficiently high temperature they are converted into vapour. The paper pattern is prepared by printing on a rotary gravure press, using disperse dyes, which have been incorporated into special printing inks. When the paper pattern is held in contact with a fabric for the correct amount of time and at the appropriate temperature, the dyes are driven from the paper and immediately attach themselves to the fabric. There is no need for any finishing treatment of the fabric, because there is a direct transfer of colour only.

The use of fibres which have an affinity for disperse dyes is, of course, absolutely necessary, but it does ensure that the colour transfer is immediate and the colours are fast to all normal requirements without any further treatment.

Fabrics made from polyester, the majority of nylon and acrylic fibre types, acetate and triacetate can be printed. Ideally, the fabric should contain 100% of these types, but blends of these fibres with natural fibres can be printed, provided that the natural fibre content is not more than about 33% otherwise the print colours are muted, although this need not always be an unacceptable effect.

Continuous piecegoods printing can be achieved by the use of specially designed calender machines. The temperatures used vary around 200°C and the contact times vary around 30 seconds. The exact time and temperature depend on the type of fabric being printed and must be accurately controlled. The contact time is governed by the speed and size of the calender and fabric can be printed at speeds of over 500 m an hour and at widths of up to 2 m.

There are several advantages of transfer printing:

1   The printer only needs to buy the presses for piece goods or garment printing. No ancillary dyeing or finishing equipment is necessary.

2   The printer can purchase either stock designs from the paper printing firms in the lengths and widths required, or can have special designs printed. There are no problems of preparing and stocking rollers or screens and very little waste in setting up new designs.

3   Printing of garments such as knitwear is greatly simplified. Multicolour designs can be applied quickly; the dye vapour penetrates into the knit structure. Solid colours can be printed by using plain coloured paper which can be quicker and more convenient than garment dyeing. Plain and print designs can be made to match exactly if the papers are printed from the same inks.

4   Patterns can be applied more cheaply by printing than by complex structures during the fabric weaving or knitting.

5   Misprints are rare providing the transfer paper has been correctly inspected. It is easier and cheaper to remove faulty paper than faulty fabric .

6   Transfer printing is a very clean process. It functions without using water or solvents and does not create any effluent problems. For clothing manufacturers the process can be fitted easily into a normal production line, rather like fusing.

As with many processes there are hazards. For example at the start it was found that fabrics made from some brands of acrylic fibre tended to turn yellow at high temperatures, so that prints with white grounds had to be avoided; also the fibres became brittle. Complete colour fastness to perspiration was difficult to achieve with nylon. But 100% polyester and high polyester blends can be very successfully transfer printed, with exceptional brilliance of colour. Yet even here there are some colour limitations, such as blue-green and bright scarlet. It is, however, exceedingly difficult to judge the finished print from the transfer paper itself, which gives little idea of what it will look like on fabric. The design is the same but the colours surprisingly different. Transfer print suppliers show the designs in fabric form rather than paper and if a customer wants to test how a print will look on another fabric, it is easy to try a small area in a table-top press which most transfer print suppliers keep on hand.

New developments in computer-controlled printing of transfer paper designs permit up to 12,584 different shades and tones, more than the eye can see. The paper can be held close to the cloth by vacuum, without pressure, using radiant heat to avoid damaging the surface, texture or pile. Continuous research is carried out on the transfer inks and dyestuffs with the aim of perfecting their use on wool and cellulosic fibres without the need for special processing of the fabric first, or in the case of wool with a washing process afterwards, for wool and other animal fibres have to be impregnated with a 'fixing' substance before being printed and it must be removed afterwards. This is a combination of 'dry printing' and wet processing normally carried out to remove spinning lubricants and to develop handle and texture.

When transfer printing first started it was thought that clothing manufacturers would install their own presses for printing rolls of fabric but in practice the majority have continued to leave printing to the textile converters. These are the companies which buy 'grey' fabric, then have it dyed, printed or finished in some other way, selling the final fabric to textile merchants or direct to the clothing manufacturers. The printers use continuous rolls of paper and fabric, whereas clothing manufacturers find the 'sheet fed' method more practical for their purpose, also easier to handle. By this method they can obtain lithographic reproductions in half tone and fine line designs. Special photo copiers using the disperse dye inks turn out transfer papers for any single colour-on-white art work ready for printing on fabric.

Several fusing press manufacturers have adjusted their presses to serve the dual purpose of fusing and printing by raising the temperature range above 210°C whereas the normal fusing requirements are from 100°C to 180°C. This means that a dress or blouse manufacturer can use the same press for either purpose. In this way the cut garment parts — perhaps the front only—can be overprinted with transfer designs to give an individual look to an otherwise basic garment. Knitwear can be printed (dependent on the fibre type) both sides at once, if transfer paper is applied on top and under, placed in a press with top and bottom heating.

In the United States the fashion manufacturers sometimes cut white fabric in bulk, holding the cut parts in stock and only printing the design on the fabric when the buyer's order is received. Often the print is designed for each garment part individually so that the pattern matches at every seam; collars, yokes, edges may have special co-ordination. They can carry out very rapid manufacture, needing only to print and stitch. Yet this 'engineered' print method has not proved so popular in Europe, possibly because of the small production runs. The printing of the paper is conditional upon a large order because the initial cost of setting up an engineered print design is more than for an all over print or for a panel print. There is also the drawback with engineered prints that a very close co-operation between garment designer and fabric print designer is essential. However, it is worthwhile for fairly standard garments such as bikini sets and shirt blouses.

Fastness of dyes

Reference has already been made earlier in this chapter to the fact that no dye is absolutely fast in all circumstances throughout its colour range and that because of this fact selection of dyestuffs to be used on fabrics depends on intended use and cost.

The main physical and chemical factors which can cause loss or change of colour in fabrics are: light, washing, dry cleaning, wet and dry rubbing, perspiration.

These are the factors which affect the general user of fabrics but in addition there are other factors which the textile manufacturer and the clothing manufacturer must consider: atmospheric fumes in storage, heat and moisture in pressing, effect of chemicals used in special finishing treatments.

Fastness to light

Exposure to daylight causes deterioration of all textile fibres and all dyestuffs to some extent, or to be more precise, the ultra-violet light in daylight is responsible. This deterioration is not usually rapid or dramatic because few fabrics are exposed to light continually without some form of protection, such as glass —which absorbs most of the ultra-violet rays. It has been found that certain dyestuffs when exposed to light for long periods change in chemical composition into compounds which accelerate degradation of textile fibres, the addition of moisture – washing for example — can complete the reaction. Large scale trouble of this kind is of course easily prevented by avoiding the dyestuffs which are known to have this effect.

The most common effect of light on dyestuffs is change of colour which is usually recognised as fading, or loss of colour strength. The degree of resistance of any dye to fading can only be measured by comparing its performance with that of standard colours under the same conditions. There are eight degrees of fastness which are measured by comparing the colour to be tested with eight blue dyes, which are accepted as the standard of comparison. Organisations such as the Society of Dyers and Colourists, the British Standards Institution, and the International Standards Organisation, have collaborated in these tests.

Since testing by daylight or natural sunlight takes a long time and, in this country, is likely to vary from day to day, most of the light testing is done artificially by using a carbon arc, or a xenon arc lamp, which gives a regular light and enables humidity and temperature to be kept under control.

Tests are carried out by exposing the sample and the standard colours together, with half of them covered by an opaque sheet so that exposed and unexposed portions can be compared at any time and the degree of colour change of the sample can be compared with that of the standard colours and the fastness number grading of the sample assessed accordingly, No 1 being the lowest and 8 the highest.

Fastness to washing

The resistance of a dye to heat, water, soap, detergent and mechanical action is an important feature for many purposes. Not only is resistance to colour loss important but also the fact whether, if colour is lost, staining of other materials will take place. Assessment of washing fastness is made by a series of five washing tests varying in severity from No 1 which is the equivalent of a 'hand-wash' to No 5 which is the equivalent of a series of severe laundering processes at near boiling temperature. In each case a 'wash wheel' or some other approved form of machine is used to enable time and temperature to be controlled and mechanical action of varying severity can be produced by placing steel balls in the canisters in which the samples are being treated. The degree of staining of other materials is assessed by stitching an undyed piece of fabric to the sample to be treated.

Colour changes are assessed by comparing the original fabric and the sample with a 'grey scale'. This enables colour loss to be measured irrespective of depth of original colour and there are five pairs of grey colours. Pair No 5 shows no change and this is the top performance. The remaining four show varying degrees of change represented by loss of colour down to No 1 which is the poorest rating.

There is a separate 'grey scale' to measure the amount of staining present on the undyed sample, and the ratings go from 5 to 1 as above.

Dry-cleaning processes use solvents with, or without, small quantities of water and detergent. Broadly speaking solvents have a less drastic action on fibres, fabrics and dyes than water and detergents. This was the main reason why the practice of dry cleaning was instituted during the nineteenth century to enable sensitive fabrics such as wool and silk to be cleaned without the shrinkage and discoloration which could occur when they were washed in water. Certain man-made fibres, however, which are not particularly affected by water, can be considerably affected by some solvents, and by heat in solvent evaporation processes (ie, drying). Loss of colour is of course only one adverse effect, but this is produced when an inappropriate solvent causes the fibres to swell and release colour which would otherwise be quite fast in water; in extreme cases actual solution of fibres is possible. Shrinkage and distortion can also be produced by unsuitable heat or mechanical treatment in solvent removal. The dry cleaner must be prepared to examine and classify all garments if processes or solvents are being used which are not safe for all fibres and fabrics.

Fastness to perspiration: rubbing

The perspiration produced by the body is a chemical fluid which can have an adverse effect on coloured fabric in regular contact with it. All perspiration contains common salt which can affect some dyes, but can vary in acidity or alkalinity according to the person.

In order to test the reaction of dyes to perspiration two chemical solutions are used which approximate to perspiration, one being slightly acid and the other slightly alkaline. Fabrics are immersed in these solutions and then heated at body temperature for four hours and examined for colour change.

Certain dyes, which are of good fastness to light and washing, are sensitive to abrasion in that the dyestuff can be removed from the fibre surface by the physical action of either wet or dry rubbing.

The reason for this is that types of insoluble dyes, such as vat dyes, or azoic dyes are developed by chemical action. Ideally this action should take place inside the fibres but in fact colour is also developed on the fibre surfaces because it is impossible to deposit the preliminary compounds entirely within the fibre and not leave any on the surface. After dyeing any loose surface colour should be removed but this is often difficult to achieve particularly with certain types of red and deep blue dyes.

Machines have been devised to test fastness to rubbing, or 'crocking', but a simple test is to rub the dyed fabric with a piece of white fabric wrapped round the finger, first with the white fabric dry and then with it wet. If the dye is not fast no rubbing it will stain the white fabric.

Fastness to bleaching: chlorine

It is necessary, from a manufacturing point of view that on occasion dyes should be used which will resist the action of bleaching substances. If a coloured pattern is required on a white ground it is cheaper and more convenient to bleach the ground after the fabric has been made— particularly with cotton. The manufacturer will be careful therefore to select colours which will resist the action of bleaching. However, many colours are used which are not intended to resist bleaching, and it must also be remembered that manufacturing processes are carefully controlled and that a colour which may resist a controlled process may be affected by an uncontrollable application such as may occur domestically .

Generally speaking the use of bleaches should be avoided where coloured materials are concerned unless the precise control of strength appropriate to the material can be guaranteed. Cellulosic fibres can be progressively degraded by bleach treatments becoming a little weaker each time until the tenderness of the fabric becomes obvious by tearing. This can happen even without noticeable colour loss and it is hastened by over-generous bleach treatments which are often administered with the false assumption that a better result will be obtained thereby.

The active ingredient in household bleach is chlorine which is a gas with a characteristic smell. This gas also has a disinfectant action—its germ-killing capacity being frequently and often dramatically advertised! It is used in water purification, particularly in swimming baths where it can often be present in obvious and often uncomfortable quantity. Manufacturers of swimwear must ensure that the colours and materials used will be resistant to chlorine.

The effects of intended use on dyestuff selection

The point has been made that no dyestuff is perfectly fast to all agencies and fastness of dyes in relation to the main consumer needs has been mentioned. There are several other considerations but as they concern the manufacturer exclusively they need not be detailed.

Selection of dyestuff is often a compromise of requirements and cost, in very much the same way that selection of fibre types, qualities and processes of manufacture are influenced. It has been shown in earlier chapters that the necessity to keep costs as low as possible can often dominate to the detriment of performance, and colour is no exception.

Since perfect fastness to light is not practicable it follows that where a fabric is intended to be exposed to light for long periods, eg, a curtain fabric, the dyes should be of maximum light fastness obtainable and that a good degree of washing or dry cleaning fastness should be possessed. Fastness to rubbing and perspiration are not highly important in this particular use. For upholstery covering light fastness is desirable but not perhaps to the degree necessary for curtains. Fastness to rubbing is certainly important, as is a good degree of fastness to washing or cleaning. For clothing a high degree of light fastness is not absolutely essential but fastness to rubbing, washing or cleaning, perspiration, etc, is important.

It will be obvious that the general properties and performance of the fabric also influence the selection of dyestuffs. If for example it is intended that a fabric or garment shall not be washed—as, for example a wool suit or costume—a high degree of washing fastness of colour would not be necessary. This is not to say that a 'loose' colour would deliberately be used but that a colour of a brightness or type that would soon deteriorate with regular washing can be used if necessary whereas if high washing fastness was necessary a less bright colour or a different type would have to be used. If a clothing fabric is not intended to be washed it follows that the fabric and colours must resist other forms of cleaning although very often an unusual fabric will be a difficult cleaning problem, not necessarily from point of view of colour fastness but more often because of structure, composition or special finish.

If a fabric is used for a purpose different from that originally intended by the manufacturer, and this is often entirely a matter of personal opinion, care must be taken to ensure that the colours are not greatly lacking in some aspect of fastness which was not considered important originally. It must not be thought that fastness of colour is the only or indeed the most important factor involved in fabric use in general or in the particular example given above; it is only one of many considerations of suitability.

On the other hand it must not be assumed that in every case the ideal types of dyestuffs have been used and that maximum fastness performance can be expected as a matter of course. In this respect a high degree of colour fastness is similar to dimensional stability, in that it can be achieved sometimes only at extra cost and if particularly requested, therefore it is not produced as a routine property.

Fugitive colours

The fastness of dyestuffs regularly used for permanent colour effects varies in degree from excellent to poor but in no case can any of these colours be classed as fugitive.

This term is reserved for colours which are intended to be temporary and easily removable, and which are used in manufacturing processes for identification purposes or to avoid errors.

For example if undyed yarns are being used in opposing ('S' and 'Z') twists alternately in sequence in either warp or weft, or both, it would be easy for operative mistakes to be made because apart from direction of twist the yarns look identical and a mistake would not be apparent until the fabric was dyed and finished. One twist will therefore be tinted with a fugitive colour to prevent confusion and the type of colour is easy to remove in wet finishing and in fact if the tinted material is left in a strong light for a short time it fades considerably and care is necessary that this doesn't happen before use or mistakes can arise.

If different types of fibres are being blended for cross dye purpose fugitive tints can be used to ensure even blending otherwise it might be impossible to check on this until too late.

VIII Basic fabrics

Fabric recognition is an important part of textile knowledge and this chapter sets out details of a number of basic fabrics covering most types. The main difficulty in conveying information on fabric recognition is that there are very few types and constructions of fabrics which enable a precise description to be given and the borderlines between similar types of fabric are not clear and mostly represent opinion rather than fact.

At one time, many years ago, fabrics could be closely identified with particular fibres so that fabric recognition and fibre identification went hand in hand. At the present time the ever-widening scope of man-made fibres adds to the number of possible variations of standard fabrics and there are very few fabrics which can now be positively identified with one particular fibre. Producers of fabrics, and manufacturers of garments, naturally wish to give an air of distinction or novelty to their products and the most common method of doing this is to evolve a 'catchy' name. This name may refer to the fibre structure, the finish or the garment style itself. It is often rather confusing to the user because it can produce a number of different items which bear the same name but which are obviously not the same as far as fabric characteristics are concerned. Some of these names achieve popularity and are given prominence by fashion writers in press and magazine articles where the constant mention of them creates the often incorrect impression that the name refers to a standard type of fabric with clear characteristics; in fact if enquiries are pursued it becomes increasingly difficult to determine exactly what the name does mean in terms of a specific fabric.

Certain basic types of fabric construction have already been dealt with and it will be found that all fabrics in present-day use are derived from these basic constructions. The possible variations are almost limitless but this chapter will deal with a wide enough selection of basic fabrics to give a reasonable idea of fabric types and a clear method of appreciation.

Appearance, texture and handle are the three important factors in recognition because these *are* the fabric. The preceding chapters have explained in general terms how the different stages of processing combine to produce these fabric properties.

The fabrics are, for the most part, described alphabetically although for convenience certain fabrics have been grouped together but are referred to alphabetically also for the sake of uniformity. References to earlier chapters and diagrams are given where considered appropriate, again, to demonstrate that the recognition factors are produced by the manufacturing processes.

Afghalaine A wool dress fabric made in plain weave using firmly twisted yarns in alternate 'S' and 'Z' twist in both warp and weft. The use of firmly twisted yarns gives a fairly crisp handle and the use of opposing twists gives a faintly crinkled appearance to the surface of the fabric. The surface of the fabric should be fairly clear of fibres. Cheaper qualities are not very crisp in handle and show more surface fibre, and may be made of a mixture of wool and a cheaper fibre.

Barathea A wool suiting or uniform fabric. The best types are fine Botany worsted fabrics, firm and compact in structure with a clean finish. The weave is a special form of twilled rib weave which in combination with the fine setting produces a finely indented fabric surface with faint regular twill lines running in opposite directions, as shown in diagram 60. The weave shown is the simplest form of barathea and there are more complex weaves used but the general effect is similar. In fine qualities this fabric makes up well in classic styles. Cheaper forms of barathea use woollen weft, and a mixture of wool and a cheaper fibre which produces a fabric with a more fibrous surface and less distinct face effect than the true fabric. Man-made staple fibres can also be used to give cheaper, lighter weight, versions of this fabric.

Bedford cord A fabric showing prominent vertical cords which are produced by a special weave structure, see diagram 50 chapter VI. It is a firmly woven hardwearing fabric, very stable, used originally for riding breeches but also used for ordinary suiting and casual trousers. Conventionally the cords are regular and of even size but different sizes can be used in stripe form for dress use. Traditionally wool, cotton or a mixture of the two was used, but man-made staple fibres can also be used for dress purposes.

Calico A plain weave cotton fabric fairly closely woven but varying in fineness and weight depending on quality. One of the basic cotton fabrics; widely used for dress and household purposes in white bleached,

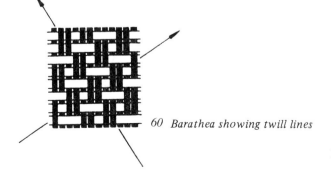

60 *Barathea showing twill lines*

plain colours, stripes and printed styles. It is more closely woven than muslin, but not as fine as lawn, nor as soft in finish as cambric.

It is also widely used in unbleached form for mattress covers and cheap coverings and lightweight types can be used as toile to make up dress patterns for stand modelling.

Cambric A fine lightweight plain weave fabric, usually cotton but can also be made in linen. The yarns are not set closely together and the finish is soft and smooth. Used for dress purposes, plain or printed and for handkerchiefs.

Cavalry twill A firmly woven fabric with a steep prominent double twill effect, produced by a special twill weave and finely set warp. Traditionally a fine wool worsted fabric, or combination of worsted warp and woollen weft used for riding breeches. Also used for suiting and sports trousers. Man-made staple fibres can be used for cheaper versions, because the traditional form of this fabric is expensive. Diagram 61 shows a typical structure.

Chiffon A soft flimsy silk fabric made in plain weave with very fine yarns and an open structure — as shown in diagram 62. Very light weight fabrics weighing 15 gm or even less per square metre are made of this type with beautiful handle and draping properties. It is difficult fabric to make up because of the looseness of structure the yarns slide very easily.

Chiffon is also made in man-made fibres, usually monofilament yarns of nylon or polyester. These are stiffer and less flexible than the true silk chiffon. Hard twist silk yarns can be used to make *crepe chiffon*, with a characteristic crinkled surface appearance (see *Crepe*).

The term chiffon is also used as a prefix to other fabric names to indicate very lightweight versions of these fabrics, eg chiffon velvet, chiffon taffeta, etc.

Checks

The traditional form of check is obtained by weaving a fabric with

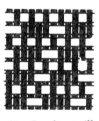

61   *Cavalry twill*

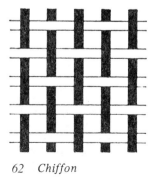

62   *Chiffon*

bold stripe colourings in both warp and weft producing a rectangular block pattern as the colours combine with each other to produce solid blocks of colour combined with blocks of mixed colour. The very wide range of Scottish Tartan designs is a typical example of this technique using solid blocks of colour and a simple weave.

Woven checks can also be produced as a combination of weave and colour (referred to in chapter VII). One of the most common examples of this type of check is the *dog-tooth* or *hounds-tooth* check produced by a pattern of four dark, four light yarns in both warp and weft on a 2/2 twill weave. The combination of interlacings and colour produces the well-known shape of check shown in diagram 63.

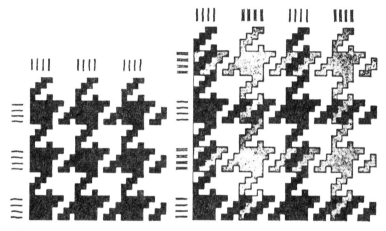

63 *Houndstooth check*   64 *Gun-club check*

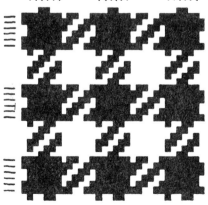

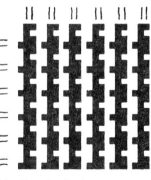

65 *Shepherd's check*   66 *Guards check*

The *gun club* check is a variation of the *dog-tooth* using two different dark colours alternating in 4 and 4 order with a light ground colour in both warp and weft. This produces a combination effect as shown in diagram 64, again using 2/2 twill.

The *shepherd* check is shown in diagram 65. In the check as shown the effect is obtained by increasing the colour sequence to five or more yarns (in the diagram six have been used) and a 2/2 twill weave. This causes the *dog-tooth* shape to be lost and produces square blocks where the colours intersect. The ordinary dog-tooth check is sometimes given this name also. This effect can also be produced on a plain weave.

If a 2 and 2 colour order is used in warp and weft on 2/2 twill a vertical line effect is produced. The *guards* check is of this type shown in diagram 66. This can be broken up by large window pane panels of colour and by slightly changing the relationship of the weave and the colour order alternate vertical and horizontal line effects can be produced in alternate panels.

The *Glen Urquhart* check is a large combination check produced by combining alternate blocks of 2 and 2 colouring and 4 and 4 colouring in both warp and weft on 2/2 twill. This produces panels of hounds-tooth check and panels of guards check separated by intermediate line effects. Large versions of this check are sometimes known as *Prince of Wales,* often with a fine contrasting over-check in red or another completely different colour (67).

Tattersal checks feature in shirtings and leisure wear fabrics. These are a copy of *horse-blanket* checks and vary in size. They are usually made using two bright colours alternately on a light ground as in diagram 68.

The above examples represent a few of the more common traditional checks. Further variety can be obtained by using coloured twist yarns instead of solid colours, by the use of different colour orders and different weaves.

Corduroy A weft-pile fabric, traditionally made from cotton, featuring pile cords produced by a special structure combined with a cutting process (see diagram 40). It was originally produced as a very hard wearing fabric for working trousers and breeches but is now produced in many forms for dress and general clothing use, in a wide variety of cord styles, and sizes. Dress styles are produced in rayon as well as cotton and elaborate cord patterns are produced by fancy cutting methods.

Crepe This term relates to the crinkled surface given to certain types of dress fabrics. Methods of producing crepe fabrics are referred to in detail in chapter VI and may be summarised as:

1 By the use of very hard twist yarns causing fabric surface distortion in finishing.

2 By the use of special crepe weaves which break up the fabric surface

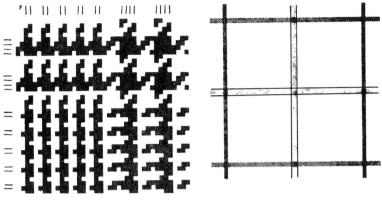

67 *Glen Urquhart check*   68 *Tattersal check*

into a random series of interlacings with no visible repeat.

3 By embossing a crinkle pattern by means of an engraved roller either into a softened thermoplastic fabric or in combination with resin.

4 By printing with a chemical paste in a pattern causing puckering of the treated parts of the fabric.

    The crepe technique is widely used as a variation of ordinary fabric types .

Crepe de chine Originally a fine silk fabric woven in plain weave, with a softly twisted filament warp and a very highly twisted filament weft, alternate pairs of weft yarns in 'S' and 'Z' twist. The effect of finishing was to cause the weft yarns to kink and crinkle the fabric. It was a fairly crisp fabric with very good draping properties—due to the softly twisted warp. It was widely used for lingerie and before the widespread use of nylon locknit for this purpose a cheaper form of crepe de chine was popular, made from viscose rayon weft and cellulose acetate warp. This type of fabric is still used for blouses and linings.

Crepon A heavy crepe effect which usually shows in the form of deep lengthways random crinkles giving a tree-bark effect. This type of fabric was originally produced by a special weave structure using high-shrinkage yarns—similar to *matelasse* but not as bold in effect. Fabrics are now produced by emboss techniques in cheaper crepon styles.

Delaine A lightweight plain weave wool fabric, made from good quality Botany worsted yarns. Soft finished and usually printed, used for dresses. Rather expensive.

Denim A hard-wearing twill fabric, traditionally made from cotton but now also made in polyester/cotton and stretch types. The weave is usually 3 x 1 twill (diagram 22) and a steep twill is produced by setting the warp yarns closer together than the weft. It was originally a protective clothing fabric but has now become accepted for leisure wear.

Doeskin A traditional West of England fine quality woollen fabric characterised by its soft handling and fine laid nap with a glossy finish. It is a *dress-face* fabric (see *Nap fabrics* page 123) and is therefore a one-way fabric. It is usually woven in a satin weave from good quality woollen yarns and the appearance developed by specialised raising techniques so that the weave is completely obscured. Used for formal tailored garments, dress uniforms, etc, an expensive fabric in its best qualities.

Dog-tooth check see *Checks*

Donegal tweed see *Tweed*

Double jersey see *Jersey*

Drill Strong hardwearing fabric, traditionally cotton similar to *denim* but better in quality and smoother in appearance. Made in warp faced twill weaves, such as 3 x 1, and 2 x 1, as in denim but also made in *satin* weave. Made in white, khaki and various plain colours and in striped styles for protective clothing, tropical clothing and uniforms, and for leisure wear. Some cotton fabrics sold as gaberdines for dress wear are actually drills.

Duchess satin see *Satin*

Faille A plain weave fabric with pronounced ribs across it. The rib effect is produced by having the warp yarns set very closely together and the weft yarns a little thicker than the warp and more openly spaced (see *Poplin*). The ribs are coarser than those of a poplin and are slightly flattened in finishing.

Originally faille was a silk fabric but it is now made from man-made filament yarns, such as cellulose acetate and is used for dresses, linings and facings.

Flannel An all-wool fabric, of the woollen type woven in plain weave, or a simple twill. During finishing surface fibre is developed so that the weave is partially or even completely obscured. The nap is normally non-directional and these fabrics are traditionally produced in white, or in wool-dyed mixtures. They are soft and full in handle, with good draping properties. The so-called worsted flannel is a fabric made from worsted yarns and though the handle is soft the surface fibre has not been developed and the weave remains visible. Cheap types of flannel are made using a cotton warp and a thick woollen weft containing re-manufactured wool.

Flannelette Is a raised cotton fabric made to imitate true flannel. It is made in either plain weave, or in simple twill and soft spun weft is used to provide the nap and the soft handle. *Winceyette* is a raised twill fabric of this type. These fabrics are made in a variety of colours in plain and printed styles. Being cheap, warm and washable they were very popular for children's wear, particularly night wear but their easy flammability led eventually to legislation designed to prevent their use for night wear unless given a durable flame resist treatment (see chapter VI).

184

Gaberdine Traditionally a fine quality wool (worsted) fabric showing a clear prominent steep twill on the face and a flat back. The steep twill was obtained by setting the warp yarns closely together, and opening the weft yarn spacing. The face twills were made prominent by arranging the loom so that warp yarns on the back of the cloth were pulled tighter than those on the face. The 2/2 twill is the standard weave, but the 2/1 twill is also used. *Union* gaberdines are made using a worsted wool warp and a cotton weft. The special construction hides the weft almost completely. Very fine construction can be used in all cotton gaberdines and fabrics of staple fibre rayon are also made.

Whilst it is primarily a rainwear fabric gaberdine is made in a variety of weights, constructions and colours for dress and suiting use; some of the cotton dress styles are made in a drill (3/1) weave.

Diagram 69 shows how the steep twill is produced. A peculiar effect of the fabric construction is that the weft lies almost straight and this can cause trouble in seams because of the tendency of the warp yarns to slide along the weft and cause a 'crack' in the fabric. This is particularly likely to happen in cheap fabrics where the warp yarns are not as closely set as they should be.

Georgette A crepe fabric made by using highly twisted 'S' and 'Z' yarns in both warp and weft and woven in a special crepe weave. This combination gives a strong crepe effect and a crisp handle and a rather springy fabric which is difficult to make up, but drapes well.

This type of fabric is made in silk, wool and rayon and is used for dress wear. It can be bonded to acetate locknit and this improves the stability and makes the fabric easier to use.

Gingham A traditional cotton fabric woven in plain weave and made with dyed yarns in stripes and checks in a wide variety of types and qualities. It is a crisp fabric with excellent washing properties because very fast dyes are normally used. Very lightweight gingham type fabrics are known as *zephyrs*.

Glen Urquhart check see *Checks*

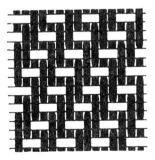

69   *Gaberdine*

Grosgrain   A fine fabric with prominent rounded ribs. The ribs are produced by weaving a plain weave with a very closely set warp of fine yarns and a more open-set weft in a thicker yarn. This is an exaggeration of the rib principle as illustrated under *poplin*. Grosgrain was originally a silk fabric and in this form it is expensive because it is rather a heavy fabric. Cheaper types are made using filament rayon or acetate for the warp and a thick cotton or staple rayon weft. The weft is entirely hidden by the close set warp and lies straight. Grosgrain is used for evening coats and for dresses and for facings. A type of grosgrain is made known as *givrine* which uses a fairly loosely folded cotton weft and the twist variations give a shimmer effect to the fabric because the ribs are not uniformly round and even.

Guards check   see *Checks*

Gun club check   see *Checks*

Haircord   A cheap lightweight cotton dress fabric with fine cord stripes produced by running two warp yarns together at small regular intervals in a variation of plain weave—as shown in diagram 70. These fabrics are produced plain piece dyed colours and in prints.

Jacquard   see page 195

Jean   A cotton fabric similar to denim, but usually lighter and finer, woven in 2/1 twill with a warp face (diagram 21) and showing a fairly steep twill, the warp being more closely set than the weft. Originally made for protective clothing and lining use but now widely adapted for leisure wear in a wide range of colours.

Jersey   This term has not, as yet, been precisely defined and can quite literally be applied to almost any knitted fabric. However, in general, the terms *single jersey*, and *double jersey* are commonly used and do have some defining meaning. Single jersey refers to a knitted fabric (usually weft knitted) made in a machine having one set of needles. In consequence the fabric is simple in structure and therefore not very stable. Mention was made of these fabrics in chapter IV where bonding techniques were mentioned as a means of adding stability to single jersey. Being simple in structure single jersey is cheaply and

70   *Haircord*

quickly made. Double jersey is taken to mean a fabric knitted on a machine with two sets of needles and the fabric can be knitted on the interlock principle (diagram 34) and patterns can be formed by interchanging yarns between face and back needles.

These fabrics are more stable than single jersey because yarns not required to show on the face are knitted into the back thus avoiding long floats and loose structure. They are slower to make and more expensive than single jersey fabrics.

Lawn A very fine plain weave fabric originally made from linen but more commonly made from cotton and now also featured in man-made fibres particularly synthetic fibres.

Lawn and cambric have similarities because both are fine fabrics but lawn is usually more closely woven and stiffer in handle than cambric. Ordinarily lawn is too closely woven to be 'sheer' but lawns made from synthetic man-made fibres have a tendency to be sheer (see definition *sheer*).

Matelasse A compound fabric with a raised or puckered design effect on the face caused by the reaction of different shrinkages of face and back fabrics during finishing (see *Piqué, blister and matelasse effects* page 131). The original type of this fabric was quite heavy and used for coatings but lighter types are now made which are perhaps more like blister fabrics than the true matelasse and the raised effect is obtained by the use of synthetic fibre yarns which have not been heat stabilised and which contract in finishing. This enables a strong back shrinkage effect to be obtained without the use of heavy compound or double structure.

Melton A woollen coating fabric with a short dense non-directional nap. These fabrics are made from all wool, or from cotton warp and woollen weft and the weave —usually a simple twill—is completely hidden by the surface fibre which is developed in finishing by milling the fabric to make it compact and then raising and cropping the surface nap. Very heavy types 930 gm per metre or more are made for overcoatings but lighter and cheaper types are used by tailors for lining the undersides of collars.

Needlecord A light-weight corduroy fabric with very fine cords, used for dresses. Made in plain piece dyed colours, or can be printed.

Organdie A thin open translucent fabric with a stiff handle, made from cotton, woven in plain weave and given a special acid finishing treatment which creates the stiff translucent effect by partially 'gelatinising' the surface of the fabric. The finish is permanent but the fabric creases easily and the same type of effect can be obtained more effectively —but not as cheaply — by the use of monofilament synthetic yarns. Organdie is used for dresses, blouses, decoration and stiffening.

Organza A light-weight, plain weave, sheer fabric made originally from fine silk yarns but now also made in man-made synthetic fibre yarns. It has a crisp handle and drapes well. Made in plain colours and in printed styles, for dress use.

Piqué A fabric with a small neat embossed-type design. Originally these fabrics were made from cotton and the embossed effect was obtained by the use of a compound structure using two warps with different tensions; the back fabric being tighter than the face thus giving the raised face effect (see chapter V) during finishing processes. This type of fabric is expensive to produce, particularly in the finer qualities and it was used for dresses, blouses and shirts either completely, or as decoration. Cheaper types of this fabric can now be made by embossing techniques using resin, or thermoplastic man-made fibres.

Plisse Originally a term describing a fabric woven in a special weave which produced pleats or folds in the fabric.

The term now refers to a crinkle effect produced on cotton fabrics by printing a stripe or other pattern in caustic soda paste compound which causes puckering of the treated parts of the fabric, or in synthetic fibres by the use of differential heat shrinkage (see chapter VI).

These methods produce cheaper and more varied crinkle effects than traditional methods such as *seersucker*.

Poplin A fine closely woven plain weave fabric showing fine ribs across the fabric. The rib effect is developed by a deliberate unbalancing of the fabric structure. The warp yarns are very closely set and the weft yarns are correspondingly opened out so that in a good quality poplin there will be twice as many warp yarns per cm than there are weft yarns. This means that the warp yarns bend round the weft yarns and the latter remain virtually straight. The warp yarn interlacings close up and almost hide the weft and the straight lines of weft produce the characteristic ribs, as in diagram 71.

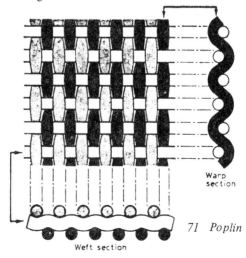

Warp section

Weft section

71 *Poplin*

In a good quality poplin warp and weft are of the same thickness and the rib is produced entirely by the imbalance of structure. Cheaper types produce the effect by using a thicker weft and a closely set warp. This can make the fabric liable to crack by the sliding of warp yarns sideways over the straight weft. A similar construction principle is used to produce the other ribbed fabrics, such as *faille, poult, grosgrain,* and *repp,* but in the case of the heavier ribbed fabrics thicker weft yarns must be used to obtain the heavier ribs and the difference in warp and weft fineness and closeness increases considerably as the ribs become bolder, eg in a grosgrain there will be four to six times as many warp yarns as weft yarns per 25 mm.

Poplin is mostly made from cotton and the best qualities are given a mercerised finish and are made from combed two fold yarns to obtain maximum smoothness and evenness. Poplin is also made from staple fibre rayon yarns. It is used for a very wide range of clothing: dresses, blouses, shirts, pyjamas, etc.

A very fine poplin can be difficult to make up because of its close structure; it can be very 'hard' to sew, particularly if it has had a resin finish and it is very susceptible to seam pucker.

Poplin originated as a ribbed fabric made with a fine silk warp and a worsted wool weft.

Poult   A plain weave ribbed fabric. The ribs are pronounced and rounded, heavier than those of *poplin* or *faille* but not as heavy as *grosgrain.* Made from a very closely set warp of filament yarns and a thicker and much less closely spaced weft. Poult is a fairly stiff fabric with a scrunchy handle. It was originally a silk fabric, but is now commonly made from man-made fibres, such as cellulose acetate; used for dresses, linings and facings.

Prince of Wales check   see *Checks*

Ratine   A woollen fabric plain weave with an uneven surface due to the use of fancy yarns usually of the spiral or loop type. These give a randomly uneven surface effect varying in coarseness according to the weight of fabric. Basically this is a coating fabric but dress or suiting weights can be made.

Repp   A prominently ribbed fabric. The true repp, which is now not commonly made, was a plain weave fabric made with two warps, one fine, one coarse, the yarns arranged alternately and the fine warp more heavily tensioned than the coarse. Two wefts were used, one fine, one coarse alternately and the weave arranged so that the coarse warp was always lifted over the coarse weft. This gave very prominent ribs. More usually the term repp is given to almost every fabric of the plain weave type having prominent ribs, made on the plain weave fine warp and thicker weft principle and of a coarser and heavier construction than poplin, faille and poult.

Repps are made in suiting weights from wool, and furnishing repps are made from cotton and man-made fibres. Some furnishing repps have different sized ribs produced by using a fancy rib weave.

Sailcloth A ribbed fabric usually made from cotton or rayon, coarser and more heavily ribbed than poplin but not as prominently ribbed as a repp. It is, however, difficult to decide just where the border-line is. Sailcloth is made in heavier weights than poplin and is used for dresses, blouses and leisure wear, according to weight. It is usually resin finished and can be quite a 'hard' and somewhat stiff fabric.

Sateen This is a weft-faced fabric (diagram 26). It is not a straight-forward reversing of a satin weave because the fabric construction differs in that the weft yarns are more numerous and more closely set than the warp yarns in order to give the necessary compactness of surface.

These fabrics are most commonly used for linings; the standard curtain lining fabric is a good example of this type of fabric, made from cotton and given a *schreiner* finish (see page 128) to produce lustre. The striped cotton linings used by tailors are often sateen cotton construction. Plain colour and printed cotton dress fabrics can also be made in this form.

Satin A fine fabric with a smooth lustrous face. It originated as a woven silk fabric and its effect depends on a special construction. A special satin weave is used which has long 'floats' of warp over weft. The warp is very closely set and there are usually at least twice as many warp yarns per cm than weft. This gives a close compact face predominantly warp. The interlacings of warp with weft should be completely hidden giving the fabric an apparently smooth featureless surface (diagrams 24 and 25). The back of the fabric is comparatively dull in contrast, because a non-lustrous yarn can be used.

Many different types and weights of satin are made from silk, and from man-made fibres for a wide variety of dress and lining use. *Duchess satin is* a very smooth rather stiff-handling satin, heavier in weight than the average dress satin, made with a very fine warp in an 8-thread satin weave, usually with a non-lustrous fairly thick weft to give the requisite firmness. *Double satin* is a very expensive fine fabric made as the name suggests with a double satin weave so that both sides are lustrous —and may be different colours — and the weft is completely hidden. *Crepe satin* features hard twisted weft yarns in alternate 'S' and 'Z' twist which cause a crinkling of the smooth surface giving a more subdued lustre. The satin weave is used in cotton and wool fabrics also, not primarily for lustre purposes but to produce a smooth surface which can be suitably enhanced by finishing processes (see *Drill* and *Doeskin*).

A satin type fabric is also produced by warp knitting by using long guide bar laps (similar to those in diagram 37); this gives the technical back of the fabric a smooth surface which is used as the face side for dress fabrics, often printed. The fabric surface is not so smooth and compact as the woven satin.

Seersucker A traditional form of cotton fabric showing crinkled stripes which may be in different colours and sizes. It is normally a plain weave fabric and is produced by having two warps, one heavily tensioned and the other comparatively slack. The crinkled stripes are formed by the slack warp and the smooth ground by the tight warp.

This is a relatively expensive method of producing crinkled effects and the chemical or heat shrinkage methods as mentioned under *Plisse* are cheaper and more commonly used.

Serge Basically a firm, compact, twill-weave worsted (wool) fabric with a clear face finish. The 2/2 and 3/3 twills are most commonly used. A wide range of fabrics is made varying in weight and quality, in plain piece dyed, yarn dyed and fibre dyed mixture colours. Woollen yarns can also be used to produce serges with a fibrous surface and cheaper types are made with a cotton warp and woollen weft. Staple fibre rayon is also used either alone or blended with wool. Conventional serge should be reasonably square in construction giving a twill diagonal of 45°. The handle will vary according to the quality of wool used. Botany wool serges are soft in handle whilst cross-bred quality serges are harder and rougher.

This is a basic suiting fabric, used extensively for uniforms particularly in heavier weights—up to about 750 gm a running metre. Cross-bred wool qualities are used where hard wearing properties are more important than softness of handle or smoothness of appearance.

Shantung This is a plain weave fabric with an unevenly ribbed surface and a crisp texture. The fabric originated in the Shantung province of China where the silkworms produced a rougher and more uneven type of silk which when used as weft gave an uneven fabric surface which became the characteristic of the fabric. *Ninghai, honan* and *pongee* are similar types of fabric but originating from different Chinese districts.

These types of fabric are now extensively copied in man-made fibres, by the use of deliberately irregularly made filament yarns. Cellulose acetate is commonly used for this type of fabric.

Sharkskin This originated as a closely woven compact twill fabric made from delustred man-made fibre yarns such as cellulose acetate. A compact form of warp knitted fabric is also made again by using long guide bar laps and using the technical back of the fabric as the effect side. The effect is that of a finely grained surface in a compact firm fabric of good weight but with good draping properties. Used for dress, suiting and sportswear.

Sheer A name given to a group of flimsy plain-weave type fabrics such as organdie, chiffon, organza, voile, where the fineness of the yarns and openness of the weave gives varying degrees of regular translucence and an even texture. The appearance of a very fine pair of ladies' stockings illustrates the textural and visual properties conveyed by this expression.

Surah The name given originally to a fine soft twill weave silk fabric used for dresses, scarves and head squares in plain or printed styles. The usual twill used is 2/2 which gives the fabric a fine appearance. Surah dress fabrics are made in cellulose acetate and triacetate fibres and these have a remarkably silk-like handle.

Taffeta Originally taffeta was closely woven fine plain-weave silk fabric with a stiff handle and which produced a rustling noise when worn as a dress or petticoat. It was a fairly square fabric so that an even surface was presented. However, increasing quantities of taffeta are made which are not square and they have more closely set warp yarns than weft yarns and this produces a faint rib effect across the fabric. Man-made fibres are extensively used and a stiff finish is usually given to the fabric to produce the authentic rustle. Some synthetic fibre taffetas are given a finish which produces a paper-like crackle and these are known as 'paper taffetas'.

Taffeta is used as a dress blouse fabric or as a lining, and in certain types of lingerie.

Tattersal check   see *Checks*

Tweed

This name can be applied to a number of different specific types of fabric and it creates a mental picture of a rough uneven fibrous woollen fabric. Whilst no one is certain as to the origin of the term *tweed* these fabrics had their origin in the rough hand-made fabrics made by the hill and mountain farmers from the strong tough wool of their own sheep. Thick lumpy fibrous yarns and simple natural dyes obtained from the roots, mosses, flowers and ferns around them gave the now accepted appearance and character to these 'homespun' fabrics. Modern tweeds are more sophisticated in colour, appearance and variety but the essential characteristics remain that they are woollen-spun from strong quality wools so that they are still somewhat coarse in terms of comparative yarn fineness and they are firm and rather rough in handle; the wool qualities being selected for strength and resilience rather than softness. The one exception to this general rule is the *Shetland tweed* which is made from soft wool of the Shetland sheep which is plucked from the animal and not shorn.

Tweeds are used for suitings and coatings and this full-handling resilient type of fabric tailors beautifully and wears very well. The roughness of the wool is sometimes too uncomfortable and in the past this has meant extra lining which tends to add to the weight and cost. However, by the use of bonding techniques the scratchiness of tweed can be eliminated and the introduction of lighter-weight qualities has helped to over-come weight objections.

True tweeds are made from virgin wool and are not cheap fabrics. Their distinctive character has inevitably led to cheaper imitations using re-manufactured wool qualities. The tweed manufacturers associations have attempted to combat this by issuing distinctive labels for authentic types of fabric, the *Orb and Cross* trade mark of Harris tweed exists and many tweeds are made which cannot be identified with any particular named variety. The four types which follow are perhaps the best known definite 'named' tweeds.

Harris tweed By law this description can only be applied to tweed made by hand weaving and processed entirely in the islands of the Outer Hebrides. This tweed is made in single width (ie 71/3 cm) and the standard type is a heavy cloth, about 340 gm a running metre for the narrow width, but two lighter weights (approx. 265 gm and 235 gm) together account for 60% of the sales on a world wide basis. The Far East and America take the lightest, which is sometimes reduced to 216 gm, whilst the heaviest weight is generally used for topcoats. The yarns are woollen spun and the wool is usually dyed before spinning so that colour mixtures in heather, lovat and brown are standard types. The weave is usually 2/2 twill either straight or herringbone and a variety of check patterns are produced. The finish is full in handle and fibrous although the weave is not obscured.

Cheviot tweed Takes its name from the Cheviot sheep bred in the Scottish Lowlands. These sheep produce a strong hard-wearing wool of which the best qualities have a fairly soft handle. A wide range of suitings and coatings is made in a variety of stripe, check and mixture styles. The suitings can be fairly fine in the best qualities and have a fairly clean appearance. The coatings can either be fairly clean on the surface showing the weave or they can be densely fibrous and milled to a firm compactness, so that this type of tweed is variable in appearance and the only constant feature is the wool quality character.

Thornproof tweed This is a characteristic type of tweed with 'salt and pepper' colouring styles. Normal woollen yarns for tweeds are single yarns but thornproof tweed is made from two-fold twist yarns and the two yarns can be either contrasting or toning in colour. The standard weave is plain and the combination of this weave and series of twist colours in warp and weft gives the characteristic sprinkled colour effect. Sometimes different colour series are used in both warp and weft so that intricate mixture effects are possible. The yarns are more firmly twisted than the average tweed and this gives a firm but porous fabric with a clean surface. If a thick pencil point is pressed through the fabric the resulting hole can be closed up again with the fingers; this property is probably the reason for the name 'Thornproof'. This fabric is used for suits and coats and has excellent tailoring and wearing properties if its harshness can either be tolerated or removed by lining or bonding.

Donegal tweed This is an Irish tweed which is characterised by its plain-weave structure composed of uneven slub yarns which contain flecks of bright colour contrasting with the ground colour. A wide range of weights and colour combinations is made for suiting and coating use. This type of tweed lends itself particularly to ladies' garments in appropriate colour mixtures. Tweeds are normally thought of as being masculine fabrics but in this type, as in the others, the designers have shown that tweed can be made completely feminine in style and colouring.

Velvet A warp pile fabric, ie a woven fabric made with two warps, a ground warp and a pile warp. A special weave construction (diagram 39) causes loops to be formed in the pile warp which stand upright and which can then be cut. The cut ends of the pile yarn form the fabric surface; the backing fabric, formed by the ground warp and the weft, holds the loops in place.

Velvet can be woven perfectly plain or a figured design can be produced by forming pile patterns on a flat ground, or by a contrast of cut and uncut loops, or different heights of pile. In *panne velvet* a design is produced by embossing or crushing a lustrous pile in different directions.

The term *velvet* refers to the construction of fabric and should not be associated with any particular fibre because velvet is made in a wide range of weights in a wide range of fibres, both natural and man-made. Usually lustrous fibres are used for the pile; the ground yarns can be completely different, silk, mohair, rayon, nylon, cotton (usually mercerised) are all used and fabrics of weights suitable for curtains, upholstery and dresses are made.

Generally speaking velvet is an expensive fabric, particularly the fine lightweight types of dress velvet such as *ring velvet* and *chiffon velvet*. It is essential that the pile should be fine and dense and firmly bound into the ground fabric. Ordinary velvets produce a 'U' construction, ie, the loops are bound by only a single weft yarn, or two weft yarns as in diagram 37. In the best quality construction the pile is bound by three separate weft yarns and the tufts of pile show a 'W' formation if they are pulled out of the fabric—this can easily be done by pulling weft yarns out. The 'W' pile is much more firmly bound and will be more durable and less likely to shed.

Velvet is a one-way fabric, care should be taken that the pile runs in the same direction throughout a garment. The direction of pile can sometimes be felt by running the finger tips lightly in the warp direction both ways but often a smooth and rough sensation cannot be perceived so great care is necessary.

Velveteen Very often this name is given to velvet made from cotton but strictly speaking it refers to a weft pile cotton fabric made to resemble velvet. A special weave is used in which one warp is interlaced with two wefts; a ground weft and a pile weft. The weave construction gives a tight ground structure of warps and ground weft, and the pile weft forms long floats similar to those shown in corduroy (diagram 40) except that an all-over pile effect is produced by cutting the pile 'floats' and not vertical cords as in diagram 40.

Velveteens are made from cotton and rayon mostly.

Velour Not a very precise term because it can be applied to either pile or nap fabrics (see *Pile fabrics* chapter V and *Nap fabrics* chapter VI). Velour is the French term for velvet but it can be given to heavy velvet or velveteen construction used for furnishing, or to fabrics with a soft, fine, dense nap used for dresses, suits and coatings, or for hats. Furnishing velours are usually cotton; dress velours are fine, soft-handling wool qualities, and hats can be made from wool, or from rabbit-hair fabric.

Voile A light, fine sheer fabric originally made from hard twisted combed cotton yarns in plain weave which gave a crisp handle to the fabric. Can be produced on plain, striped or printed styles, used for blouses and dresses. Can also be made in man-made fibres.

Whipcord A firm compact fabric with a prominent, indented, steep twill. The steep twill is produced by having the warp closely set and the weft more open, and a special weave in which the twill interlacings are 'stepped-up' two weft yarns to give a steeper twill line. Diagram 72 shows the effect produced.

Winceyette A soft, medium-weight twill fabric with a raised finish made from cotton (see *Flannelette*) made in white, plain colours, and in printed styles. Used extensively for children's wear because of its cheapness, warmth and washability. A highly flammable fabric unless treated.

Types of loom

The name Jacquard is associated with the production of elaborate

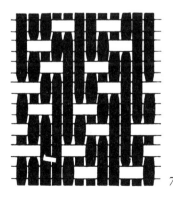

72   Whipcord

figured fabrics with large repeats containing hundreds or even thousands of different interlacings. This revolutionary machine, first exhibited by Joseph Jacquard at the Paris Exhibition of 1801, was the culmination of efforts made by a number of French inventors during the 18th century, to improve the figuring capacity of the loom without the use of cumbersome equipment and weaver's assistants.

Simple interlacings in a conventional loom are produced by using shafts, or heddles, containing rows of eyes through which warp yarns can be threaded. Plain weave requires two shafts and the warp yarns are threaded alternately through them. To make the two basic interlacings of plain weave the first shaft is lifted, dividing the warp. The weft yarn is passed through, the shaft then descends and the first interlacing is then formed. The second shaft is lifted, the weft passes through, the shaft descends and the second interlacing is formed, and so on, repeating the sequence.

More elaborate interlacing patterns can only be produced in the conventional loom by distributing the warp yarns over a greater number of shafts eg the 3/2/1/2 diagonal weave illustrated on page 93 would require 8 shafts because this weave requires independent control of each of 8 warp yarns for each repeat.

Dobby machines used in modern looms can enable up to 48 shafts to be used but as the number of shafts increases so do weaving problems, such as the weight of the shafts and the space they need to work effectively so that maximum capacity is seldom exploited and this method is utterly impractical for very large designs.

Jacquard improved on the efforts of his predecessors and produced the first really successful mechanism for figure pattern weaving.

A typical small Jacquard machine would have 200 'hooks' arranged in 8 rows of 25. This would give individual control of 200 warp yarns in a repeat and they would be lifted in any required sequence of interlacings. The interlacings would be produced by using punched cards, one card for each weft yarn inserted, and these cards were laced together in a continuous loop. The cards were punched in a separate machine in accordance with the interlacings of the design. Larger machines, or a number of machines linked together on the same loom, can extend the available number of interlacings into thousands.

The selection and control of machine movements by the use of a continuous pattern chain of some kind has led to the use of the name *Jacquard* in other forms of fabric production, such as knitting and embroidery. Magnetic tapes, micro chips and other electronic forms of control represent the updating of this remarkable invention.

Modern *Rapier* looms and *Water Jet* methods do not use shuttles. Yarns are projected through the warp threads by pointed carriers or high pressure water jets.

IX Fabrics in use

The whole object of acquiring fabric knowledge is to make the work of selection and use of fabrics more deliberately effective and less haphazard.

It is obvious from the preceding chapters that fabrics are designed and that the whole sequence of manufacturing processes is directed to producing a specific type of material. In other words fabrics do not just happen; much care and thought go into their production, not always primarily from the point of view of aesthetic beauty, often the attention is directed mostly towards efficiency and speed of production because most fabrics are works of manufacture rather than works of art.

It is not suggested that one should perpetually stand in awe of the whole procedure of fabric manufacture and treat every fabric as if it were an irreplaceable part of the original Bayeux Tapestry. If the user of fabric is *aware* of the elements of fabric manufacture and the effect that these can have on properties and behaviour and has some conception of the basic intentions of the manufacturer in producing fabrics — which the preceding chapters have set out to explain, the chances are that selection and use of fabrics will at least be more positive and purposeful even if not always perfectly efficient.

A textile fabric is raw material for some other purpose, rarely is it suitable or usable as an end in itself although it is often usable and beautiful with relatively simple methods and does not always need complicated handling. The graceful flowing and draping effect of an Indian sari is achieved merely by winding and draping a length of fabric about the wearer. It would be both undesirable and impracticable to create all garments in this manner but it illustrates the point that simple methods of use which fully utilise the main properties of the raw materials can be effective and that effectiveness does not necessarily increase with complication. The adaptation of a fabric, a predominently two-dimensional structure, to the subtly variable three-dimensional human figure is, from a scientific standpoint, a very complex procedure and many aspects of it have not been fully explained and rationalised. This does not, and never has, prevented the designing and production of beautiful, attractive and useful garments by the use of 'flair' or instinctive appreciation of fabric-garment relationship. Certain technical aspects of designing, for fabrics and for garments, are tedious in that the conversion of the idea into material and the exploration of various methods of attaining a visualised effect means expense of time. Mechanical, or electronic, aids such as computers have been adapted to save time in these operations with some degree of success. In the same manner computer control enables a complex knitting machine to produce a complete sequence of garment parts, already shaped, needing only to be fitted together. This is in no way suggesting that the machine is *creative* and does *everything* but that methods of translating ideas into material shape are constantly changing and that whilst these changes can and do affect ideas it is the *creative idea* which is the beginning and these ideas are more likely to flow when the originator is fully aware of, and sensitive to, all aspects of the raw material.

Certain originators of unconventional clothing designs are often alleged to owe their success to the fact that their ignorance of technical considerations made them unaware that certain things 'could not be done' and they just went ahead and did them. This is often a gross oversimplification and the real importance is that creative ideas and technical knowledge are both important and are really compatible if neither becomes too rigid and implacable to change. Some creative designers have achieved such status that they can confine their activities to the production of ideas leaving the technical development of them to others but it is a complete fallacy to suppose that they are either ignorant, or negligent, of the practical aspect of their ideas.

Knowledge of fabric properties and garment construction principles is an asset to anyone whether concerned with merely the using of clothing as a consumer, or as a designer, or a maker of garments in an individual capacity or as a business.

Initial selection of fabric

This paragraph heading pre-supposes that a fabric is being selected for making up into a garment. The comments which follow would apply also to a ready made garment except that the composite completed article is more difficult to check than the individual components.

Usually the governing factor in selection of either fabric or garment is *price*. It would be ideal if unfettered personal choice was available without thought of cost but very few people are so fortunate. Having accepted the ruling of price the next thought is to obtain the best value for money. It is as difficult to be completely objective about price and value in textile fabrics as it is about any other commodity and there is no easy rule of thumb method of establishing the true monetary value of a textile fabric.

Price alone is not the main consideration either, but it must be allied to *suitability*.

It is desirable that a fabric shall be suitable in colour, appearance, weight, and type and these properties influence the price. In textiles the adage 'You get what you pay for' is as true as in any other commodity. One can only learn about prices by continual comparison based on knowledge. For example, a fine cotton voile may cost over twice as much as a plain dyed cotton calico fabric. Why is this? Cotton is a cheap fibre, both fabrics are plain-weave and appear simple in construction; cotton is a cheap fibre, in its ordinary qualities, and calico is thoroughly representative of the ordinary exceedingly useful properties of cotton and the manufacture of it represents all the convenient aspects of cotton. Voile is made from very fine firmly twisted yarns which require a very good quality of cotton, much superior to the ordinary quality used for calico. The spinning of very fine even yarns involves extra processes such as combing in order to develop the essential fineness and smoothness of yarn, this takes extra time and involves extra costs.

The weaving and finishing of calico is routine and poses no special problems, but the weaving and finishing of a delicate fabric like voile necessitates special care all the way through. Imperfections which would not be noticed in an ordinary calico would be immediately obvious in a fine voile. All this adds up to extra cost which is reflected in the finished fabric. Fabrics which need special qualities of fibres and special processes in yarn and fabric preparation and in finishing will always be more expensive than ordinary fabrics. This aspect has been referred to in the earlier chapters from the note on qualities of fibres in chapter II onwards.

The *weight* of a fabric has a distinct bearing on cost, suitability and durability, as mentioned early in chapter V. Judgement of weight by handle alone is extremely difficult within close limits without considerable experience but its effect on suppleness of handle and drape is noticeable. Broadly speaking as fabrics increase in weight they become coarser in appearance and less supple in handle unless special constructions, or special qualities of fibres and yarns have been used. A heavy, supple, fine-looking material will assuredly be expensive.

Obviously weight requirements will vary according to the garment and the season. Durability requirements will also vary but this property is linked in general to weight of fabric in conjunction with the type of fibre used. Very light-weight fabrics made from strong fibres such as nylon, polyester, silk and cotton, and linen are reasonably durable, but those made from the weaker fibres such as wool, viscose rayon, cellulose acetate and triacetate are not as strong. It will usually be found that these latter fibres are not made in very light-weight structures anyway because of the strength limitations of the fibres.

Where purchases of large quantities of fabrics are involved the weight of the fabric is very important and must be determined accurately in the sample, by actually weighing it, and then the bulk fabric must be checked to ensure that the weight is correct and not lighter than it should be; it is very rare that a fabric will be heavier than the sample. The amount of allowable tolerance varies according to the weight and type of material but should be within 5%.

The *width* of a fabric is also an important factor in fabric making-up, and should never be taken for granted. In the case of individual garments the width is not always important but even so it is always wise to check this point to enable just the correct amount to be purchased because so many different widths of fabrics are available (see chapter V).

Again where large quantities are involved the width is extremely important —in conjunction with the weight — in that it should not vary greatly either within a piece or from one piece to another. Usually the required width is specified because economical cutting of a large number of garments in a number of layers of fabric demands constant width throughout to avoid excess wastage. For example if a fabric was delivered 25 mm or more narrower than expected the whole system of pattern cutting would have to be re-organised and this would certainly affect tight costings adversely. Some types of fabric are traditionally difficult to control in width, wool fabrics and crepe fabrics in particular.

Effect of finish

As shown in chapter VI the finishing processes can play a major part in the appearance, handle and performance of a fabric. Two similarly constructed fabrics can differ widely in these properties due entirely to differences in finishing processes. These differences may either be deliberate or they may represent undesirable and unintentional variations between different batches of pieces or even within the same batch. Every textile manufacturer and processor tries by every quality control means available, to produce consistent and uniform quality fabrics but in spite of this variations do occur. One of the most common finish variations is that of width—referred to above. Certain types of fabric are extremely difficult to produce consistently even in texture and appearance. The effect of the raising process on nap fabrics has been referred to in chapter VI, in that the process is critical from the point of view of weft strength, and if raising is prolonged unnecessarily even for a short time, the durability of the fabric can suffer. This weakening is not always obvious but it can sometimes be detected if a piece of fabric is torn in the warp direction (ie across the weft yarns) and the resistance, or lack of, to tearing can be gauged. Low-priced raised fabrics are often questionably durable because they usually contain a high proportion of re-manufactured wool. The fibres are therefore quite short and being loosened by the raising process, are easily rubbed out in wear leaving a bare and sometimes rather 'thin' fabric. Sometimes, in order to consolidate to hold the short fibres the fabric is 'milled' to cause felting. This has a stiffening effect on the fabric and makes the drape less supple and the handle firmer than a similar fabric of good quality, but it does improve the strength and wearing properties. This is perhaps preferable to a misleading initial softness which may prove disappointing in wear.

Pile fabrics are difficult and expensive to make and finish so that a dense fine even surface, which completely hides the ground fabric, is produced. In view of this special handling arrangements are necessary even to the extent of rolling the finished pieces in 'star' frames to avoid fabric surfaces touching and causing crush marks. This procedure is only adopted with very heavy or very delicate velvets because it produces very bulky packages which are difficult to handle. Even if they are not treated with the above care all velvet fabrics are rolled at full width and are *never* folded. In selecting and using velvets care should be taken that the fabric is free from crush marks and is not shaded by uneven cropping. Velvet is not a cheap type of fabric and cheap qualities often lack regularity of appearance and the pile cover is often sparse so that the ground fabric can be clearly seen. In a cheap velvet the pile will not be as securely bound firstly because the fabric will not be closely set and secondly because a fairly simple structure will be used and the loops of pile will only be secured by one weft yarn. The pile fibres should be resilient otherwise recovery from crushing will be poor or very slow. Cheap velvets are made by using rayon or cotton for the pile. Rayon can be given good recovery by crease-resist treatment and if the pile is adequately dense and of reasonable length an attractive useful material can be produced. Cotton velvets are perhaps more suitable for furnishing use, curtains in particular, where their lack of crush resistance is not as noticeable. The finest dress velvets are unquestionably those made from silk, their appearance, handle, drape and resistance to and recovery from crushing are excellent *but* these fabrics are expensive.

Resin finishes

A very wide range of dress fabrics is made from fibres—mainly cotton and rayon—which have been given some form of resin treatment. Reference has already been made to this in chapter VI to the fact that, particularly in the case of cotton fabrics, resin can lower the strength of a fabric.

This is an important fact to be borne in mind particularly where light-weight resin treated fabrics are involved. The main effect of this lowering of strength is a lowering of tear-resistance often to a dangerous point. Naturally a tremendous amount of research and development has been directed to the cure of this and definite improvements have been made but at the same time it must be borne in mind that resin problems have not been ideally solved as yet and most resin processes are a compromise between efficiency of treatment and lowering of fabric strength. The weakening effect of resin is often visible in wear on the edges of collars and cuffs, or wherever the material is sharply folded; these points rough up first. Intense resin treatments, such as embossed effects, are particularly susceptible to tear, weakening and papery handle, particularly in cheaper types.

The effect of resin when used for crease resistance in rayon fabrics has also been mentioned in chapter VI in that it does not seriously weaken the fabric. If the treatment is carried out efficiently a reasonably supple handle can be produced together with good crease recovery. But where low priced fabrics are concerned the resin application can produce an undesirable stiffness and hardness which makes the fabric initially difficult to handle in making up and these types of fabric often become disappointingly limp in wear or after a series of washing or cleansing treatments and soon rough up.

The problem of gaseous formaldehyde released into factory atmospheres from resin finished fabrics is being studied worldwide. Formaldehyde can cause skin irritation and respiration problems which may have adverse effect on staff health and morale. There are accepted threshhold limits which vary from one nation to another. Britain, the USA and East Germany permit more than the majority of countries, except for France which allows considerably more than any other. The Shirley Institute is undertaking an investigation to quantify the relationship between atmospheric formaldehyde and fabric formaldehyde levels. Gaseous formations and dust levels are being monitored in three factories.

Fabric grain

Reference was made in chapter I to fabric grain particularly with reference to stability. Another very important reference to fabric grain concerns finishing in particular and the use of fabric in making up.

It is worth reiterating here that the grain of a fabric is the relationship of its structural elements to vertical and horizontal lines.

Grain is easily appreciated and illustrated by the example of a woven fabric where in ideal conditions warp direction represents the vertical line and weft direction represents the horizontal. Warp and weft interlace at 90° so that in a correctly made and finished woven fabric grain and structure are square with each other.

Finishing processes involve the handling of long lengths of fabric, often in a wet state, under tension in both width and length. Squareness of fabric can only be achieved by accurate balance of tensions in length and width and this can be difficult in the case of light or extensible fabrics.

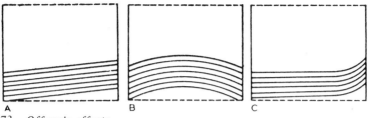

73   *Off grain effects*

Fabrics can be produced, therefore, which are off grain in themselves due to uneven or incorrect tensions in finishing processes. The result is easiest to illustrate in woven fabrics. Diagram 73 shows the three common off grain appearances.

At 'A' the weft is off square in that the line is straight but not at 90° to the warp.

'B' shows a bowing effect in that the weft shows a curve from selvedge to selvedge. 'C' shows a skew effect, the weft being straight for part of the way and then curving to one selvedge.

In each case it will be noted that the warp is quite straight and it is extremely rare for this to be otherwise because the weight and tension of a long piece of fabric will automatically ensure this but the width cannot always be so controlled.

A small amount of off grain can be adjusted during making up of the garment, ie, say, less than 2 cm in 90 cm width. Greater deviations are impossible to adjust locally and the fabric needs re-finishing.

Fabrics should be examined for this defect before purchase but it is not always easy to spot, particularly with knitted fabrics because unless the fabric is clear finished or has a regular design which gives the horizontal line the grain lines will not be easy to see. Checks show any off grain effects very clearly and it is important because the effectiveness of a check design in making up is in the matching of the checks and this may be impossible because of distortion. Light-weight fabrics are the chief offenders although off grain is not entirely confined to them by any means.

Printed fabrics should be carefully examined because sometimes although the pattern is square and true the basic fabric has been distorted and the grain of the fabric does not correspond with the grain of the print.

The distortion in an off grain fabric will have been temporarily 'set' by finishing; that is why it is difficult to adjust normally in making up. If a fabric is cut with disregard for the distortion it will re-adjust itself eventually—usually after washing when the set is released—and the garment will become distorted as the weft straightens.

Similar grain considerations apply to knitted fabrics made from regular yarn constructions. Some types of fabric such as very open woven structures, springy crepe fabrics, single jersey fabrics, lace and net constructions are unstable and can easily be distorted in cutting and must be supported in some way. The simplest way is to pin or tack to a thin sheet of paper and the technique of bonding referred to in chapter V helps in this respect. Clothing manufacturers who may be cutting many layers at once have to adopt elaborate precautions to prevent this distortion in laying up the layers of fabric and in cutting them.

Deliberate off grain cutting is sometimes essential particularly in woven fabrics in order to obtain necessary fabric 'movement' for shaping or styling. Conversely the taping or otherwise stabilising of certain garment seams is necessary to prevent movement or stretching. This is often necessary where perhaps a woven fabric has been cut 'on the bias' to obtain movement or shape in one part but another part may need to be kept fairly rigid, or in a straight seam in a knitted fabric where the natural movement of the fabric is too great for the necessary rigidity of the garment.

Certain very closely woven fabrics, such as fine poplins, are often difficult to seam smoothly, particularly if the seam follows the straight warp line. The reason for this is that the weft yarns are rigid due to the compactness of the fabric, and quite literally, no more space is available even to insert a sewing thread between them without causing puckering—even if all other conditions such as fabric tension, needle size and thread size are correct. A lockstitch machine working at 15 stitches per 3 cm will be attempting to interpose 30 thicknesses of thread, in a correctly balanced stitch, between already rigidly spaced weft yarns. Normally the natural displacement of yarns accommodates this extra quite easily but a close compact fabric will not and puckering is the result. If the fabric is cut slightly on the bias the sewing threads are not being placed between the weft yarns in a direct straight line and some displacement takes place and the sewing thread can be accommodated in a flat seam. Unfortunately some garment styles do not lend themselves to deliberate off grain cutting and, also, many makers of clothing are reluctant to deliberately cut in this manner.

One way fabrics, matching

Reference has already been made to the one way aspect of certain nap fabrics, and of pile fabrics in general.

Where a fibrous surface, be it nap or pile, is directional, there is a distinct difference in colour effect according to the direction in which light impinges on the surface fibres.

To begin with, it is impossible in practice to produce a large quantity of directional nap or pile fabric with all the fibres at exactly the same angle of inclination. Theoretically pile fabrics should be symmetrical in fibre arrangement—diagram 39 suggests this—but in practice the finishing processes, cropping and brushing, impart a direction to the pile which cannot be kept uniform over a large area. This is visible if a large area of plain Wilton carpet is examined. Patches of different colour can be seen where the pile angle differs—even if all the strips have been carefully and correctly arranged.

In clothing the areas of fabric are not large enough to produce patchy areas but the movement of a garment causes colour changes to be constantly visible. It is important therefore that the direction of fibres in all garment parts is the same. Dressmakers usually prefer the pile of a fabric to run upwards as this gives a richer colour effect, but obviously directional nap fabrics are made with the nap running downwards. The colour changes due to differing light reflection referred to above make colour matching of pile fabrics with each other and with conventional fabrics very difficult and at times it appears that a perfect match is impossible and that a compromise is all that can be achieved. It does mean that great care must be taken in matching nap or pile fabrics with plain textured materials, and with each other.

The matching of checks has already been referred to partly in grain considerations but it should be appreciated that woven checks can on occasion differ appreciably in their length dimension. This should not be so but certain types of loom can become erratic in this respect and with checks of any size it is advisable to examine the fabric with this in mind *before* cutting.

Certain check, and stripe, weave and colour effects are also directional—the Glen Urquhart check in diagram 67 demonstrates this—so that close attention should be paid to the detail of the colour effect and not merely the superficial general effect which *may* be symmetrical.

The same considerations apply to print designs; these are usually more obvious but where a design is not 'all over' and has directional aspects it should be examined carefully.

Compatibility of fabrics

So far most of the references to fabric have been related to the top or outer fabric of a garment. But as a garment is a composite of different types of material reference must be made to the other materials, often hidden which are also part of the garment.

Failure to ensure that linings and interlinings are compatible in performance with the outer fabric can absolutely nullify careful selection of the main fabric. This seems an obvious statement but it is surprising how often incompatibility occurs in commercially made garments. Often this is caused by false economy in the use of inferior materials on the lines of 'what is hidden doesn't matter'. But equally it is plain that many manufacturers who take great care in selection of main materials do not feel that equal care is necessary in selection of subsidiary materials.

Those who do know that it pays in time and trouble and proof of this is shown in the way in which specifications are laid down for *all* materials which go into durable press garments. The main fabric, linings, interlinings, trimmings, sewing threads, zip-fasteners and even buttons must reach a certain standard of performance, particularly in respect of the high temperature curing which is necessary.

This is admittedly an extreme case but it illustrates a principle which has over and over again been shown to be well worth extending.

For example it would seem obvious that a garment designed to be washed regularly would need to be made from a fully shrunk, or otherwise shrink resist material. It should seem equally obvious that there is little point in using interlinings and linings in such a garment which has received no antishrink treatment at all because the distortion caused by its shrinkage will spoil the garment even if the outer fabric does not shrink. The shrinkage of a sewing thread can cause distortion of a seam so that a non-shrink sewing thread should also be part of such a garment.

If a garment is made from drip dry material intended as an easy care garment it might again seem obvious to state that linings and interlinings should be drip dry also, but this requirement is often ignored as if the outer fabric had the power somehow to communicate its properties to the other materials.

Stretch fabrics need special consideration as to whether some garment areas should be prevented from stretching or matched with equally stretchable interlinings. Non-wovens and fusible interlinings can also raise compatibility problems. The correct weight and type should be carefully selected; most manufacturers publish booklets advising on the uses of their qualities because the majority of the complaints they have dealt with were the result of incorrect quality selection rather than faulty material. Some qualities are washable, some are not, some fusible types can be dry cleaned satisfactorily, some cannot. The use of fusible interlinings raises certain difficulties. Some types are treated with a resin which will discolour a white top material and therefore are not suitable for all fabrics. Some man-made fibre materials are dyed with dyestuffs which 'sublime' under heat and the use of heat to fuse interlinings can cause a colour change which may or may not reverse when the fabric cools. A number of fabrics shrink in dry heat or steam.

It is impossible to cover every aspect of compatibility but the user of fabrics should be thoroughly aware of the need for all components of a garment to behave similarly under reasonable conditions.

Cutting and sewing

Many points of cutting have been covered—chiefly those concerned with fabric stability and grain. Fabrics must always be cut in a relaxed, flat, perfectly straight state and if a fabric is difficult to maintain in this manner it should be stabilised by contact with paper or other fabric. Sharp scissors, or knives, are necessary for all cutting and particularly so for fabrics made from synthetic fibres because these are tough and need sharp cutting edges. Often where high speed cutting knives are used by clothing manufacturers constant sharpening maintenance is necessary and lubrication to prevent too much heat developing and fusing layers of fabrics together.

Fabrics which are loose, open in structure, or made from slippery filament yarns need a generous seam allowance to avoid seam slippage when sewn. Reference has already been made to cutting with a slight degree of bias to prevent seam puckering in the case of a closely woven poplin. The same technique is often recommended with woven filament fabrics to avoid slippage of seams. If they are cut in line with the warp there is always a danger that smooth filament warp yarns will slide sideways and cause the seam to gape when tension is exerted on it. With one way fabrics it is often useful to have some system of working (on the back of the fabric) showing direction so that if any pattern pieces are symmetrical in shape there is no doubt as to which way up they go. It is often difficult to assess accurately nap or pile direction in a fairly small piece of cut fabric although it might be obvious if it is sewn in incorrectly!

Sewing primarily involves attention to several points: needle size; thread type, size and tension; and stitch frequency are the most important. These vary according to the type of fabric being sewn. The needle must pierce the fabric rapidly and accurately without damaging it. If a needle persistently cuts or breaks continuous filament yarns as the fabric is sewn a line of fibre ends sticking up like bristles will be visible down the seam and will spoil the smoothness effect. Fabrics made from synthetic filaments are particularly susceptible to cutting so that needles with a fine cloth or ball point should be used and the finest needle size should be used. Different manufacturers have different methods of needle sizing but the normal Singer range of sizes 10 to 12, or Continental sizes 70 to 80, are common suitable needle sizes for synthetic fibre fabrics.

The choice of a suitable thickness and type of sewing thread is important but as a general rule the finest thread size consistent with adequate strength should be selected since the majority of seams or at least the stitches in them are required to be as unobtrusive as possible. Cotton covered polyester sewing threads are acceptable for most purposes but for synthetic fibre fabrics, and where particularly high strength and resistance to shrinkage is concerned, synthetic fibre sewing threads are preferable. Tension of thread in needle and spool should be as low as is consistent with a balanced stitch, ie the crossing of spool and needle thread should take place *in* the fabric and not either on the back or on the surface. Synthetic threads are very strong and elastic and if fed into the machine at too great a tension they can actually draw the seam together in a pucker when the tension relaxes.

Correct seaming requires control of the stitch interval. This varies from about 15 to 19 or 22 stitches per 3 cm. It is desirable that a seam should have the same lengthways amount of give as the fabric otherwise it will have a binding effect and will be subjected to strain which could cause it to snap. Seams for extensible fabrics should contain more stitches to the cm than seams for close and firm fabrics because they have more elasticity. Similarly seams for light and open fabrics should be close in order to hold the fabric securely and prevent yarn slippage.

The pressure of the machine foot should be only as heavy as is necessary to enable the fabric to be gripped by the feed mechanism. If it is too heavy it will cause puckering of the fabric layers and gathering.

Industrial sewing machines are capable of sewing speeds up to 8000 stitches a minute. At these high speeds the adjustments referred to above are extremely important and in addition the feed dogs in the plate underneath the machine foot are adjusted to give the correct amount of fabric movement. With these high-speed machines the problem of needle heating can arise and sufficient heat can be developed actually to melt thermoplastic threads and fabrics so that a greater degree of attention to needle size and type, thread size and tension must be paid; needle lubrication used where necessary and in some cases restriction of speed to avoid breakage and damage due to heat.

Where knitted fabrics are being sewn, seams which are necessary for garment stability, are usually taped or supported by binding. With firmly woven fabrics curved seams usually require frequent notching of the inlay to give the required suppleness and evenness of curve. Neatening of seams is essential in the case of filament yarn fabrics and loosely woven staple fibre fabrics, particularly those of rayon, to prevent untidiness through unravelling of fabric. The overlock machine is used extensively by clothing manufacturers for this purpose as well as for the general sewing of knitted fabrics.

Pressing of fabrics

The operation of pressing, ie the use of physical pressure, combined with heat or heat and moisture, forms an essential part of garment making and garment maintenance. It is a form of temporary setting whereby fabrics are either set into a crease or are set flat and unwanted creases removed. Heat, or heat and moisture, prepare the fibres for the physical pressure exerted by the sole of an iron or the plates of a press. All the physical factors in pressing must be controlled to prevent either outright damage to the fibres, or unwanted effects on the fabric and it is perhaps better to examine the factors individually although they do act in combination.

Heat All textile fibres are affected by heat in some degree. The natural cellulosic fibres, linen and cotton, have a very good resistance and can withstand higher temperatures than any other clothing fibres although they will ultimately 'yellow' and scorch if the temperature is consistently raised. An important factor in conjunction with heat is time, a prolonged exposure to heat is much more damaging to a fibre than a short one. In pressing of any kind there is heat loss and a time lag between the passage of heat from the source, ie the iron sole or the plates of the press to the fabric.

The longer the fabric is in contact with the source of heat the higher is its temperature raised and if the source is heated to a temperature above the limit for the fabric, prolonged contact will damage the fabric, but a short brief contact will probably have no harmful effect because of heat loss between the surfaces and the fact that the fabric is not in contact long enough for the temperature to build up to a dangerous point.

In most pressing operations precise control of temperature is not possible so that an adequate safety margin must be allowed to prevent the time factor from becoming too critical. Domestic irons are light in weight and are designed to heat quickly. A consequence of this is that the sole plate tends to vary in temperature according to the distance of any particular part of the plate from the heating element. If the iron is kept in prolonged contact with the fabric the area of the sole plate nearest to the heating element can quickly become too hot locally and can cause damage thereby. Most domestic irons are controlled by a thermostat which is named with settings appropriate to various fibres. These thermostats vary in efficiency and that together with the temperature variation mentioned above makes it advisable to keep the iron contact period as brief as possible, repeated short pressings being preferable to long contact. Commercial equipment is heavier and tends to be more even in heat but even so the same considerations apply.

Short contact does not necessarily mean sliding movement of the iron because with thermoplastic man-made fibres this action can cause glazing of the surface even if the reverse side of the fabric is being treated. To prevent this happening too easily fabrics should always be pressed on a resilient padded surface—particularly where seams are concerned otherwise the face of the fabric will show an imprint of the seam and glazing is more likely where extra fabric thickness can suddenly increase the pressure effect. All thermoplastic fibres, ie all the synthetic fibres and cellulose acetate and triacetate are sensitive to heat damage and should be treated carefully. Acrylic fibres are particularly sensitive to distortion and glazing and should always be pressed by dry heat only at the very lowest temperature setting and with light pressure and minimum of sliding movement.

Heat and moisture

Steam irons and steam presses, or the use of an ordinary iron and a damp cloth combine moisture and heat. Steam presses are supplied with steam under pressure, usually about 4.5 kg per square cm. This gives a theoretical temperature of about 145°C but the heat lost as the steam heats the top and bottom press surfaces brings the temperature down to 100° from 110°C. This temperature is safe enough for most fibres—except acrylic fibres where a lower temperature than 100°C is necessary to avoid damage. Heat and moisture applied locally by steam iron or damp cloth and iron keeps the temperature in the 100°C region which again is safe enough for most fibres – except acrylics. Cellulose acetate can be delustred inadvertently by injudicious heat and moisture treatment and acrylic fibres should never be treated with heat and moisture together. Certain types of resin glaze are also sensitive to heat, or to heat and moisture because of the thermoplastic nature of the resin and these types of fabric and indeed any type of fabric of which the reaction is in doubt, should be tested on a spare piece before a garment is treated.

Fabric surface and structure

The weight, structure and surface finish of a fabric have an influence in pressing in addition to the actual fibre content already mentioned.

Light-weight fabrics require additional care because whatever sensitivity the fibre itself may possess is intensified by fine yarns and fine structure.

Crepe fabrics, ie true crepe fabrics made from hard twisted yarns, require very careful pressing treatment with a minimum of moisture to prevent excessive shrinkage.

The neatening effect of pressing does not always involve the flattening of a fabric surface. In the case of certain nap fabrics, and in all pile fabrics, flattening is undesirable. This can be avoided by pressing the reverse side lightly on a very soft surface or by the use of a needle board, ie a pad with a surface composed of wire points closely set together which allows the pile fabric to remain upright whilst the back of the fabric is pressed.

Fabrics with a rough or an embossed surface also require light careful treatment on the reverse side on a soft surface to prevent undue surface flattening or glazing. Where it is essential for pressing to take place on the right side of a fabric, great care must be taken to avoid producing glaze or lustre where not required. The use of moisture is a help in this respect, except in acrylic fibres, and the surface of a pile fabric will often respond to the use of steam alone without any pressure.

Permanent heat setting

The permanent setting of synthetic fibres—in creases, pleats or shapes – should never be attempted domestically, or without the correct equipment. Efficient heat setting requires much more precise control of temperatures and time than is possible with ordinary pressing equipment. Special presses are used which can be accurately controlled at temperatures from 150° to 200°C together with timing devices which open the press. Theoretically synthetic fibres can be set at 100°C but higher temperatures give a more durable effect but need strict time control to prevent damage.

If permanent setting is attempted without this equipment it will not be sufficiently durable, even if it is achieved at all. When synthetic fibres are being pressed ordinarily care must be taken to avoid pressing in unwanted creases because these may be very difficult to remove completely.

Moulding and shape setting

The moulding of near-seamless bras and pantie girdles has been well established throughout the USA and Europe since the early 1970s, with the cup shapes set on positive/negative metal moulds heated to a high temperature. Half the bras sold on the European continent are produced by this method. Fabrics used for moulding normally contain a high percentage of thermoplastic fibre such as polyester or nylon and the special fabric finish is a critical factor. Woven fabrics incorporating elastane fibre, laces or warp knitted fabrics in a fairly tight construction are the main types for this shaping technique.

Research and development for outerwear moulding have now reached an advanced stage in the USA, Germany, Czechoslovakia, Japan and Britain but factory production has been spasmodic, largely through lack of support from the industry. Clothing manufacturers are not yet convinced of the economic need to make a complete change in the method of making clothes. This situation will remain until they can see the economic advantage of setting a shape into fabric instead of cutting flat garment panels, then stitching them together, with all the extra work involved. There is less advantage for outerwear to have the smooth seamless shape which is the main selling point of the moulded bras and girdles.

Moulded outerwear such as trousers, skirts and jackets can be shaped by several moulding methods but the basic essential common to all of them is the creation of a well shaped mould which will imitate the best points of a 'well cut' garment, ie it must include the drape, flare and shaping of a flattering smart garment. If the mould is badly shaped, then all garments moulded from it will be equally badly shaped. The positive part of the mould is all that is required for outerwear moulding; the pressure exerted by a negative mould onto the positive shape is not generally necessary.

Jersey tubes of suitable diameter, knitted in a firm construction and containing at least 70% polyester, preferably more, can be pulled over the garment mould and heat-set at approximately 180° -190°C for a few minutes, in order to make the shape permanent through washing and dry cleaning. Pockets, collars, zips, etc, can all be stitched into the garment before moulding—or afterwards. If there is any risk of shade change through the high temperature all parts should go through the oven at the same time. Fabrics containing up to 30% cotton or wool may be moulded by this method, providing the remaining percentage is polyester, or other suitable thermoplastic fibre; then the percentage of natural fibre gives the moulded garment a soft natural handle. 100% polyester can be moulded very successfully, becoming fractionally firmer after moulding but at the same time gaining considerably improved crease resistance.

Other methods of moulding are based on woven fabrics containing a small percentage of elastane yarn which enables the fabric to stretch over the mould wherever required. A high polyester content is also needed to provide the main fibre to be heat-set, for although elastane answers this description, as little as 2% can produce the required stretch (and because of its high cost it should be kept to a low content) needing polyester to make up the necessary 70% or more of thermoplastic fibre, blended with wool, cotton or viscose.

Shrinkable polyester fibre is sometimes included in woven or knitted fabrics, being shrunk to fit the mould shape, instead of being stretched. 100% wool fabrics can be moulded by steam under pressure in an autoclave but the resultant shape is not permanent through 'hot' dry cleaning or washing unless the fabric has first been impregnated with the MEAS solution used for permanent pleats and creases in wool, before moulding takes place. Equally the Koratron process can be used to achieve moulding of knitted fabrics with high cellulosic content, blended with 30-50% polyester. The fabrics are sensitised with the cross-linking agents used for this shape-setting permanent press technique; they are cured during the moulding process in a dry heat oven. Polyester/wool fabrics can also be moulded in the same manner, using the different Koratron chemicals for this type of blend.

The potential of these methods will be realised when labour costs become too high to justify cutting up fabric into small parts and stitching them together again to obtain a shape which can in reality be heat-set in the first place. Style features can be added after moulding in order to make individual ranges of fashions look quite different from each other.

Physiological aspects

There are three possible ways that heat can be transferred through textile clothing materials: (1) by conduction through the fibres (2) by convection through moving air and (3) by radiation. In most countries one of the main purposes of clothing is to protect the body from heat loss. Even in the desert it is bitterly cold at night and countries on the equator have their colder months. But it has been found that *still air* is the best possible insulator, which plays a very important part in retaining body warmth. There is trapped air between the yarns and fibres of a fabric, also within the kinks and curls of textured filaments, and in any brushed or pile surface, all of which increases a fabric's warmth virtually by the way the air is used. There is a very large volume of air in most fabrics as, for instance, in a blanket where more than 90% of the bulk is occupied by air. But *moving air* can be used to cool the body, which if over-heated must get rid of excessive heat, in which case insulation has to be removed in order to permit air to circulate and assist evaporation of perspiration.

In order to provide insulation the entrapped air must be immobilised, and therefore under windy conditions the outer layer of the clothing assembly should be almost impermeable to air. Although fabrics can be constructed to have very low permeability, no woven or knitted fabric can ever be completely impermeable. This can only be achieved by laminating the fabric to a plastic film or coating. But very closely woven cotton fabrics, or polyester and cotton blended, using fine yarns set very closely together so that air and wind have difficulty in passing between them, form a reasonably good insulating outer layer, particularly if finished with a showerproof treatment.

To assess the value of air gaps between clothing layers, tests conducted on a man wearing a vest, shirt and jacket show that out of the total thermal resistance for the whole assembly, 66% is due to the garments and 34% to the air gaps between them; such air gaps between garment layers can contribute significantly to the warmth of a clothing system. Yet because fibres in a textile fabric occupy only a small fraction of the total volume, the difference in thermal conductivity between one fibre and another is unimportant in clothing for average climates. Those with low conductivity, often used for internal layers of cold weather clothing, are polypropylene, polyester and polyvinylchloride. Wool, acrylic and cellulose acetate are higher than viscose and polyethylene. Cotton has the highest thermal conductivity, ie produces the lowest heat retention. The thermal insulation of air is about one thirtieth of most *fibres* and about one sixth of most *fabrics*.

Textiles can protect the body from excessive radiant heat such as the sun's rays, or the heat of a furnace. In this case a dense fabric construction is necessary in order to gain maximum protection. Colour can also divert radiant heat from the body by means of reflection. White provides good heat reflection whereas black is the least effective. Thick fabrics coated with aluminium foil give a high protection against radiant heat, although aluminium paint is less efficient. In addition to protecting the body against excessive heat from the outside, it is necessary in cold climates to protect it from radiant *heat loss* from the body into the clothing assembly or the outside atmosphere.

Under normal conditions of atmospheric temperature and humidity (the amount of moisture in the air) and of body activity, the entire human body is continuously producing perspiration in order to regulate the body's temperature, which evaporates within the skin layers and is emitted in the form of water vapour, which is invisible. This is referred to by physiologists as 'sensible' perspiration which is liquid sweat normally only appearing when the temperature and humidity of the air is abnormally high or the individual indulges in strenuous exercise. A third form of perspiration is the apocrine sweating from certain glands which can contribute to offensive body odours; this can be either acid or alkaline. But as long as the normal perspiration remains insensible— that is, in vapour form—a person will feel reasonably comfortable. Yet if water vapour cannot escape quickly enough through the clothing, the percentage of relative humidity at skin level will increase, making the wearer feel clammy and if the conditions and type of clothing are such that the relative humidity within the clothing is increased to 100%, liquid moisture is formed on the skin and sometimes on the garment, by condensation of the water vapour, and the discomfort is increased. To be comfortable the skin must be kept in a dry condition and the body temperature should be constant, not too high or too low — between 35°C and 40°C, preferably at 37°C.

The need for fabrics to allow transmission of water vapour is generally understood but it is often confused with air permeability. Air and water vapour pass through a fabric in different ways. All textile fibres irrespective of their chemical composition are impermeable to air and therefore the passage of air through a fabric can only take place through spaces between the fibres, called the *interstices*.

The water vapour, on the other hand, passes through fabric in several ways, sometimes through the interstices and sometimes right through the fibre itself, evaporating in the process, which can cause cooling of the skin. Every fibre has a different ability to absorb and evaporate moisture. For example, PVC fibres, polypropylene and polyethylene fibres have none; polyester and nylon have very little; wool has reasonably good ability, whilst linen, viscose and cotton are very good for this purpose. Water vapour can pass through all absorbent fibres, but some have better facilities for moisture evaporation than others. It is possible to have a fabric with very low air permeability but with high moisture vapour permeability, dependent on the fibre used.

For tropical clothing the fabrics should be made of open weave to allow air permeability and to be absorbent with high evaporation ability. Also the air between the body and the layers of clothing should be kept circulating. Open necks and sleeves, shirts left loose at the hips, not belted or tucked in, enables the air currents to pass through the garment. Conversely, to provide extra warmth in the same garment, the collar can be buttoned closely at the neck, the sleeve cuffs fastened round the wrist and the waist belted tightly, which stops the air currents and creates still air insulation round the body, providing as much extra warmth as putting on an additional lightweight garment.

Thermal underwear

'Wickability' is a term used to describe how moisture can run along a fibre which in itself may be totally non-absorbent. This helps with evaporation of moisture into the atmosphere. Although moisture may sometimes appear to be absorbed by the fabric, it is only held within a spun, crimped or textured fibre formation, resting on the surface of the fibres. If moisture is not absorbed the fabric dries more quickly, ie the moisture is wicked along the fibres either to become evaporated or to be absorbed by outer layers of clothing.

This wicking property is claimed for Rhovyl *Thermovyl* chlorofibre (polyvinylchloride), Montedison's *Meraklon* (polypropylene) and Du Pont's *Thermax* (polyester) which are used for thermal underwear, so that when garments made of these fibres are worn next to the skin, the theory is that the skin is kept dry through the wicking action of the fibre, transferring body moisture into a more absorbent garment worn on top. There are opposing opinions on whether it is more comfortable to have absorbent fabric or non-absorbent fabric next to the skin, and wearer trials have been used to prove both cases, which is a curious situation. Some wearers report that damp absorbent fabric held next to the skin is more uncomfortable than a less sympathetic non-absorbent fibre which gets rid of the damp quickly, whilst others favour some absorbency next to the skin, preferably with some wicking action as well. The synthetic fibres are spun into yarns which are soft, almost cotton-like in handle so that there is no question of a clammy fabric next to the skin.

However, most thermal underwear seems to rely on almost total lack of 'moisture regain' which helps to limit the thermal conductivity of the fibre. If the construction of the fabric provides a layer of still air over the body it will prevent the entry of cold from the outside and the loss of heat outwards from the body. The fabric construction and the garment layers play an important part in creating the necessary insulation properties.

An additional factor is a negative electrostatic charge generated by chlorofibre which is regarded as therapeutic. It has been found to relieve pain and is believed to help retain body warmth by producing a barrier of air which is electrostatic. Researchers at French and Italian

	Thermal Conductivity (Relative air 1.0)	Moisture Regain (20°C & 65% RH)	Specific* Gravity
Polypropylene	4.8	0.05	0.91
Polyester	5.6	0.40	1.38
Polyvinylchloride	6.4	0.10	1.39
Wool	7.3	15	1.32
Acrylic	8.0	1.50	1.17
Viscose	11.2	12	1.52
Cotton	17.5	8.50	1.54

Starts sinking in water at 1.00

74 Fibre properties compared

universities and hospitals report that these tribo-electrical properties of polyvinyl chloride have beneficial effects on patients suffering from various conditions such as neuralgia, sciatica and rheumatism, with 50% of patients showing full recovery or considerable improvement.

Hollow fibres

Relying on the theory of using still air for warmth, several textile producers have engineered fibres to be completely hollow, extruding them as very fine micro-tubes, air-filled along the length of fibre, at the same time making them appreciably softer and lighter warm fillings. For pillows Du Pont's *Comforel* takes the form of small fibre balls, claimed to be the synthetic version of duck's down..

In the case of Courtauld's *Viloft*, basically a viscose fibre, the thermal insulation, absorbency and wicking ability are good, and when blended with polyester this produces easily washable garments which fulfil all the requirements of thermal underwear, especially the degree of absorbency which Courtaulds consider to be necessary for this type of garment. It is a theory in contrast with the one put out by the synthetic fibre producers but Courtaulds maintain that independent wearing trials and the volume of sales confirm their claim.

Du Pont's *Hollofil* Dacron polyester was one of the first hollow fibres, intended to provide bulk without weight, improving the fillings for anoraks and continental duvets, also the fillings for soft upholstered chairs and settees. Du Pont's name *Fiberfill* covers a range of six Dacron fibre types, some hollow, others self bonding, including specially soft fillings for slimline warm quilted fashion coats. One of the advantages of polyester waddings or 'battings' is that when wet, the water runs through the fibres and dries quickly, without forming a soggy mass. ICI also produces a hollow polyester fibre for the same type of softer warm fillings.

Linings

The texturing of polyester filament fibres has provided a number of practical advantages for linings. The fabric can be made very strong and light without being transparent. It can withstand all the processes of 'engineered' clothing production such as automatic pressing and, having easy care properties, is suitable for washable garments. The wearer feels reasonably comfortable since the texturing appears to absorb body moisture and the wicking theory applies, dispersing the moisture into the outer fabric. These linings tend to wear longer than viscose or acetate and the fabric is strong enough for pocket bags.

Some linings are made with spun polyester yarns in the weft, with a textured polyester warp, to gain a more cotton-like handle. They can be printed, either roller or transfer methods, with small geometric motifs, plaid designs in single colour or the logos of the clothing manufacturer or a retailer, providing that sufficient quantities are ordered to keep the price reasonable.

On the other hand polyester linings are not as cool to wear as viscose linings and do not help the 'hang' of a jacket because they are light. Yet in the case of viscose the shrinkage can be a disadvantage, being unsuitable for washable garments. For women's linings there is usually a very wide colour range in acetate poults and taffetas, also triacetate taffetas, but their wear-life is not as long as viscose, nylon or polyester. Nylon taffeta, if made for linings, would have to be very closely woven to avoid seam slippage, which makes the fabric very warm to wear. Nylon locknit is cooler and, in special constructions, strong enough even for pocketings, which makes it a popular choice for multi-purpose linings.

Identification: labelling

Identification of fabrics, ie of the fibre composition is an important part of fabric knowledge because the care and treatment of fabrics, either during making up or in actual use, is influenced considerably by the composition as well as by the type of fabric.

In view of the number of different types of fibre available and the number of processes and finishes which can be applied to textile yarns and fabrics, the general aspects of which have been dealt with in this book, identification is a special study on its own and cannot be dealt with satisfactorily in a superficial manner. There was a time, many years ago, when the composition of fabrics could be identified by handle and appearance, with possibly a burning test in addition. But the greater complexity of fibre blends, and treatments in use now makes simple methods very unreliable. Details of fibre identification methods will be found in the books listed at the end of this chapter. Two of them, the Textile Institute publication, and *Textile Fibers* contain detailed analysis procedures which go far beyond general identification needs and equipment facilities. Normally it is only necessary to determine the type or types of fibre in a fabric so that a simpler identification scheme as set out *Man-Made Fibres* will be adequate.

A wide background of textile knowledge is an asset in fibre identification because the type of fabric often indicates the type of fibre and practical experience of fabric handling helps tremendously in preliminary assessment.

Any system whether detailed, or general, will always advocate the collection of known samples; these can be handled, examined and burnt in comparison with the unknown fabric and provide a very useful indication. It is extremely valuable for instance to know whether a fabric is thermoplastic or not. This can easily be determined by burning a small piece and noting whether or not it melts and whether it leaves a hard residue when the flame has been blown out and the material allowed to cool. This does not constitute detailed identification but it is useful information in regard to treatment. Even if the fabric is a blend of thermoplastic and non-thermoplastic fibres the thermoplastic content will be noticeable in hard residue and if a fabric contains thermoplastic fibres it must be heat-treated accordingly, irrespective of the non-thermoplastic content. Ignorance of this fact has resulted in many garments being given glazed seams in pressing.

The really satisfactory answer to problems of identification and care is of course sensible *labelling* of fabrics and garments. It is easy to say this but there are many problems connected with labelling which have not yet been ideally solved.

Any effective labelling system must be simple and comprehensive. Large wordy labels, or collections of small labels, are tiresome to read and eventually are ignored and defeat their object. Labels in durable press garments represent the ideal in that they give information as to fibre content and precise and concise information on care. The provision of these labels is no problem because as explained in chapter VI these garments are made to precise quality standards, on the garment manufacturer's responsibility and under his control so that all the components of the garment are compatible and it is made with a specific object — durable press — in mind. Whatever variety of material is used in providing a range of garments it is all directed to this object and labelling becomes rationalised and straightforward.

Now that composition labelling is compulsory by law, in accordance with a directive of the EC, the responsibility of specifying the exact percentage of fibre under its correct EC generic name lies with the manufacturer or importer, ie the supplier from which the retailer purchases the garment. Yet it is the retailer's duty to ensure that the product is correctly labelled.

Although the basic intention is to provide information for the purchaser, the directive was also intended to co-ordinate the names of fibres throughout the EC countries. The scheme applies to outer fabrics and linings but excludes all interlinings, backings and trimmings.

The sale of textiles is also covered by this order in addition to made up garments. But a ticket attached to a roll of fabric is sufficient, providing the invoice and other relative documents include the necessary information. These regulations apply to all items in which textile fibres constitute an important part. A tolerance of 10% of 'other fibres' is allowed, according to type of product, without the need to identify them by name. The percentages quoted on the labels of each garment are to be based on the weight of each fibre content. As long as the appropriate percentage with the fibre's correct generic name is stated on the label, other names may be *added*, such as brand names for the fibres and traditional descriptions such as botany wool, Shetland wool, Sea Island cotton, Irish linen, etc. The terms 'fleece wool', 'virgin wool' and 'pure new wool' may be used providing none of the fibres has been re-processed from previously manufactured textile materials.

However, the use of such a label carries no guarantee as to the precise quality of *wool* which goes in and these types of fabric can vary considerably in this respect. This is by no means suggesting that inferior wool qualities are deliberately used but that content labelling can become a minimum of quality standard which can be confusing to a fabric user who mistakenly assumes a quality standard. Due to the confusion which has existed on this point, large fibre producers have initiated quality tested schemes of various kinds which do link performance and durability to content labelling. Some confusion of opinion has also been found over the 'Woolmark' initiated by the International Wool Secretariat. This mark can only be used when a fabric is made from virgin wool without any adulteration and it was originally intended to be a simple statement to that effect. However, as an illustration that the apparently simple may not be *quite* so simple, confusion has arisen because, as set out in chapter II, virgin wool is produced in many different *qualities* and success in any fabric use depends on the correct *quality* being used, and this is a different consideration and not connected with mere statement of purity of content. In any sphere of activity there are always those who will take advantage of ambiguity and this can adversely affect a whole scheme. For this reason it is essential that certain 'performance' guarantees are incorporated into content labelling and this is being done by some organisations but it is by no means universal.

In the case of garments made from more than one outer fabric, eg with yokes or sleeves in contrast, the textile composition must be specified for each fabric constituting 30% or *more* of the product's total weight. Obviously it may be advisable to specify the fibre used for parts forming *less* than 30% if they require a different after-care treatment from the remainder of the garment, but this is not compulsory. For instance where the body of the garment is made from a fibre which is known to be washable but the collars and cuffs are only dry cleanable, it means that the whole garment should be dry cleaned and should be labelled accordingly if the supplier wishes to avoid later complaints. There is considerable ignorance about the best methods of cleaning different types of fabrics and finishes. Taking labelling to its logical conclusion there should be a statement on whether the garment has been showerproofed or given other special finishes which may affect the manner in which it should be treated.

Any claims for special fabric properties such as Flame Retardance (see page 152) should be carefully considered in view of the 1987 Consumer Protection Act which puts the liability for defective products onto the manufacturer without the consumer having the need to prove negligence. Heavy financial claims could therefore result from over-optimistic statements. Any description of fitness for purpose should be carefully worded.

The Home Laundering Consultative Council (HLCC) evolved a system of care labelling a number of years ago, with the emphasis on home laundering to cover all washable fabrics and garments. Now a simpler system of eleven basic labels has replaced the original series of recommended methods which were numbered from 1 to 9. In the new system only the temperature of the wash is given, inside a different washtub, with examples of application. A bar under the tub indicates reduced machine action and a broken or double bar for 'wool wash' 40° stresses the need for extra care involving minimum machine action. The absence of a bar means that normal or maximum machine action can be used, as for cotton wash. Labels usually contain space for special instructions such as 'do not bleach' or 'do not boil'. Articles which cannot be washed satisfactorily by any of the ten procedures should come under the eleventh label type 'DO NOT WASH'. The HLCC wash methods are usually shown on detergent packs.

Some manufacturers label their garments DRY CLEAN ONLY as a safety first measure to cover HANDWASH and DO NOT WASH but purchasers have sometimes assumed they can use a mild wash, with unfortunate results. It is better to be quite specific, using the DO NOT WASH label. Whilst it is not legally necessary for suppliers to attach care labels, if they do so there is a legal requirement that the garment is fit for the treatment recommended.

It is claimed that these eleven basic labels form the simplest combination of requirements, with the minimum of special instructions. The design and content of the labels have been discussed and agreed by representatives of the textile industry, the domestic appliance industry, washing product manufacturers, distributors and other allied interests. The new scheme is now covered by the British Standard Code of Practice for Textile Care

Labelling (BS 2747: 1986) which contains a number of new features approved by GINETEX, the international textile care labelling association of which the HLCC is a member.

Fortunately the International Textile Care Labelling Code provides symbols for garment labels to standardise care instructions. The symbols cover three different temperature ranges for ironing by means of dots on the iron base (no dots means cool), three different dry cleaning solvents, together with crossed symbols to indicate 'Do Not' for each; advice on bleaching and tumble drying is similarly depicted. The washing symbols are included in the scheme.

Whereas fibre content labels are required by law, from January 1989 it became unnecessary to specify Country of Origin. Such labelling used to be compulsory in the UK but there was always considerable argument on this subject within the European Community, with several countries objecting to origin labelling because they use many other areas of the world for production processes, sometimes cutting the cloth within the EEC but sewing in factories thousands of miles away, yet packing and despatching again in the original country. They argued that it is inappropriate and often impossible to determine a single country of origin; eventually their arguments successfully influenced EC laws. But in the UK origin must still be stated in cases where misrepresentation appears, eg the flags or emblems of a different country.

In conclusion it remains for users of fabrics to know what they are purchasing and using, in order to obtain maximum value for money.

Bibliography

Matthews Textile Fibers, 6th edition, John Wiley and Sons New York and Chapman & Hall London

Man-Made Fibres, 6th edition, R W Moncrieff, Newnes Butterworth 1975

Standard Handbook of Textiles, 8th edition, A J Hall, Newnes Butterworth 1975

Technology of Textile Properties, M A Taylor, Forbes Publications

Handbook of Textiles, 3rd edition, A M Collier, Wheaton 1980

Handbook of Textile Fibres Nos 1 and 2, J G Cook, Merrow

A Students Textbook of Textile Science, A J Hall, Allman 1963

Introduction To The Study of Spinning, 3rd edition, W E Morton and G R Wray, Longman

Worsted, A Brearley, Pitman

The Woollen Industry, Brearley & Iredale, Wira 1977

Woven Cloth Construction, A T C Robinson and R Marks, Textile Institute, Butterworth

Knitting, H. Wignall, Pitman

Warp Knitting Technology, D F Paling, Columbine Press

Non-Wovens, P L Kerr (ed) Textile Trade Press 1971

Introduction to Textile Finishing, J T Marsh, Chapman & Hall

Textile Finishing, A J Hall, Heywood

Thames and Hudson Manual of Dyes and Fabrics, J Storey, Thames and Hudson 1978

Identification of Textile Materials, Textile Institute

Index

Supplementary to table of contents

223